PRESIDING LIKE A WOMAN

Edited by
NICOLA SLEE and STEPHEN BURNS

T0316301

First published in Great Britain in 2010

Society for Promoting Christian Knowledge
36 Causton Street
London SW1P 4ST
www.spckpublishing.co.uk

British Library Cataloguing-in-Publication Data
A catalogue record for this book is available from the British Library

ISBN 978–0–281–06186–0

1 3 5 7 9 10 8 6 4 2

Typeset by Graphicraft Ltd, Hong Kong
Printed in Great Britain by MPG

Produced on paper from sustainable forests

Contents

Contents

Contributors

Alastair Barrett is a priest in the orders of the Church of England, serving in the diocese of Birmingham, UK. He was a contributor to *The Edge of God: New Liturgical Texts and Contexts in Conversation* (co-edited by Stephen Burns, Michael N. Jagessar and Nicola Slee, 2008) and has published a number of articles in *Modern Believing*.

Andrea Bieler is Professor of Christian Worship at Pacific School of Religion in the Graduate Theological Union, Berkeley, California, USA. She is an ordained pastor in the Evangelical Lutheran Church in the USA. Her publications include *The Eucharist: Bodies, Bread, Resurrection* (co-author with Luise Schottroff, 2007) and *Embodying Grace: Proclaiming Justification in the Real World* (co-author with Hans-Martin Guttmann, 2010).

June Boyce-Tillman MBE is Professor of Applied Music at the University of Winchester, UK. She is a priest in the orders of the Church of England. Her publications include *A Rainbow to Heaven* (2006), *The Creative Spirit: Harmonious Living with Hildegard of Bingen* (2006) and *Unconventional Wisdom* (2007).

Veronica Brady is Emerita Professor of English at the University of Western Australia, Perth. She is a Loreto Sister. Her publications include *The God-Shaped Hole* (2007).

Stephen Burns is Research Fellow in Public and Contextual Theology at United Theological College, Charles Sturt University, North Parramatta, Australia. He is a priest in the orders of the Church of England. His publications include *Worship in Context: Liturgical Theology, Children and the City* (2006), *Liturgy* (SCM Studyguide, 2006), *Exchanges of Grace: Essays in Honour of Ann Loades* (co-editor with Natalie K. Watson, 2008), *The Edge of God: New Liturgical Texts and Contexts in Conversation* (co-editor with Michael N. Jagessar and Nicola Slee, 2008), *Christian Worship in Australia: Inculturating the Liturgical Tradition* (co-editor with Anita Monro, 2009), *Christian Worship: Postcolonial Perspectives* (co-author with Michael N. Jagessar, 2010) and *Not Behind Our Backs: Feminist Questions and Public Theology* (co-editor with Anita Monro, forthcoming). He is editor of the series *Renewing the Eucharist* (2008–).

Barbara Darling is Bishop of the Eastern Region of the Diocese of Melbourne in the Anglican Church of Australia. She was the second female bishop to be appointed by the Anglican Church of Australia.

Susan Durber is Principal of Westminster College in the Cambridge Theological Federation, UK. She is an ordained minister in the United

Reformed Church. Her publications include *Preaching Like a Woman* (SPCK 2007).

Alison Green is a priest in the orders of the Church in Wales, serving in the diocese of Monmouth. Her publications include *A Theology of Women's Priesthood* (SPCK 2009).

Mary Grey is Emerita Professor of Pastoral Theology at the University of Wales, Lampeter, and Professorial Research Fellow at St Mary's University, Twickenham, UK. She is a lay member of the Roman Catholic Church. Her publications include *The Wisdom of Fools: Seeking Revelation for Today* (SPCK 2000), *The Outrageous Pursuit of Hope: Prophetic Dreams for the Twenty-first Century* (2001), *Sacred Longings: Ecofeminist Theology and Globalisation* (2003), *To Rwanda and Back: Liberation Spirituality and Reconciliation* (2007) and *Crying for Dignity: Caste-based Violence Against Dalit Women* (2010).

Gillian Hill is a priest in the orders of the Church of England, serving in the diocese of Portsmouth, where she is also Advisor on Women's Ministries.

Ann Loades CBE is Professorial Fellow of St Chad's College and Emerita Professor of Divinity in the University of Durham, and Honorary Professor in the University of St Andrews, UK. She is a lay member of the Church of England, and a member of its doctrine commission. Her publications include *Feminist Theology: Voices from the Past* (2001), *The Truth-Seeking Heart: The Writings of Austin Farrer* (co-editor with Robert MacSwain, 2006) and *Christology: Key Readings in Christian Thought* (co-editor with Jeff Astley and David Brown, SPCK, 2009).

Dorothy McRae-McMahon AM is minister of the word in the South Sydney congregation of the Uniting Church in Australia. Her publications include *Liturgies for the Journey of Life* (SPCK 2000), *In This Hour: Liturgies for Pausing* (SPCK 2001), *Liturgies for Life's Particular Moments* (SPCK 2001), *Liturgies for Daily Life* (SPCK 2004), *Liturgies for High Days* (SPCK 2006), and *Liturgies for the Young in Years* (SPCK 2007).

Rachel Mann is a priest in the orders of the Church of England, serving in the diocese of Manchester. She was a contributor to *The Edge of God: New Liturgical Texts and Contexts in Conversation* (co-edited by Michael N. Jagessar, Nicola Slee and Stephen Burns, 2008) and has contributed to numerous collections of poetry and essays.

Anita Monro is minister of the word in the Armidale congregation of New England presbytery of the Uniting Church in Australia. She is a member of both the doctrine and worship working groups of the Uniting Church. Her publications include *Resurrecting Erotic Transgression: Subjecting Ambiguity* in *Theology* (2006) and *Christian Worship in Australia: Inculturating the Liturgical Tradition* (co-editor with Stephen Burns, 2009).

Julia Pitman is a candidate for minister of the word at Uniting College for Leadership and Theology at Adelaide, Australia. She was a contributor to *Women and Ordination in the Christian Churches* (co-edited by Ian Jones, Kirsty Thorpe and Janet Wootton, 2008) and *Christian Worship in Australia: Inculturating the Liturgical Tradition* (co-edited by Anita Monro and Stephen Burns, 2009).

David Plüss is Professor of Homiletics and Liturgy at the University of Bern, Switzerland. He is a minister in the Swiss Reformed Church. His publications include *Gottesdienst als Textinszenierung: Perspektiven einer performativen Ästhetik des Gottesdienstes* (2007), *Theologie und Geschlecht: Dialoge Queetbeet* (co-editor with Heike Walz, 2008) and *Im Auge des Flaneurs: Fundstucke zur religiosen Lebenskunst: Festschrift fur Albrecht Grozinger* (co-editor with Tabitha Walther and Adrian Portmann, 2009).

Nicola Slee is Research Fellow and Co-ordinator of the MA in applied theology at the Queen's Foundation for Ecumenical Theological Education, Birmingham, UK. She is a lay member of the Church of England. Her publications include *Faith and Feminism: An Introduction to Christian Feminist Theology* (2003), *Women's Faith Development: Patterns and Processes* (2004), *Praying Like a Woman* (SPCK 2004), *Doing December Differently: An Alternative Christmas Handbook* (co-editor with Rosie Miles, 2006), *The Book of Mary* (SPCK 2007), *The Edge of God: New Liturgical Texts and Contexts in Conversation* (co-editor with Michael N. Jagessar and Stephen Burns, 2008) and *Seeking the Risen Christa* (forthcoming).

Natalie K. Watson is Senior Commissioning Editor for SCM Press, London, UK. She is a lay member of the Church of England. Her publications include *Introducing Feminist Ecclesiology* (2002), *Feminist Theology: An Introduction* (2003) and *Exchanges of Grace: Essays in Honour of Ann Loades* (co-editor with Stephen Burns, 2009).

Val Webb is adjunct professor of religion at Augsburg College, Minneapolis, Minnesota, USA. She is a lay member of the Uniting Church in Australia. Her publications include *Florence Nightingale: The Making of a Radical Theologian* (2002), *Why We're Equal: Introducing Feminist Theology* (2006) and *Like Catching Water in a Net: Human Attempts to Describe the Divine* (2007).

Lucy Winkett is Rector of St James's, Piccadilly. With degrees in history, theology and as a trained soprano, she writes, speaks and debates on a wide range of issues reflecting on culture, gender, music and religion. She is a regular contributor to 'Thought for the Day' on Radio 4's *Today* programme and wrote the Archbishop of Canterbury's Lent Book for 2010, *Our Sound* *is our Wound* (2010). She was a contributor to the best-selling *Why I am Still an Anglican* (2006) and contributed to *Seven Words for Three Hours* (2005). She is a founder adviser to Theos, a public theology think tank launched in 2006 and is Chair of the Governors of St Mary Magdalene Academy, Islington.

Foreword

Multi-tasking is something many women are used to, if not always brilliant at doing. This foreword is a result of multi-tasking - taking parts of the book to New Norcia to look at while undergoing a retreat; reading some in between sermon preparation and visiting parishes, numerous diocesan meetings, moving house, adjusting to a new role as a regional bishop, and reflecting on what it means to be a woman in ministry, let alone trying to understand where our various writers are coming from. It was an enjoyable challenge to read the book and to follow through many distinctive ideas and thoughts that arose when digesting its pages.

This book is a real smorgasbord. Some writers are from my more biblical and historical background; others are from different kinds of feminist perspective; some are rather foreign to my own framework and experience. Some I identify with *so* clearly as they bring back memories of earlier days, struggling to be recognized as women in ministry. The personal anecdotes are eminently readable, striking at my heart and the depths of my emotions at times. Contributors focus in a variety of ways on theology alongside music, gesture, different experiences, things in common between women and men, and at times highlight what might be our distinctive qualities.

In Melbourne we have been very fortunate to have a group of men and women, lay and ordained, who have spoken out boldly to enable women to be ordained at each level in our Anglican Church. Despite a court case in Canberra holding back ordination, followed by a bomb-scare in our cathedral and some very vocal opponents to women being ordained as deacons, great was the rejoicing when this occurred in 1986. We had hoped with the support of our Archbishop David Penman that women would go on to be ordained as priests by the late 1980s. However, Archbishop David's grave illness and then death meant we took years to elect a new archbishop and then had various church legal battles and debates in General Synod.

After six years of being 'ladies in waiting' we eventually had the legislation passed by the General Synod and the Melbourne Synod. Twenty-nine women went into retreat, hoping and praying that it would lead to being priested. We were warned by Archbishop Keith Rayner at the eleventh hour that there was going to be a legal challenge in the service. There was, but their claim that being women made us ineligible was not deemed to be a legitimate reason against being ordained. So on 13 December 1992 the first 12 women clergy in Melbourne who were in positions of leadership in the Church were ordained as priests, followed three days later by another group. (By the end of 1992 there were 92 women priested in Australia.)

As minister in charge at Ascot Vale I was ordained in the first group. The following night my parish church was full to overflowing with parishioners, friends, photographers and others coming to the first service after my ordination where I presided 'like a woman'. It was the most incredible feeling, after four years of having 'rent a priest' males coming to take the service, to be able to preside at the Lord's Supper. It felt rather overwhelming, but also so right. The joy on the faces of the parishioners, who had walked with me on this long and sometimes difficult journey, was just so wonderful to see.

After the initial euphoria came the settling in and trying to work out just what was important in celebrating and leading the liturgy – what could we do differently and what was best to leave as had been. I believe we are still at that phase in many parts of the Church – working out what is really necessary, what is helpful and what is optional. As more and more women are ordained, we see different styles and different theologies emerging.

One of the vivid memories in my first few years when priested and presiding, was of hearing a parishioner describe how her eight-year-old daughter came skipping into the kitchen one morning, wearing a tea towel draped side saddle over her shoulders. When her mother asked her what she was doing, she explained that she was going to church and being like Vicar Barbara, taking a service. She didn't want to be a teacher or nurse when she grew up – she wanted to be a priest like Vicar Barbara! This gave her mother and me great joy, as we realized that now for the first time young girls had a role model and a new possibility and horizon to pursue as they grew up. This is one of the delights in being a bishop too – to show to women and men and girls and boys the new possibilities and new gifts and talents of having women in equal leadership roles.

There is good news here – but there is also sad news. My heart went out to the women in this book who wrote from a position where their church is still unable to accept the leadership roles of women in ministry – and yet women have offered their church so much.

I hope that, like me, you will be stimulated, encouraged and challenged by these chapters and the people behind them. Some of the chapters are beyond my comfort zone and they have indeed challenged me, but have also opened my eyes to how others have been formed theologically. I look forward to going back and reading the chapters again, pondering on the different truths and perspectives that emerge.

Thanks to the women (and a few brave men!) who have provided this book for our pondering, our 'possibility thinking' and for our prayers. May God enable us to grow in understanding of the ministry of all God's people, so that men and women add new dimensions in mutual ministry.

Bishop Barbara Darling, Melbourne, Victoria

Acknowledgements

As ever, with a book of this nature, there are many people we are glad to acknowledge and thank, both the obvious ones and those who might have no consciousness of the debt we owe them or of the part they have played in bringing this book into being. In the 'obvious' category, first and foremost we are grateful to all the contributors who have offered their work, between them bringing a rich diversity of perspective and a profound measure of insight into the questions we are seeking to address. There are others who, while unable for a variety of reasons to contribute to the collection, nevertheless formed part of our conversations and ideas in the early stages of developing our proposal: Mary Caygill, Helen Stanton and Jione Havea have contributed to the spirit, if not the final content, of the book.

We are grateful to Ruth McCurry and Lauren Chiosso at SPCK, who have helped to steer the project through the inevitable pitfalls and doldrums that beset any major publishing undertaking, and to Jennifer Wild for copy-editing the text with intelligence and humour. Doris Klein's beautiful, fluid image, 'Fire of urgency', is used with our grateful thanks to the artist: it is an image which we hope signals both openness and urgency and captures something of the energy and passion which women bring to the work of presiding.

We acknowledge permission to use copyright material from Stainer and Bell for June Boyce-Tillman's hymns (© Stainer & Bell Ltd, 23 Gruneisen Road, London N3 1DZ, UK <www.stainer.co.uk>). Susan Durber's service is used by permission of the United Reformed Church.

Beyond the obvious, there is a great roll-call of women – and some men – who, at different stages of our respective lives, have inspired us with a vision of what it could mean to 'preside like a woman', although some of them might be surprised to know that they have played such a role. Their actions, gestures, voices, styles of leadership, ways of creating space and sharing power – above all their values and the way they live their lives – have helped to shape our own work and ministry, and to inform the vision that this book seeks to honour. It is a moot question how far an individual forms and shapes a community and how far it is the other way round – so it is not only individuals we seek to recognize, but groups, networks and communities which have in some sense gestured towards the kind of collaborative, empowering and enabling forms of leadership we see as truly feminist. Although it does not seem appropriate to name particular individuals and groups in a publication of this nature (not least because we are bound to leave some out who ought to be included), we are conscious of the debt we owe to many friends, family members, our partners, colleagues, teachers and students, children and godchildren, scholars and practitioners, church congregations and institutions of theological learning in a variety of places – from whom we have learnt whatever we know about feminist leadership. Some of these individuals and groups are represented in the pieces that follow, and we hope that those who are not may guess who they are and recognize our gratitude to them.

Nicola Slee
Stirchley

Stephen Burns
Parramatta

To the women who forge new ways of presiding
To the men who unlearn old ways and discover
new ones alongside their sisters
To each other, who have helped to midwife this book,
and the Spirit, in each other
To the ones yet to come who will birth ways
we cannot yet imagine

Introduction

NICOLA SLEE AND STEPHEN BURNS

In much feminist liturgical and theological discourse, concepts of priesthood and presidency have been strongly critiqued if not all together repudiated – and for good reasons.[1] But just as, in recent feminist discourse, both praying – in its widest range of meanings – and preaching have been explored and reappropriated,[2] in this book we are seeking to offer a forum in which similar kinds of questions might be asked of women's ministry of presiding, primarily within liturgical contexts but not excluding other settings. We are not necessarily expecting to offer any answers – certainly not any definitive ones. Rather our purpose is to point to the importance of the topic, to try to ask some good questions about it, highlight some resources to help us think into the questions, and invite women who are presiders (as well as those who experience and receive their ministry) to articulate answers of their own.

We have invited a range of contributors, lay and ordained, women and men, from different Christian traditions (though with a strongly Anglican focus), and largely from our respective contexts of Britain and Australia, to ponder on a range of questions:

- What does it mean to 'preside like a woman', if anything?
- Do women do it differently and, if so, how and why?
- What do we mean by the notion of eucharistic – and other related kinds of – presidency?
- Is this a notion worthy and capable of feminist reclamation, or is it a hopelessly patriarchal concept?
- From where and whom do we derive our understandings of presidency? What are the sources and traditions upon which we can usefully draw?
- How do we enquire into the nature, form and style of presiding 'like a woman'? Whom do we ask? Where do we look? What are the significant questions, and what might they tell us?
- What do women's relatively recent experiences of presiding offer by way of insight, critique, questions and meanings?
- How do women and men (both lay and ordained) experience women's priestly ministry in the liturgical assembly and at the eucharistic table, as well as more widely? What do these varied responses suggest about the meanings of ministry as reflected in women's liturgical presidency?
- What are the differences, if any, between lay and ordained presidency?

- How can presidency be shared and experienced as a truly collaborative, enabling form of leadership?
- What is the significance of body, gesture, voice, presence, authority and so on in the exercise of presidency?

Our contributors have responded, as we hoped and expected, in a wide range of ways: from their diverse contexts and perspectives; in a variety of registers, styles and discourses – telling stories, offering poems, hymns and liturgical texts, drawing on histories and elaborating theoretical perspectives; and pushing at the boundaries of the questions we sent them, thinking new questions and opening up avenues of enquiry we had not originally envisaged. In editing and arranging their offerings, we have not in any way attempted to smooth out the different styles and perspectives but rather to accent them in the hope that readers will be stimulated by the differences and enter into conversation with the contributors.

Presiding Like a Woman is the third in what has become a kind of unofficial 'series' instigated by Nicola's *Praying Like a Woman* (SPCK 2004), and taken up by Susan Durber (also a contributor to this collection) in her *Preaching Like a Woman* (SPCK 2007). There was no idea of a series at all to start with, yet the 'like a woman' phrase seems to have sparked off some kind of resonance for other writers in offering a suggestive yet spacious notion around which to explore what might be distinctive in different aspects of women's liturgical ministry and leadership. It is a phrase that eschews essentialist meanings of gender: men can, potentially, pray, preach or preside 'like a woman'. It does not assume any one meaning of what it means to be a woman, and invites contextualization and narration from different perspectives and settings.

One of the things we hope this book does is to reflect something of the variety and diversity of settings and forms within which women preside, not only in the liturgical assembly but in other places too: in the particular, unique, human/female bodies that women inhabit, with our own particular, inflected voices – or with our own distinctive silences and bodily gestures; as old or young women, differently abled, in 'every place where human lives jostle, mingle, struggle, despair, survive', as Nicola's poem[3] has it. Women give and receive leadership and presidency in as many different ways and forms as women do anything, depending on their context, histories, multiple identities (of which, of course, gender is only one, and not necessarily a straightforward one) and commitments.

Nevertheless, while there is no essentialist or universal way of talking about women's exercise of presidency, a feminist perspective on 'how women do it' looks to retrieve traditions and meanings, rooted in diverse women's experiences, that have been lost, marginalized or ignored in mainstream, patriarchal constructions. Women, like men, have presided, if not in Christian assembly then certainly in the spheres in which they have worked and wielded influence, some of which of course they have only very recently entered, some of which have long been regarded as the habitat of the feminine. In boardrooms, in kitchens, at table, in operating theatres, in parliamentary committees and city councils, in concert halls, in classrooms, in gardens, in bedrooms and waterpools, as well as 'in church' – these are just some of the places in which women have occupied the seat of authority, exercised superintendence, direction or control, conducted or directed the company (as the Oxford English Dictionary defines some of the meanings of 'preside').[4] But, of course, the traditions of women's presidency, like women's priesthood, remain largely hidden, rendered invisible in patriarchal histories that focus on the achievements of men and are based on narrow, very partial notions of leadership and authority. If this collection of essays does nothing else, we hope it may open up for critical scrutiny some of these notions, and begin to sketch, however inadequately, some alternative traditions and conceptions of presidency which emerge from the perspective of women's different, and differing, experiences.

No one account can hope to be comprehensive or fully inclusive, but by offering the particular accounts that we do, from our own particular perspectives, we can each contribute to a fuller, richer account of the way things are (or could be). Rather than trying to speak for each other, we speak with the unique voices that are ours, *to* each other, making the effort both to speak as clearly and responsibly as we can from out of our particular context and experience, *and* to listen to the other as she or he responds out of her or his context and experience, and thence to build up the conversation that can criss-cross many diverse settings and perceptions and work towards a more adequate account of women's experiences than any one, or two, or three, of us could offer alone.

We are conscious of our audacity in editing this book as a lay woman and a male cleric respectively – and that is, in itself, we hope, indicative of the creative and collaborative nature of what we endeavour rather than to be seen as any kind of arrogant presumption to speak for others who can very well speak for themselves. Perhaps our very status as ordained male on the one hand and lay woman on the other gives us a freedom and impetus to create the space in which important critical questions can be asked about the style and nature of women's liturgical ministries and leadership. We also want to say: such questions belong to all of us, lay and ordained, women and men, 'High' church or 'Low' – because they are questions about the nature of the ecclesial community and the ways in which we relate to and interact with one another, the manner in which and the reasons why we 'handle holy things' and create sacred space together, the forms in which we seek to exercise enabling power and be present to one another in the presence of the holy.

Although essays in a collection have to take some kind of linear order, there is no one right or obvious way of reading this book, and readers will find their own ways through it. We wrestled with a variety of ways of structuring the material and in the end had to opt for one order rather than another. Nevertheless, we prefer to think of the contents of the book as a kind of carousel of offerings which can be spun in different directions, items taken out in different orders, shuffled and rearranged to suit different situations and needs. We are conscious that our varied reflections arise out of different contexts, including Sydney, where the local brand of Anglicanism is marked by a long-term and still active resistance to the full equality of women in the Church, although part of a national Anglican Church which now includes the ministry of women as bishops (including Barbara Darling, whom we are delighted to have write the Foreword to this book). Above all, we hope that the diversity represented here can resonate with, against and between each other as pieces are read alongside each other in different clusterings and orders.

As it stands, the sequence we have chosen follows a loose clustering of trajectories and themes, although we are conscious that there is a lot of overlap and blurring of boundaries between these perspectives. We begin with two contrasting pieces of our own – a poem by Nicola which intends to celebrate and name some of the many different contexts and ways in which women have presided and do preside, and an essay by Stephen which looks to a number of feminist theological and liturgical resources to begin to articulate some theological perspectives on what it might mean for women to preside. These pieces are placed at the beginning of the collection, as a kind of framing of what follows, partly because they were sent out to all contributors as a way of beginning to formulate the kinds of questions we were hoping to address in the book. The use of two very different forms and styles – a poem on the one hand, an essay on the other – was also deliberate, as a way of encouraging our contributors to speak in whatever form and style they deemed most appropriate.

Following on from these two opening pieces are four reflections, from Dorothy McRae-McMahon, June Boyce-Tillman, Susan Durber and Mary Grey, which are shaped in strongly narrative and autobiographical forms. Dorothy and June tell their own distinctive stories of their respective journeys to ordained ministry, and what they have discovered about presiding from their own experience as ordained women. Susan Durber, an ordained Reformed minister, reflects on crafting and using an order of communion intended for all-age use, as well as some of the reaction to this rite from within her own denomination. In contrast to these three reflections from ordained women, Mary Grey offers an autobiographically informed lay perspective from the exiled edges of her Roman Catholic tradition, in which, among other concerns, she pushes towards recognition of the multiple ways in which women have presided when liturgical presidency is denied them.

Next, three essays offer historical perspectives from the last couple of centuries, tracing something of women's recent traditions of presiding, sometimes making reference to a number of persons who now feature in the churches' calendars of saints. Val Webb paints vivid vignettes of some Victorian women who, in different contexts and ways, presided: Queen Victoria, Florence Nightingale and Catherine Booth. Julia Pitman widens the perspective to consider trends in the nineteenth-century movement towards women's ordination in North America, Britain and Australia, highlighting the roles of a number of individual women such as Constance Coltman and Maude Royden. Ann Loades considers changing attitudes towards religious tradition in the nineteenth, twentieth and twenty-first centuries, and how this has shaped thinking around women's priesthood, focusing some of the shifts through a case study of C. S. Lewis.

A further cluster of reflections turns from primarily autobiographical and historical approaches to other theological, theoretical and literary analyses of women's experiences of presiding (though the autobiographical context of some of these pieces is strongly marked). Veronica Brady reflects on the need for her own Roman Catholic tradition to 'return to the people' the gift of priesthood and presiding, and what this might mean. Lucy Winkett offers a striking meditation on her experience of singing the eucharistic prayer in St Paul's Cathedral, analysing ways in which women's traditions of song are, quite literally, giving new voice to theological conceptions of women's ministry. Andrea Bieler and David Plüss expound and discuss performative notions of gender (drawing particularly on Judith Butler), and explore what this might suggest for female presidency. Anita Monro also looks at the performative aspects of presiding, arguing that, when women preside at the Eucharist, meanings of the sacrament are disrupted and desta-bilized in ambiguous but potentially enriching ways, ways that present the stark and messy reality of the incarnation in women's bodies.

Finally, we end with a number of pieces which, in different ways, broaden and challenge the central focus maintained in most of the book on women's eucharistic and liturgical presidency. Rachel Mann speaks as a trans-woman of 'presiding from the broken middle', challenging any fixed or simplistic notions of gender. Natalie Watson speaks as a lay woman about what it means, not to *preside* as a woman, but to *receive* as one. Gillian Hill, rather than analysing the eucharistic assembly, considers instead some of the rich feminine symbolics of baptism, and argues for a reappropriation of maternal theology in the conduct of baptismal liturgy. Nicola Slee offers an extended meditation on presiding as a woman, not in the liturgical assembly, but in the classroom, suggesting ways in which women's leadership in the educational sphere might provide insight into women's leadership in the liturgical assembly. Alastair Barrett writes as a feminist man who is also a father, and combines reflection on the ways in which children can extend our experience and thinking about presiding with some nuanced readings of New Testament narratives.

A number of the reflections offered in this book draw on the image of the Christa, or female Christ, to speak of presiding '*in persona Christae*' rather than '*in persona Christi*'. To close the book, and bringing us back full circle to the eucharistic assembly, Nicola's poem, 'At the table of Christa', attempts to image something of the inclusive, non-hierarchical, embodied nature of the ecclesial gathering which, in many different ways, underlies all of the pieces in this book.

Notes

1 See Stephen's contribution to this collection, pp. 9–18, particularly his discussion of Ruether and Russell.
2 For feminist considerations of prayer, see, for example, Procter-Smith, M., *In Her Own Rite: Constructing Feminist Liturgical Tradition*, 2nd edition (Akron, OH: Order of Saint Luke, 2000), and *Praying with Eyes Open* (Nashville, TN: Abingdon Press, 1995); Morley, J., *All Desires Known*, 3rd edition (London: SPCK, 2005); and Slee, N., *Praying Like a Woman* (London: SPCK, 2004). For feminist approaches to preaching, see Smith, C. M., *Weaving the Sermon: Preaching in a Feminist Perspective* (Louisville, KY: Westminster John Knox Press, 1989); Norén, C. M., *The Woman in the Pulpit* (Nashville, TN: Abingdon Press, 1992); and Durber, S., *Preaching Like a Woman* (London: SPCK, 2007).
3 See pp. 7–8.
4 *The Shorter Oxford English Dictionary on Historical Principles* (Oxford: Clarendon Press, 1993), p. 1661.

Presiding like a woman

NICOLA SLEE

This is how we do it:

In boardrooms, working skilfully so that all the voices can be heard.
In kitchens, standing over steaming saucepans, following recipes
    passed down by our grandmothers.
At the table, gathering the day's news from children, guests;
lighting candles, feeding titbits to the cats.
In operating theatres, administering with precision the deadly wounds that
    will heal.
In parliamentary committees and city councils,
trying to find another way of doing business,
wielding power that enables and includes.
In concert halls, at the rostrum, bringing all that unruly creativity
    into one living, breathing music.
In classrooms, warming to our subject, encouraging the slow and
    quick-witted learners, drawing out incipient wisdom.
In gardens, clearing weeds, making space for things to grow,
planning colours in their right times and seasons.
In bedrooms and at waterpools, leaning over the women about to give
    birth,
holding their sweating hands, looking into their eyes, saying
'Yes! Now! Push!'

In our own voices – elegant, educated; rough, untamed; stuttering or
    eloquent;
in all the languages that God gives.
Or sometimes without voice, silently, through gestures:
the nod of the head, lifting of an arm, sway of our bodies,
the way we move around a space.
Sometimes with permission, mostly without.
Recognized for the priests that we are or, mostly, not.
Never alone: always in the company of sisters,
brothers, children, animals who call our gifts into being
and offer their own for the making of something
that includes everyone and yet is beyond us all.

Seated, standing, lying propped up in beds or couches,
from wheelchairs and walking frames,
proud of our bodies, bent with the burdens we've carried all these years
or youthful, resilient, reaching after what's yet to come.

In shanty towns, under rickety roofs made out of tarpaulin,
and high-rise council flats in the centre of sprawling cities.
In remote rural monasteries and out of the way retreat centres;

in hospitals, prisons and shopping centres,
factories, office blocks and parliamentary corridors;
in women's refuges and hostels for the homeless,
old people's homes and kids' nurseries,
on death row and in the birthing wards:
every place where human lives jostle, mingle, struggle, despair, survive.
In the desert cave and the hermit's hidden cleft,
where land and sky and the company of saints are the congregation.

This is how we do it:
not really thinking how we do it but doing it;
not naming it for what it is but sometimes, in flashes,
recognizing the nature of what it is we do:
the calling, the gathering, the creating of community,
the naming, the celebrating and lamenting of a people's sorrows and joys,
the taking of what human hands have made,
offering it with thanksgiving and blessing,
the breaking, the fracturing of so many hopes and expectations,
to discover something unlooked for, new, beyond the brokenness;
the sharing of what has been given by others;
the discovering that, even out of little, hungers are fed,
hurts healed, wounds not taken away but transfigured –
the bearing, the manifesting of the body of God,
the carrying in our bodies of the marks of the risen One;
seeing the light reflected in each others' eyes,
seeing Her beauty mirrored in each one's softened face.

'Four in a vestment'? Feminist gestures for Christian assembly[1]

STEPHEN BURNS

James Lee Byars's installation art *Four in a Vestment* (1996)[2] is a circle of linen cloth, eight metres in diameter, with four holes for the heads of its wearers in a square around the centre. It is an intriguing image with which to begin reflection on feminist gestures for Christian assembly – clearly reminiscent of a chasuble, it is worn not by one, but four; it singles out no one, but covers several equally; it de-centres each person who wears it, requiring their equality. So far as I know, *Four in a Vestment* has never been worn by (a) presider(s) at the Eucharist – though I would like to see it. It has, however, been worn by a couple – she, Asian, he, European – during their wedding ceremony, their differences gathered up in the huge cloth. Yet it is so huge that its symbolism may also swamp the particular persons enrobed in *Four in a Vestment* – its wearers may be reduced to tiny heads bobbing about in a mass of white fabric. And apart from that, it is entirely impractical, not least in having no holes for arms to extend out of it. (If the married couple exchanged rings, it is not clear how that might have happened, at least so as to be witnessed.)

I see *Four in a Vestment* as being resonant both with feminist aspiration for Christian assembly and the felt sense of discomfort and incongruity that female presiders, and those who celebrate – or refuse to celebrate – with them, sometimes articulate as women step into roles which had long been withheld from them. *Four in a Vestment* provokes my reflections on female presidency and feminist gestures.

Praying, preaching, presiding

Susan Durber's *Preaching Like a Woman*[3] draws attention to Nicola Slee's *Praying Like a Woman*[4] in which Slee states her intent to 'sing and stutter and shout all we've been aching to say' as a feminist theologian and poet.[5] Durber asks, 'If you can pray like a woman, can you not preach like one too?'[6] With *Four in a Vestment* in mind, Slee and Durber's praying and preaching shape up my questions about presiding. What is the significance of gender in styles of 'sitting in front of'[7] a Christian assembly? If praying and preaching are two distinctive liturgical ministries that may seemingly be reflected upon and taken up in distinctively gendered ways, how do we enquire into what embracing a third liturgical ministry, presiding, 'like a woman' may involve?

I am curious as to why there has as yet been such scant reflection on the question of how women (might) engage in liturgical presidency. Is one possible reason that (mainly Protestant?) women get caught up in a wider ecclesial dynamic that accents the primacy of word/s, and so consequently underplay the alliance between word and gesture, art and environment, or the latter apart from verbal expressions? And that for other (mainly Catholic?) women, there is less expectation of women ever coming into eucharistic presidency and, not unrelated to that, a lack of precedents? The problem of a lack of precedents for women presiding is powerfully apparent in Susan White's *A History of Women in Christian Worship*.[8] Its very chapter headings – such as 'Finding Women in the History of Christian Worship' with its subheadings like 'The View From a Distance' and 'The Persistent Elusiveness of Women' – indicate the enormity of the challenge White undertakes. And the inside back flap is a signal indicator of the acute lack of examples of women in vocal and focal leadership in liturgy: it mentions

> the many roles women played in Christian worship, including the ways in which they prepared their households for worship; the cloth they donated to their churches for particular uses; the requests noted in their wills; the records of their living and dying set down in journals, hymns, prayers and plaques; their participation in various liturgical arts and crafts; their care of the bodies of the living and dead; their leadership in temperance movements and in convents, in tending wayside shrines, and providing meeting space, spiritual leadership, and hospitality.

But, of course, *presiding* in liturgy is not on the list. For obvious reasons, neither does the index include any reference to 'presiding'. Certainly, until very recently at least, the lack of instances of women presiding has not simply been a 'Catholic problem'.

In my contemplation which follows, I first explore insights from the literature of feminist theology broadly about worship. After that, I draw in some key points from the literature of liturgical renewal.

Returning to some feminist forebears

Rosemary Radford Ruether's *Women-Church* is of major significance for feminist construction of liturgical tradition. It speaks of the need for new texts, it proposes new metaphors for worshipping the divine, and it depicts feminist use of space (the 'celebration center', the 'conversation circle', etc.). It includes a wide range of innovative rituals around what have traditionally been recognized as sacramental moments as well as ones that syncretize, challenge or in some other way enlarge the tradition – a ritual of divorce, covenant celebration for a lesbian couple, croning, menstrual and new moon liturgies, among others. Yet it includes very little constructive discussion of what kinds of presidential *style* are appropriate to feminist Christian assembly.

There are reasons for this: clearly, Ruether thinks what is needed is 'an understanding of ministry as originating from the community and continually based in it'[9] instead of 'hierarchical clericalism', which she sees as being built upon patriarchalism, and which must therefore be dismantled.[10] She attacks the view that 'only the male can represent Christ[, that t]here must be a physical resemblance between the priest and Christ', noting that this is not understood to mean 'that the priest should look Jewish. It means that the priest should have balls, male genitalia, should stand erect as the monument of phallic power.'[11] She is particularly disparaging about the idea that presiding at the Eucharist might involve any art: she states her view that 'Since the actual sacramental actions of the Eucharist are rather simple, and anyone could learn to do them in an hour, this is obviously not a matter of special skills or expertise.'[12] Elsewhere, she reiterates this view:

> Presiding at the liturgical gathering, which involves blessing the Eucharistic symbols and administering them to others, requires the fewest special talents. This came home to me dramatically a few years ago when I had been asked to preach at Old Cambridge Baptist Church. The pastor of the community, a woman, asked me to share in blessing the Eucharist and administering the cup to the community. She did not ask me if I knew how to do this; she simply assumed that I could do it without instruction.[13]

However, I want to lift up the view that it is not just possible, but prudent, to hold another view about presiding; indeed, one which involves patient reflection and the conscious nurturing of a skills base.

As I hope is obvious, this is by no means to disregard Ruether. I am especially interested in her conviction that ministry is 'the community symboliz[ing] its common life',[14] and that it is crucial, from a feminist standpoint, to 'reappropriat[e] to the people what has been falsely expropriated from us'.[15] Her own outworking of this reappropriation involves her suggestion to rotate the role of blessing, breaking and giving bread to others – what she calls 'communalizing these roles'.[16] My point is that *however* the roles are understood, the details of how they are enacted constitute and communicate an active and visual theology that is so powerful that it cannot be assumed that they can be done without instruction or sustained scrutiny. So my appeal is for thought about how presiding – *including communalized presiding* – might be embodied in a consciously gendered way, one which celebrates what women may bring to contest so much of what Ruether dislikes.

Rosemary Radford Ruether is not the only feminist to reflect on worship and in doing so to suggest sometimes luminous ideas and ideals. Perhaps as influential as *Women-Church* is Letty Russell's *Church in the Round*,[17] with its key image of a round table. Russell's focal notion implies at least a certain decentring of one particular person – the presider. So it is perhaps not so surprising that Russell does not reflect on how one person presiding might be reimagined. What is strange is that she does not reflect on how its communization might be enacted. Russell, like Ruether, is vague about how her ideals – in her case, the round table – might be *manifest in liturgical practices* around the table. My appeal is for attention to be given to practices – use of gestures, arrangement of seating, adoption of posture, donning of vesture, engagement with environment and art, use of the hands – and more – and how these might cohere with, amplify and confirm the ideals of round table talk. Otherwise, I fear, these things may well subvert it, thereby making it mute.

Still, Letty Russell argues in ways that begin to explain why she may have chosen not to discuss particular aspects of presiding style. It is evident that she regards traditional restrictions about who may officiate at sacraments as a lamentable means of 'fenc[ing] the table'.[18] At several points, she reiterates her conviction that ordination is problematic: it has had 'disastrous effects on producing a class-division between "upper-class" clergy and "lower-class" laity'.[19] Moreover,

> No matter how much we all emphasize that there is only one ministry in Jesus Christ and that we all share in this ministry, the clerical structures continue to reinforce structures of hierarchy and domination, whether or not the particular clergyperson is female.[20]

Perhaps, then, she broadly coheres with Ruether's view that ministry must be communalized, or 'organized contextually'?[21] It seems so from her vignette about a particular funeral mass, which conveys that whatever she understands by organization does not exclude spontaneity:[22] at the mass, members of the congregation both 'began to stand up and give homilies and testimonies', and also joined in the 'consecration and commemoration'[23] – that is, presumably, that they voiced the Eucharistic Prayer. (Here is a subversive tactic to complement the perhaps better-known feminist turns to 'bestow ourselves to silence', to borrow a chapter heading from Marjorie Procter-Smith.[24])

In their different and related ways, Ruether and Russell raise the question of whether 'presidency' in the sense of being held by one particular person, is a feminist approach at all. This challenge should not be underestimated. Letty Russell does, however, discuss some differences she perceives between patriarchal and feminist styles of leadership, which are one aspect of what I am suggesting needs to be thought about. Russell talks about postures, contrasting a patriarchal exercise of authority as 'standing above' and a feminist style of 'standing with' others.[25] The latter she sees as expressing partnership, shared authority and as depicted in circular, as opposed to hierarchical, imagery – not least the round table itself. Here are insights that surely need to be related not only to the physical bearing of the presider(s), and others, but to issues about their distance from one another, and the direction they may or may not face. Russell also cites Sam Keen's comment that 'the symbol of power is the chair',[26] so that 'we need at least for the moment to get rid of chairs at the table, so there is no limited seating'.[27]

Embodying feminist convictions

Here are numerous insights about space and symbolism that need to be expanded in consideration of what it might mean to preside like a woman, even in the company of other (women?) presiders. One person who pushes further than either Ruether or Russell into judgement of actual liturgical practices in feminist liturgy is Janet Walton. Her comments about feminist Christian assembly are not specifically about presidency, but they do most certainly apply to it. She affirms 'horizontal gestures' suggesting 'equality and interdependence', with out-flowing implications for style, space and ceremonial:[28] 'Generally we do not look up to find God.' Furthermore, she asserts, 'we pray with our eyes open and without bowing our heads.' Bowing gestures the body into a 'non-reciprocal action' that reinforces male domination, just as kneeling may yield to misplaced power. And, she remarks sagely, 'closing one's eyes is dangerous in an unjust society'. In short, Walton's view is that 'feminist liturgies intend to provide occasions to practise resistance and expressions of shared power'.

Consider, then, the following conviction, from no less of an authority on feminist liturgy than Gail Ramshaw:

> Much of what the 20th-century liturgical movement advocates corresponds to feminist concerns. Both movements value many of the same goals: circular rather than rectangular space; participatory rituals rather than passive attention to leaders; a re-evaluation of the role of the clergy; multiplicity of voices in the assembly . . . In fact it can be argued, not that feminists have been influenced by the liturgical renewal movement, but the opposite: that the ecumenical liturgical renewal movement is yet another demonstration of the rise of feminist consciousness.[29]

My hope is that Ramshaw's mapping together of feminist theology and liturgical renewal might point to a number of further resources to help us consider how presiders might gesture themselves before God – and the assembly – in a way which embodies and amplifies feminist perspectives.

Strong, loving and wise

I am interested in feminist presiding, with or without official sanction, communalized or otherwise, and in light of my citation from Ramshaw, I want to juxtapose my explorations of feminist theology of worship with literature on liturgical renewal and consider how they might read together with an eye to 'presiding like a woman'.

Robert Hovda's presider's manual *Strong, Loving and Wise* challenges long-standing notions of presiders acting in a 'depersonalized'[30] manner – oftentimes a consequence of perceiving themselves to be acting *in persona Christi*. Hovda counters thus:

> The presider's function, ordinarily a clergy function, has become depersonalized over the course of many centuries. Persons could perform them 'with their eyes closed,' so to speak. It is clear in these early stages of basic ecclesial reform and renewal that a new situation requires a radical break with habits and customs of long (and 'good') standing. A whole new job description is involved.[31]

As Hovda expounds it, what is required by the renewal of worship involves presiders emphatically jettisoning any temptation towards presenting a 'sacred alias' in sacramental celebration (likewise a 'pulpit tone'[32]). The positive qualities to which he calls attention, again and again, are the personal, yet elusive, manifestation of 'spirit',[33] 'feeling',[34] 'soul',[35] 'consciousness', 'awareness',[36] of which he speaks in different and related ways. The manifestation of such spirit is a crucial matter of style: 'with that spirit, techniques are indispensable and highly useful. Without that spirit techniques are dangerous.'[37]

For Hovda, the presider is one who yields focus, and prompts, and guides, not least in communalized planning, which he stresses. About as close as he comes to an actual definition of presiding is this: 'the loving tendering of one person while one endeavours to minimize peculiarities and idiosyncrasies';[38] but minimizing quirks by no means entails erasure, but rather fully, consciously and actively sensate, embodied, and synaesthetic experience. In Hovda's vision, the presider is adept at listening;[39] and as important for Hovda as listening is looking: 'we need the life and encouragement of other people's eyes and expressions', 'to look in their faces, that we may revive one another'.[40] Such emphases mean that

> The presider in liturgy has a very special need to become a body person, at home in the flesh, moving gracefully and expressively, gesturing spontaneously, saying something to people by style in walking as well as in talking, communicating by the rhythm and articulation of the whole person, knowing how to dress up and wear clothing, etc. You can call it 'soul,' as many do. Whatever you call it, our liturgical experience is in desperate need of it.[41]

I think that there is much here to attract, engage and amplify feminist sensibilities. What can engage in his pressing attention to the centrality of the 'feeling' of presiding? And turning Hovda's words, another way to ask the question of how to preside like a woman might be: how does a woman preside as a body person, at home in her flesh?

I also want to celebrate how Siobhán Garrigan, as a woman clearly sympathetic to feminist sensibilities, elaborates on Hovda's themes.[42] In her essay on 'the spirituality of the presider', she highlights the need for presiders to become adept at 'paradoxical capabilities: passion and stamina, patience and quick-wittedness, vulnerability and a thick skin'.[43] But she especially focuses on the presider's *voice*: 'tone, words, cadence, timing, timbre, your sounds, your voice's pauses and silences',[44] each of which contributes to the way that presiders 'proclaim, invite, dedicate, pray, teach, sing, lead, chant, dream, lament, challenge, cry'.[45] It is not at all that she disparages senses other than sound, and as if testing her own convictions, she names her own sense of the importance in worship of the likes of sign-language, choreography of gesture, eye-contact, pouring, censing, and circle-dancing.[46] Her point then becomes one about how presiders pour 'presence' into one or more of these sensate, embodied experiences, and she engages in some fascinating semantics that deepen the usual association of presiding and 'sitting in front of' others:

> 'Preside' is based on the root *sed* which means to put down. The root evolved in three main ways, marking the putting down of: the buttocks (stopping, sitting, dwelling); the feet (walking, going); or the fists or weapons (yielding).[47]

Our word 'presiding', she suggests, 'is mostly about the buttocks': 'From its Sanskrit meaning of *sitting beside* through its Greek for *seat* (and thus our word *cathedral*) and *sitting together* (Sanhedrin) and a possible Latin overtone of sitting down to eat together (*sitos*: meal), it comes to us laden with associations of abiding a while and dwelling together'.[48] She comes, then, to emphasize sitting, with its resonances of 'abiding', to correct an imbalanced understanding of presiding as primarily 'standing', with its resonances of activity. The dimension of 'abiding' which she wants to recover has an obvious continuity with Letty Russell's prescriptions for feminist Christian leadership, cited earlier. And in her own way like Ruether and Russell, Garrigan also wants to communalize presiding, so she speaks of a 'presidership'[49] that includes: greeters, musicians, lectors, 'the ragtaggle group of us who process the gifts',[50] as well as the clergy voicing the Eucharistic Prayer. Even a flower arrangement might exercise presidership, in the sense that it 'exercises a certain control on the gathering', being for Garrigan 'the main vehicle of the service',[51] at least on occasion. Garrigan suggests that these reflections are 'an extension' of Hovda's emphasis on the people as the presider's focus,[52] of the presider's yielding. According to Garrigan, presiding/presidership is emphatically an 'interactive', 'integrated witness', a 'mutual relational' reality.[53] What, I wonder, do these reflections evoke from women who are presiders – either in the stricter sense, or Garrigan's more expansive perspective?

15

In persona Christae!

I want to draw to a close by pressing for special consideration of two specific liturgical practices that are widely considered as close to the heart of presiding, and widely allied in the tradition to the presumption to preside *in persona Christi*. Both concern ways in which actions and the mediation of the senses relate to choices by the one praying the Eucharistic Prayer – or part of it, the 'institution narrative'. The first is that cluster of gestures sometimes known as the 'manual acts' (taking, blessing, breaking, giving) – itself a construct based on the 'Last Supper' narratives that has been mapped onto the eucharistic rite in different ways in different traditions, at different times. My question in relation to such manual acts focuses on the extent to which a feminist presider might want – or not – to associate her/himself with Jesus, as certain 'performances' of manual acts inevitably do, as do other sensate dimensions of celebration such as recitation of the supposed words of Jesus slowly (think: Darth Vader), which is commonplace in some traditions. Such actions, and such a tone of voice, might, in my view, unhelpfully single out just one celebrant as ally of Jesus, whereas the strain of feminist sensibility in the readings I have cited is perhaps more to accentuate, in one way or another, the *assembly* as Christic community. A counterpoint to this, however, is perhaps that it might well be considered crucial that women do embrace a kind of 'mimicry' of Jesus in order to defy a longstanding tradition that says that they may not do so! Of course, the incompatibility of these perspectives is central to my question: so just how is the incompatibility to be negotiated by women presiders in the gestures they choose, the tone they adopt? Whatever, perhaps presiding like a woman may well involve not so much of *in persona Christi*, and more, if I may, of *in persona Christae*, my reference here being to that female Christ-figure who has been to some such a shocking subversion of liturgical art. The cross-reference to Christa here is both an invitation to feminist presiders, and *a warning*: that presiding like a woman – however particular stances and tones are chosen – might seem unconventional, perhaps shocking, and might well, and perhaps ought to, disturb assumed norms. Whatever might be made of the *Four in a Vestment*, I hope to have suggested that shaking up assumptions about practices of presiding such as standing, sitting, eye-contact, tone of voice, silence, distance, the gestures of the hands, head and body, and perhaps their decoration, needs to take place. All of this is in addition to texts, and in my view, none of it can simply be 'adopted as unisex'.[54]

Notes

1 Portions of this chapter originally appeared as Burns, S., 'Presiding Like a Woman: Feminist Gestures for Christian Assembly', *Feminist Theology* 18 (2009), pp. 29–49.

2 For images and commentary, see Crumlin, R. (ed.), *Beyond Belief: Modern Art and the Religious Imagination* (Melbourne: National Gallery of Victoria, 1998), pp. 170–1.

3 Durber, S., *Preaching Like a Woman* (London: SPCK, 2007).

4 Slee, N., *Praying Like a Woman* (London: SPCK, 2004).

5 Slee, *Praying*, p. 3; Durber, *Preaching*, p. 12.

6 Durber, *Preaching*, p. 12.

7 Burns, S., *Liturgy*, SCM Studyguide (London: SCM Press, 2006), pp. 169–75.

8 White, S. J., *A History of Women in Christian Worship* (London: SPCK, 2003).

9 Ruether, R. R. *Women-Church: Theology and Practice* (San Francisco, CA: HarperCollins, 1985), p. 75.

10 Ruether, *Women-Church*, p. 89.

11 Ruether, *Women-Church*, p. 70.

12 Ruether, *Women-Church*, p. 78.

13 Ruether, *Women-Church*, p. 90.

14 Ruether, *Women-Church*, pp. 86, 87.

15 Ruether, *Women-Church*, p. 87.

16 Ruether, *Women-Church*, p. 91.

17 Russell, L., *Church in the Round: Feminist Interpretation of the Church* (Louisville, KY: Westminster John Knox Press, 1993).

18 Russell, *Church in the Round*, p. 142.

19 Russell, *Church in the Round*, p. 50.

20 Russell, *Church in the Round*, p. 51.

21 Russell, *Church in the Round*, p. 51, here employing for herself a phrase coined by Lynn Rhodes.

22 Russell, *Church in the Round*, p. 144.

23 Russell, *Church in the Round*, p. 144.

24 Procter-Smith, M., *Praying With Our Eyes Open: Engendering Feminist Liturgical Prayer* (Nashville, TN: Abingdon Press, 1995), pp. 41–54.

25 Russell, *Church in the Round*, pp. 56–7.

26 Russell, *Church in the Round*, p. 149.

27 Russell, *Church in the Round*, p. 67.

28 Walton, J., *Feminist Liturgy: A Matter of Justice* (Collegeville, MN: Liturgical Press, 2000), pp. 37–8.

29 Ramshaw, G., 'Christian Worship from a Feminist Perspective', in Best, T. F. and Heller, D. (eds), *Worship Today: Understanding, Practice, Ecumenical Implications* (Geneva: WCC Publications, 2004), pp. 208–13, at p. 212.

30 Hovda, R., *Strong, Loving and Wise: Presiding in Liturgy* (Collegeville, MN: Liturgical Press, 1976); the critique starts on p. 1, and runs on.

31 Hovda, *Strong, Loving*, p. 1.

32 Hovda, *Strong, Loving*, pp. 56–7.

33 Hovda, *Strong, Loving*, p. 2.

34 Hovda, *Strong, Loving*, p. 3.

35 Hovda, *Strong, Loving*, p. 31.

36 Hovda, *Strong, Loving*, p. 3.

37 Hovda, *Strong, Loving*, p. 3.

38 Hovda, *Strong, Loving*, p. 43.

39 Hovda, *Strong, Loving*, p. 24.
40 Hovda, *Strong, Loving*, p. 48. Elsewhere, we need mutual 'interested, compassionate, encouraging looks ...' (p. 76).
41 Hovda, *Strong, Loving*, p. 31.
42 Garrigan, S., 'The Spirituality of Presiding', *Liturgy* 22 (2007), pp. 3–8.
43 Garrigan, 'Spirituality', p. 3.
44 Garrigan, 'Spirituality', p. 4.
45 Garrigan, 'Spirituality', p. 4.
46 Garrigan, 'Spirituality', p. 5.
47 Garrigan, 'Spirituality', p. 5.
48 Garrigan, 'Spirituality', p. 5.
49 Garrigan, 'Spirituality', p. 6.
50 Garrigan, 'Spirituality', p. 6.
51 Garrigan, 'Spirituality', p. 6.
52 Garrigan, 'Spirituality', p. 6.
53 Garrigan, 'Spirituality', p. 7.
54 Ramshaw, 'Feminist Perspective', p. 209.

My fervent, feminist heart

DOROTHY McRAE-McMAHON

Stirrings in the womb-space of life

When I contemplated writing this essay, I began by thinking that maybe I had little to say, other than the reality that to preside at the Eucharist is virtually central to my life and that maybe it is no different to the presiding of men. Then I realized that, underlying my presiding is actually a story which engages with many moments of deepening and clarifying both my life and my understandings of the moment when I may preside.

I began my life as a Christian feminist in 1968, when I was pregnant with my last child. I remember feeling that within the womb-space of my life many ideas and possibilities were stirring and that I would need to carry them faithfully and bring them to birth through a pathway filled with both pain and labour. Under the leadership of Dottie Pope, an American woman who was shocked by the lack of feminist awareness among Australian women, twelve of us decided to invite women from our churches to gather and listen to us reflecting on Easter. We were amazed when hundreds of women packed our venue and delighted to find that we did have something to say about the journey of Easter – both that of Jesus Christ and our own journey.

I discovered that I had a voice and over the next decade, during the period when I was on the staff of the New South Wales Ecumenical Council working in the area of international aid, I found myself being invited over and over again to preach around the state. I enjoyed doing that and felt that maybe I was contributing something to the thought that one day women might be able to be ordained – given that our capacity to be lay preachers was being recognized.

Journey to ordination: returning to the people what is rightfully theirs

The years passed and our fervour for the ordination of women and a greater participation in the leadership of the churches in general was gaining strength. As women, including myself, participated in the negotiations which led to the formation of the Uniting Church in Australia we could see that we might well achieve ordination for women in its charter. This new church was the uniting of the Congregational, Methodist and Presbyterian Churches in our country. The Congregational Church had been ordaining women since early in the twentieth century, but only a very few women had taken up that opportunity and the other two churches were moving towards ordination for women but had not at that stage affirmed it. Even though I was one of the women pushing for its incorporation into the plans for the Uniting Church, I still did not see that I was fighting for myself.

In 1975, I was appointed as one of the seven delegates from the Methodist Church of Australasia to the World Council of Churches Assembly in Nairobi. I had several roles in the Assembly, including being a speaker to a plenary session on 'Women in a changing world'. I enjoyed the worship and the debates and all the privileges in meeting with churches from around the world. Then we came to the great Eucharist which, at this Assembly, was placed in the hands of the African Churches. We were sitting in the front row of the Assembly as countries were seated in alphabetical order. I watched while the preparations were made for the Eucharist. Then, one by one, the leadership for the liturgy processed up onto the stage which was being used as the sanctuary. There was not one woman – not a reader, not a server, nothing.

It is hard to describe what happened to me as I saw that unfold before me. It wasn't anger or indignation coming from my fervent feminist heart. It was a deep grief and pain as I saw the Eucharist being incomplete in some profound way. Tears ran down my face and I found myself quietly sobbing through the whole service. When the elements were offered to me, I received them and, in the depths of my soul, I knew that I must be part of the completing of the Eucharist. The Great Thanksgiving needed the wholeness of humanity in both men and women, just as God was our Loving Parent – Mother and Father, Christ represented all people and the Spirit of Wisdom could be imaged as female as well as male.

When I returned home, I wondered aloud among my Christian feminist friends whether this experience was a call to the ordained ministry. In spite of our having been working for the equality of women and men in the church, most of them firmly told me that the ordained ministry was an institution of male hierarchy and not for feminists. My particular friends hadn't been strong on the struggle for ordaining women. I didn't argue – just quietly put my thoughts aside and decided that possibly I should do some theological training anyway. I told myself that it would be useful for my work.

A few months went past and the then principal of our theological college, Gordon Dicker, was invited to preach at our local church. The reading he chose was the story of Zacchaeus climbing the tree to see Jesus (Luke 19.1–10). I hadn't, at that moment, the faintest idea why that passage had anything to do with my ordination. All I knew was that when I heard it, I had another sense that I needed to prepare myself. As I shook his hand at the door of the church, I asked Gordon whether it was possible to study part-time at the college. I knew that, with my family and work responsibilities, I couldn't do full-time study. He said firmly that there was no provision for part-time study. I set my thoughts aside again.

Then I met the new principal of the college, Graeme Ferguson, when we were sitting on some church council together and drawing near to the inauguration of the Uniting Church in Australia. I casually asked him whether it would be possible to study theology part-time. He said that of course I could do that, and I began my formal journey towards presiding at the Eucharist. While there had not been a strong eucharistic focus in Methodism, which was my church at that time, I still knew that there was something about it that was very critical to my life and faith.

I juggled family, work and study for the next six years. About four years into that period, two critical things happened. A lecturer from the USA came to our college to give a series of studies on ordination and he was really questioning whether it was appropriate and good for the Church. I listened with respect and felt anxieties stirring within me. I began to try to discuss with my lecturers, many of whom were also my friends and colleagues on church committees, whether they believed that ordination was a good thing. I was really searching my own heart, but many of them responded as though I was attacking them and I found it hard to go deeper into any further reflection on the issue.

Then a couple of truly brave women friends, who I am thankful to say are still that, sat me down and faced me with the fact that, in speaking, standing up in all sorts of courts and councils of the church and society to claim the ground for women, I was actually often feeding my own ego now. With what I can only describe was an agony of heart, I decided to finish my study but not proceed to ordination. I believed that ordination would simply feed my power and that I would be dangerous to myself and others in having that happen. I informed the college principal, who was dumbfounded, I told my feminist friends, who cheered, and my family, who said that I must make my own decisions. I felt brave and determined as I moved on in my life.

I then placed myself under the wonderful guidance of Betty Kennedy, a Catholic Sister of Mercy, for spiritual direction. She immediately picked up the issues of my struggle with power and ego and took me down into a painful and honest pathway towards the truth. I made many decisions not to respond to invitations to leadership positions in both church and political life. With each of these decisions came an extraordinary lightness of being. My soul soared in freedom and peace and I knew that I was on the right track. The one decision which did not give me that sense was my determination not to proceed to ordination. I decided that it was probably because that was the ultimate temptation for me.

In my final year of study, I chose the history of liturgy as one of my subjects and became fascinated with the grand traditions of the Church and its evolving of eucharistic life. In my relatively 'low church' Protestant environment, I found myself committed to at least holding to the main elements of liturgy, including the assurance of pardon which was not commonly used at that stage in Protestant liturgy. I began to imagine using seasonal colours rather than the Uniting Church blue scarf over an alb and reflecting that in cloths on the communion table as though I could at least imagine presiding at the Eucharist.

Then one day, with a feeling of desolation, I attended the lunchtime Eucharist of an Anglican church in the centre of Sydney. I sat there sadly as the priest took us through the liturgy, then went forward to the communion rail to receive the elements. The priest put the chalice in my hands and as I looked at it, with breathless wonder, I could see a light around it. The priest took the chalice from me and the light stayed in my cupped hands. I heard an inner voice which said to me, 'I now place the cup into your hands, Dorothy.' I knelt there for the blessing and returned to my seat as though in a dream.

The story of Zacchaeus came back into my head and I, at last, realized its significance for me. When Zacchaeus met Jesus and sat at table with him, Jesus asked him to return to the people what was rightfully theirs. I had now returned, as best I could, the power which I had taken to myself which belonged to others. It didn't mean I would never fail in that area again. On the contrary, the area of power and ego would always be an area of temptation for me. However, it was now safe enough for me to proceed to ordination and maybe try to model a presiding which would give to the people what is rightfully theirs – the real presence of the Christ.

If I share this part of the story, it is to make the point that I do not believe that presiding at the Eucharist should ever be about personal power. I distinguish power from authority and will discuss that later.

Ordination and after

The day of my ordination approached after I had received my call to take up ministry with the Pitt Street parish in the centre of Sydney. My younger brother John was to be ordained in Melbourne in the same week. Interestingly, when he told our mother and Methodist minister father of his intentions, our mother said that, from his birth, she had always felt he was destined to be a minister. When I told my parents of my decision to move to ordination, my dear mother wrote, 'But what about your children?' Those were the days!

The time for my ordination arrived. I had embroidered my own stole with an ecumenical World Council of Churches symbol on it and a symbolic shape which represented a God who was like a womb-space for all creation, rather than buying one with a Uniting Church logo. I wanted my presiding to be joined with the universal Church and all its rich tradition of the Eucharist.

Betty Kennedy read the lesson and, quite apart from celebrating her wise guidance of me, I wanted her to take part because she linked me with a more Catholic understanding of the Eucharist. My father was there as one who would be among those laying hands on my head at the moment of ordination. One of my theological teachers gave me the 'charge'. I was moved to find that he charged me to 'be a priest' in a church which never called its ministers priests. When I knelt to receive the sacred moment and the hands of the presiding clergy were placed on my head, I experienced a strange mixture of sensations. At first the weight of their hands felt as though the weight of the world was resting on my head and then, as I was ordained and blessed, that somehow translated itself into a fullness and wholeness which I had never before experienced.

I rose to move into presiding at the Eucharist. As the moment approached when I would take, bless and then break the bread, I suddenly entered this dark place of fear. Would my woman's hands destroy the Eucharist for the people? I had heard that for so long – not put in quite those words, but the message conveyed through all manner of opposition to the ordination of women. In faith, I took a deep breath and held out my hands for the bread. As soon as I took it, a great peace was given to me and a sure knowledge that my hands would only ever be the vehicle for the real presence of Christ. The life of Christ was independent of me and I was simply the one who had been called to faithfully offer it to the people. My spirit sang with joy and hope.

At that time, I was in a parish which customarily served the Eucharist with little glasses and tiny squares of bread but I had asked that we use a common cup and break a loaf of bread. The chalice was already for me the symbol of our common humanness and the corporate gift of the life of Christ among us. The bread needed to be torn apart as a symbol of Christ's willingness to experience an ultimate torn apartness as he entered our human journey with all its struggles and realities. I still find it hard to find that imagery in either individual glasses and wafers or little squares of pre-cut bread.

Priestly power and priestly authority

As I entered my ministry to the city of Sydney, I found myself wrestling with the difference between priestly power and priestly authority, both in the Eucharist and in parish ministry. I decided that the appropriate power is that which is delivered within an authority to offer eucharistic gifts to the people for their healing, forgiveness and peace and for the expanding of just and loving community in the world. I saw it as my sacred calling never to leave them without the Word.

I believed that inappropriate power takes power from the people and adds ego to one's own life. It can also sometimes be an avoiding of the costly and brave moments in ministry to which we are called when the clergyperson needs to say 'Enough' to people within a parish who are dominating and misleading the people – when the Word becomes distorted by tyrannies carried out by powerful families and cultures which overwhelm faithful life.

As I preside, I always use what I believe is a firm voice of authority when I announce that 'Our sins are forgiven!' I know all too well, from my experience in ministry over the years, that many, many people find it hard to believe that they are forgiven, including sometimes myself! When I come to the words of the institution narrative, I always emphasize the word 'betrayed' when I say 'On the night when he was betrayed . . .' because I have so often heard those who preside say that word so very casually as though it means little. We will never know who is waiting to hear that Jesus deeply experienced betrayal and yet still exercises hospitality to us all and walks on towards the cross. The table of Jesus Christ is truly open to all who come in hope, humanness and trembling faith. My own receiving of the bread and wine always reminds me of that truth.

I often wonder why those who preside do not learn words of the institution narrative off by heart. We say them week after week, year after year. For me it makes a profound difference to see the presiding person lift the chalice and the bread high towards the people and say the words looking them in the face. The words are addressed to the people and it is in the Eucharist that they are said with engagement, hospitality and authority. The great Prayer of Thanksgiving is prayed, in my view, with a sort of reflective dwelling on the privilege of presiding as your hands lie over the elements. I pray that prayer each time as a great act of faith for everyone there – that they will know the real presence of the life of Christ that day. I could not do it while reading the words as it never seems focused enough to me.

I love to set the table with the same care with which I would prepare the table for guests at home. The cloth must be clean and straight and everything arranged on it with grace and as much artistic merit as I can bring and a sense of genuine celebration to come. I can't bear cloths with visible marks of wax and dirt – as though they lie on any old table. I don't like crosses or chalices that are not polished and carefully carried and placed. This is, for me, the sacred table of Christ's hospitality to all people as well as that which bears divine life. Only the best will do to carry all that to the people and honour the Christ who graces us with a holy presence.

The mystery of the Eucharist

In all my years of presiding at the Eucharist, I have never ceased to be moved and surprised by the miracles of grace and the gratitude of all sorts of people as they are gathered into the community of faith around the holy table. The mystery of the Eucharist is still profound for me, alongside my small and privileged part in bringing it to those who wait in longing.

When I ministered with the people at Pitt Street in Sydney, we rebuilt the tiny congregation together into a strong community of faith and, at the centre was our eucharistic life. During the years when we were taking our stand against racism, homophobia and anti-Semitism and were being regularly attacked by a neo-Nazi group in ways which were frightening and sometimes life-threatening, we looked at each other as we formed a great circle of love around the church and passed the bread to each other and held it while we waited for the wine. We knew that the mystery of a Christ who walked towards the destructive powers of his day was with us and our spirits lifted in courage and determination. The Eucharist was for us a moment when we were sure that all that we were and could be was gathered together in Christ. As I presided, I knew that in my hands lay the infinite and eternal gift for the people of God.

Now, in my retirement, I work in one of the toughest areas of Australia with many people who are disadvantaged, abused or rejected – many of them wounded by attitudes which they have found within the Church – and who have often been isolated in the community. As we form a circle around the holy table we know that we are one in Christ Jesus and that none of us is less worthy or more worthy of receiving the body and blood of Christ. As people are invited to be servers, so often I see the rapt look of wonder at being trusted to give to others the elements of Christ's life.

I come from a tradition in the Protestant churches which often regarded the Eucharist as primarily a memorial meal – a re-enacting of the Last Supper which would remind us of Christ's promises to be with us. My experiences in the Ecumenical Movement, especially in the Orthodox 'feast of heaven' (the liturgy) and the Catholic and Anglo-Catholic masses, have influenced me in the way I have now long viewed the Eucharist.

Do I really preside like a woman? I don't know. I feel as though this journey has taken me through many processes and reflections which would not have happened to most men. People have come to me on numbers of occasions and asked if I would bring them the Eucharist because they think a woman may be kinder to them – people who have been wounded by the judgements of the Church. Some have commented that I seem to have a special joy as I preside, and that may well arise from the fact that I originally thought that I might never be allowed to do so; and it is also possibly related to the fairly struggling pathway towards my ordination.

My woman's heart and soul has never been loath to believe that there are more things in life and faith than we can ever see. I suspect that this was encouraged in us more than in the enculturation of most men in Anglo societies. My Celtic forebears knew better.

I never have a moment of doubt that, when I preside at the Eucharist, I am inviting all present to believe that the real presence of Christ is in our midst and that it is offered to all who will come in faith. The fact that I may lead them towards that reality is a privilege and responsibility beyond naming. Thanks be to God!

Colouring outside the lines

JUNE BOYCE-TILLMAN

The context

I was brought up in rural Anglicanism with its emphasis on a middle way – not too High (which was papist) and not too Low (which was chapel) – at St Winfrid's, Testwood, Hampshire. I always went to adult worship and longed to be in the processions that characterized it but not even the choir was open to me – even though I sang better than the boys who were in it. I loved the Passion play organized by Miss Biffin, the lady church worker, where there seemed to be a great number of parts for women around the entombment and resurrection of Christ. They were older women and they moved beautifully to Samuel Barber's music, dressed in pastel colours. It left an unforgettable impression on a young child.

The journey

In 1986 in Tooting I became involved in interfaith dialogue, organizing an act of sharing in our church during an interregnum. It brought me into closer contact with other faiths and their elaborate rituals than ever before. It has been an extraordinarily rewarding journey that still continues. As I did it, however, I became aware that the dilemma of women's authority characterized most faiths. I think I wondered as I started the journey through different belief systems and worship styles if I would change my faith allegiance, but I found similar problems for women within them all (it was only much later that I discovered the Wiccan tradition). I decided to continue my own faith journey on the playing field with which I was familiar, Christianity.

Alongside this exploration I encountered liturgy groups, in particular Catholic Women's Network and the group that met at St Mark's, Wimbledon. These opened up a whole new world for me – of feminist theology and inclusive language and the capacity to create liturgy rather than use ready-made services. I wrote liturgies for special occasions such as the healing of the wounds of abuse and the consequences of abortion. The process of creating relevant contemporary liturgy had already started for me when I worshipped with Methodists in Notting Hill in the 1960s and 70s when there was a great deal of worship experimentation as a response to the recent race riots.

The priesthood

During this time I was a member of the Movement for the Ordination of Women (MOW) but my own vocation was quite well hidden under the stress of a failing marriage and two growing children. I was also involved in Women in Theology, which was beginning to publish liturgical material by women including (in co-operation with Stainer and Bell) *Reflecting Praise*,[1] concentrating on women's contribution to hymnody. It was around this time that I started writing hymns myself, initially versifying Celtic hymns so that they could be sung to metrical tunes. It was for a service organized for the Southwark Ordination Course by Nicola Slee in Southwark Cathedral that I wrote the hymn that has become closely associated with MOW (but it has also been used for a wide variety of situations including weddings and funerals and a service for World AIDS Day in Westminster Abbey). It is set to the traditional Irish tune often called *Danny Boy*.

1. We shall go out with hope of resurrection.
   We shall go out, from strength to strength go on.
   We shall go out and tell our stories boldly,
   Tales of a love that will not let us go.
   We'll sing our songs of wrongs that can be righted.
   We'll dream our dreams of hurts that can be healed.
   We'll weave a cloth of all the world united
   Within the vision of a Christ who sets us free.

2. We'll give a voice to those who have not spoken.
   We'll find the words for those whose lips are sealed.
   We'll make the tunes for those who sing no longer,
   Vibrating love alive in every heart.
   We'll share our joy with those who are still weeping.
   Chant hymns of strength for hearts that break in grief.
   We'll leap and dance the resurrection story
   Including all within the circles of our love.[2]

When I was going through the elaborate process of becoming a priest, I knew that for some in my congregation I could never be the traditional black-robed man – the image of the priest with which they were brought up. But gradually I feel I have acquired a new and maybe different authority with these older members of my congregation. I work and struggle for women's authority and have done so for a long time. I long for a woman bishop to bless me, and wrote this 'hymn for women bishops' for WATCH (Women and the Church)[3] at the time of the 2008 Lambeth Conference:

1. Tides come flowing claiming freedom
   Spreading over sand and rock;
   So is truth engulfing falsehood

In a flood that will not stop.
Christ, our Justice, presses onward,
Guiding like a shining sun,
Moving forward, glowing strongly,
Showing how God's will is done.

2. Jesus' words ring clear through history
Calling 'Mary, I am here.
Be the voice of my disciples;
Make my message very clear.
I have sanctioned women's witness,
Valued their authority,
Made them chief of my apostles,
Broken chains and set them free.'

3. Listen hard, my Christian brother,
Can you hear your sister's sighs?
How she longs to be your pastor
As a woman who is wise.
How long will it be till all men
Know God's pow'r cannot be tamed,
And leaps up in women's knowing
As eternal Wisdom's flame?

4. Then the Church will start reflecting
God's truth of equality –
Where each person finds acceptance
Of their special ministry.
So the Church will show Christ's kingdom,
Counter-cultural, welcoming
All who hear the call to freedom
Promised in their Christening.[4]

The final word can be changed to 'baptism' but the use of the word 'christening' suggests an entry into Christ which is very appropriate for this hymn.

The faith

I have in the course of my faith explored a number of Christian traditions – the middle-of-the-road Anglicanism of my upbringing, the low evangelicalism at St Aldate's and High Anglicanism at Pusey House while at Oxford University and then living in a community in Kensington associated with the Community of the Resurrection. But it was feminist theology and in particular the work of Mary Grey that became the place where I really felt at home. It gradually made me increasingly unhappy with the substitution theology associated with the crucifixion and a theology of sacrifice in which

God, to some eyes, becomes a child abuser. This made entrance to the Anglican priesthood very difficult as this theology runs through all our Eucharistic Prayers. I was heartened when, as a Visiting Fellow at the Episcopal Divinity School at Cambridge, Massachusetts, I heard Carter Heyward use the word 'sacrament' in place of 'sacrifice' in a Eucharistic Prayer. It caused a stir there, but it echoes through my head all the time that I now stand at the altar and consider the significance of what I am doing. I tried to encapsulate it in this poem:

Agnus Dei

Why did you die,
Jesus who is called the Lamb of God?

Certainly not for me
who was, at the time of your death,
but a collection of genes
scattered around the Mediterranean or thereabouts.

The logic on which your sacrifice is based is unthinkable –
rooted in a God
so thirsty for human flesh
that this hunger can only be assuaged
by becoming an abuser of his own child.

Why did you die?
Just like many today and whole sections of the planet –
you died because of unjust and inflexible structures,
institutionally violent systems
operated by men whose deepest fear
is that their systems will be overturned –
as you overthrew the tables of the money changers.

The structural violence of Rome
is now replicated across Church and State
and the innocent and vulnerable are still killed.

You died – a symbol of innocent human suffering
and a model of human survival.

Your wounds flower with compassion;
your suffering gives us insight
into trillions of woundings through the ages;
your resurrection is a model of the depth of creativity within our
    fragile world,
a world at once broken and transfigured.

Beneath my fingers
the bread snaps and cracks
as ancient lambsong fills the church.

Here within this tiny bowl
is the brokenness and the glory
of the world.[5]

The end of this poem refers to my first experience of presiding at a Eucharist. In this, I was completely bowled over by the moment of the Fraction – when the priest breaks the bread. I broke the bread and the choir started to sing the Agnus Dei, 'Lamb of God'. As the music circled around me and I broke the bread into smaller and smaller pieces, it was as if all the suffering in the world was in the small plate at that moment and that it was both broken and transfigured with glory at the same time. The experience was one of such deep emotion that I felt close to tears – pain and beauty intertwined.

The Eucharist is central to my faith. A weekly Eucharist has been a part of my rule of life from my middle twenties. In this hymn I tried to encapsulate some of my theology around it:

1. The wounds are human wounds;
   The tears are human tears;
   Two loving friends beside a cross
   Pour love in spite of fears.

2. In broken human form
   That Christ still lives today,
   And human love can still be poured
   To wipe the pain away.

3. The loving joy of God
   Is poured out in our wine;
   The bread reveals our brokenness,
   Christ's body in the vine.

4. In sharing grief and pain
   And joyful, laughing love,
   We are a priesthood here on earth
   Reflecting God above.[6]

I have used the Eucharist for my own personal healing and strengthening for a long time. At the bread I offer the pain and at the wine the joy of the week just past. I receive them back in a transformed form that will enable me to live the next week with integrity and understanding.

In presiding I feel that I am making clear an ongoing celebration at the very heart of the cosmos:

1. Deep inside creation's mystery
   Stands a table set with bread,
   And a cup of grapes' rejoicing,
   Love full-bodied, sparkling red.

2. Hands reach out across the cosmos;
   Each is gladly taking part,
   Off'ring deeply all their being
   In this Eucharistic heart.

3. Rocks and stones rejoice together;
   Insects, birds can join the song;
   Flowers leap up and clouds are dancing;
   All are joined and all are strong.

4. Human voices join the chorus;
   Chant and jazz and mystic prose,
   Hymns of fellowship all make the
   Counterpoint of One who knows.

5. Life-transforming celebration
   Cent'ring eccentricity,
   Shape our dancing, keep it rooted
   In love's creativity.

6. We all bear the marks of loving
   In our hearts. That is the plan.
   In our own truth we shall find that
   Truth in Whom we all began.[7]

The body

My attempts to be true to my eco-feminist liberation theological position made the ordination course on which I trained a struggle for me and I found myself constantly wrestling with the orthodox positions. Having reached the moment of ordination I nearly stumbled at the final hurdle – the clothes. I am a large woman and the straight-down garments – alb and cassock – were designed for bodies that had shoulders wider than hips. In order to get the garments to fit my bust and hips they hung loosely from my shoulders. The cassock and surplice were the worst for not only did the cassock fall off at the shoulders but the surplice, made of polyester cotton and designed for someone at least a foot taller than me and thinner, made me look like a giant balloon. When I tried a pleated cotta which looked much better it was associated with a different liturgical tradition from the one in my church and I was told by a close clerical friend that it was not correct choir dress. I very nearly despaired until I found a man with a tape measure who found a less gathered garment of an appropriate length.

The clerical shirts were no better. I was determined not to wear black because of the way it drags the colour from an ageing face. Again they were all in polyester cotton, an ungrateful material for the larger woman's body.

It was my interfaith group that came to my rescue – indeed they were one of the most supportive groups in my journey to ordination. As I described my dilemmas, the Sikh member said that Paramjeet, a member of her gurdwara, could help me. So I took myself to her house and explained the design of the neck of the shirt. She made me the most wonderful shirts of amazingly colourful silky Indian fabrics that draped themselves beautifully over my curvaceous hips. They are admired by many fellow clergy and I was able to keep my natural approach to colour and be a priest.

From the work of Lisa Isherwood and Elizabeth Stuart[8] I had learned a great deal of body theology and the use of our bodies liturgically. I decided that in the Eucharist we already had a wonderful series of gestures hallowed by tradition and my High Anglican background suited me fine. I learned from Yvon Bonenfant, one of our performing arts lecturers at Winchester University, about the softness and gentleness of gesture and gained his help in forming these in such a way that will make them express the loving embrace of God. It has become a great joy to me to wear the beautiful chasubles and use them for gestures of love.

The language

Inclusive language is a huge problem. I have been greatly supported in my journey by Ianthe Pratt and the Association for Inclusive Language.[9] As an Anglican priest I have sworn to use the prayers that are approved and there is little that is inclusive about their language for God, who is mostly Almighty and/or a father. I use 'creator, redeemer and life-giving Spirit' for blessings and often use some of my own inclusive language hymns. I often create my own propers for services – like the collect, post-communion prayer and blessing – always in inclusive language, when I can draw on my long experience of constructing liturgies for particular contexts.

My desire for inclusion has led me into great sadness about the exclusion from the communion of members of other faiths. I experience a similar sadness when I am excluded from receiving communion when worshipping in Roman Catholic and Orthodox contexts. I cannot imagine Jesus excluding anyone and I tried to encompass an atmosphere of inclusion in this hymn:

1. We gather here together
   From different ways of faith.
   Your Myst'ry calls us forward
   Into the heart of grace.
   We know Your Truth is wider
   Than all we can expect;
   So here we seek communion
   In love and with respect.

2. We own our faith in Jesus
   Who made Your essence known;
   And hope we have been faithful
   To what we have been shown.
   We share our partial insights
   And find You are our rest.
   And so become empowered
   With love and with respect.

3. Your Spirit flows between us
   And makes Your Being clear.
   Diversely reuniting
   We sense Your presence here;
   And so Your Church can mirror
   The world You resurrect,
   As gently we draw nearer
   In love and in respect.[10]

I have had great support from my Roman Catholic brothers and sisters and it was a great delight to play for the service ordaining women priests in Canada. It strengthened my own vocation as I found my complex way through the vagaries of Anglican ordination training. Sometimes I celebrate with and for Roman Catholic friends in informal contexts. It is one of my greatest delights to work across that terrible schism in our faith.

In one of these contexts the stole is sometimes given to the presider by a member of the congregation saying, 'We know that we are all priests here. But just for this service will you lead us?' I long for the day when I have the courage to do this with my own congregation. I love it when I am free of the restraints of Anglicanism and can create my own liturgies like the one for the international gathering of evangelical gay, lesbian, transsexual, transgender and intersex groups from Europe in 2007 at London Colney. Here we had clowns expressing the laughter of Ascensiontide as we danced in around the cloister in procession:

1. See the cosmos comes to birth;
   Christ returns to heaven from earth,
   Bearing our humanity
   Deep within the Trinity. Alleluya, Alleluya.

2. Now divisions fall away
   At the dawning of the day
   When the heaven's gates swing wide
   And outsiders flock inside. Alleluya, Alleluya.

3. Angels sing celestial psalms;
   Saints and prophets wave their palms;
   Christ's procession enters in;
   All creation starts to sing Alleluya, Alleluya.

4. Christ's ascension has revealed
   How our hurts are being healed,
   How our nature forms a part
   Of the deeps within God's heart. Alleluya, Alleluya.

5. All our hopes and all our fears,
   All our joys and all our tears,
   All our visions and despair
   Nestle in God's shelt'ring care. Alleluya, Alleluya.

6. Heav'n and earth are interlaced;
   God has shown that interface;
   How our true integrity
   Glows within the Deity. Alleluya, Alleluya.

7. Let the feasting now begin;
   Clowns and creatures tumble in;
   In God's loving we are free;
   Let us claim our liberty! Alleluya, Alleluya.[11]

We also had origami birds/cranes receiving our prayers and thanksgiving and I and a Baptist minister concelebrated. There was such joy here. At Holy Rood House in Yorkshire[12] I get a similar feeling when I share in the wonderfully poetic liturgies created by Elizabeth Baxter. Here I feel free and at home.

The liturgy

I love presiding at the Eucharist and finding ways of bringing it alive. My interest in ecotheology has made me think of ways of linking what is going on inside the church with the natural world. When I greet people I always refer to the season and the state of the growing world; for example, 'Welcome to St Paul's on this fine spring morning when it looks as if all the trees are springing into life.' My placement during my ordination training at St James's, Piccadilly[13] was seminal in my thinking. Here was a church that really manages to make liturgy live. The breaking of the bread at the four corners for other faiths, the poor, the earth and our own brokenness, I now use at our family services. I enjoy making services as appropriate as I can for purpose, asking people about their beliefs and trying to get services like weddings and funerals as close to their understandings and requests as I can. I enjoy this process immensely. I love it, for example, when I am called to a Caribbean household at the death of a family member and they are all gathered. I know that all I have to do is to start a time of prayer and all the women in particular will have *Daily Light* or other poems or devotional materials in their bags and that I have no need of more material. I can simply guide their own process of liturgy construction.

Preaching I have always enjoyed. I am a professional storyteller and largely use stories. I have moved gradually towards a position where I preach mostly with few if any notes. A member of my congregation commented: 'I love it when you preach, June, because you do it like Jesus. You tell us a story and then help us understand it.' Although I would not define my feminist theological position as clearly in my situation as a non-stipendiary priest in a South London parish, it runs through all my thought; I have been amazed at how these ideas have found such a ready acceptance within my congregation, which is a great mix of culture, ethnicity and educational background. It is as if they have been thirsting for someone to express the ideas that they (particularly the women) have been thinking for a long time and have never had the courage or the means to articulate. This has been a particularly rewarding part of my ministry at the Eucharist.

Epilogue

I will sometimes sing as part of the celebration. A song that I will often use during the clearing away and washing up of the communion vessels is one I wrote in France which encapsulates my belief in a supporting and supportive God. This little chant has become one of the most moving that I have written; I remember using it in a context where one member of the congregation was ill in bed in another room and the communion was taken to him. The song reached and included him in our gathering:

> I will hold you in the hollow of my hand, my hand, my hand,
> I will hold you in the hollow of my hand,
> I will hold you in the hollow of my hand, my hand, my hand,
> I will hold you in the hollow of my hand.
>
> I will hold you on the ripples of the sea, the sea, the sea,
> I will hold you on the ripples of the sea,
> I will hold you on the ripples of the sea, the sea, the sea,
> I will hold you in the hollow of my hand.
>
> I will hold you in the flowing of the air, [etc.]
> I will hold you in the hollow of my hand.
>
> I will hold you in the laughter with your friends [etc.]
> I will hold you in the hollow of my hand.[14]

I am not sure if this is like a woman, but it is like me. I have developed a variety of performance skills over my somewhat complex life. If I can use them (drawing on models from the twelfth-century Hildegard of Bingen[15]) to make God's all-encircling love more clear to a congregation, I will.

Notes

1 Boyce-Tillman, J. and Wootton, J. (eds), *Reflecting Praise* (London: Stainer and Bell and Women in Theology, 1993).

2 Boyce-Tillman, J., *A Rainbow to Heaven* (London: Stainer and Bell, 2006), pp. 80–1.

3 Women and the Church website: <www.womenandthechurch.org>.

4 Written for Christina Rees and WATCH; June Boyce-Tillman, March 2008; unpublished.

5 Boyce-Tillman, J., July 2008; unpublished.

6 Boyce-Tillman, *Rainbow*, p. 69.

7 Boyce-Tillman, *Rainbow*, p. 21.

8 Isherwood, L. and Stuart, E., *Introducing Body Theology* (Sheffield: Sheffield Academic Press, 1998).

9 The Association for Inclusive Language, c/o 36 Court Lane, London SE21 7DR.

10 Boyce-Tillman, *Rainbow*, p. 76. (To the tune *Thornbury* usually used for 'The Church's one foundation'.)

11 The tune for this hymn comes from the medieval festival of the donkey (*Adventavit Asinus*) celebrating Mary and Joseph's escape to Egypt to avoid Herod's slaughter. It was discontinued because the celebrations got out of hand! The Alleluya originally reflected the braying of the donkey.

12 <www.holyroodhouse.freeuk.com>.

13 <www.st-james-piccadilly.org>.

14 Boyce-Tillman, J., August 2007; unpublished.

15 Boyce-Tillman, J., *The Creative Spirit: Harmonious Living with Hildegard of Bingen* (Norwich: Canterbury Press, 2006).

An inclusive communion order for a denominational worship book

SUSAN DURBER

Introduction

This is the story of how I came to write a feminist order for communion for the URC worship book. Even though nobody actually asked for one. 'We don't have a set liturgy' is the kind of thing you'll hear often around the United Reformed Church. In 1662 several thousand dissenting ministers in England were 'ejected' from their livings in parish churches because they refused to conform, partly at least by not using a particular service book. Since then, we have had an aversion to 'set liturgies'. We publish worship books, including orders for communion, but they are never prescribed. For some of our ministers and worship leaders it would be regarded as a failure of nerve not to compose your own prayers each time and to frame them creatively in relationship with the Scripture readings for the day and with an eye to contemporary events and resonances. But the orders in our worship books stand as a witness to what might be honoured as norms and templates within our tradition. They have a kind of authority as a 'norm', though they should not be seen as wholly representative of actual practice in our churches.

Creating an all-age communion rite

Whenever a worship book is to be published (and there is always a debate about whether we should have such a thing at all) a committee is gathered, writers are commissioned and texts are critiqued and edited rigorously. The orders are published under the name of the denomination, the principal author(s) remaining anonymous. They are offered to the churches, with the affirmation of General Assembly, but not in any sense really 'authorized'. But of course, to say that they are not authorized does not mean that they have no authority or significance or that such texts cannot be highly con-tested or provoke controversy. A careful study of the succession of service books in our tradition would reveal how, for example, the liturgical and ecumenical movements have had an impact on our worship forms. An opportunity to write for such a book represents a chance to have influence. As in any community of faith, what happens in worship, and particularly at the communion table, is profoundly important. Perhaps, in a denomination like ours, where the structures of authority are often subtly obscured because so many want to deny that they really exist, it is not always easy to give an account of the way in which things like worship texts and practices are produced and, however gently, 'authorized'.

In such circumstances, I was a member of the committee that oversaw the publication of the most recent service book (*Worship: from the United Reformed Church*) in 2003 and, in its latter stages, chair of the committee. I was writer for a number of texts and had not expected to write a communion order, those commissions generally going to more prestigious writers than me. But when a commission for an order for communion for all ages floundered for various reasons, I volunteered to produce a draft at short notice. The need was for an order that could be used when people of all ages are present for communion.

As I wrote I had a number of things in mind. I wanted to use vocabulary that was simple, yet put together in beautiful phrases, to create a liturgy that was inclusive in terms of accessibility, but not unredeemed by poetry and beauty. It was a high priority in my own mind to make this service 'oral' in form, so that anyone who couldn't read (whether for reasons of age or otherwise) could participate fully in responses. So I used repetition and familiarity to create an order which invited voices to join in without having to use a printed order of service. I also wanted to produce a service that would interpret what we do at communion not only through the lens of the Last Supper, but through the feeding miracles, the stories of Jesus' table fellowship with sinners and outsiders, and through his honouring of children as exemplars of discipleship.

But I also had my own, unspoken, hopes. I wanted to produce an order that would embody the Christian faith in gender-inclusive language and that would offer our children and adults words to pray that did not carry the faith to them in patriarchal language. I wrote of humankind and of God in language that I hoped was faithful, simple, beautiful, accessible, and inclusive, subversive even of the patriarchal language which has come to seem almost inevitable in anything like an 'official' or 'authorized' liturgical text. There has often seemed to be an unspoken acceptance that feminist liturgies may exist at the edges of the Church, or as secondary options, but that when the Church is being most official and most itself, the traditional and so-called orthodox language has to be used. I was used to leading worship drawn from my feminist standpoint week by week in my own congregations and had learned that it can be done in ways which do not draw attention to themselves. I knew that the committee would never have been persuaded to commission a feminist order for communion. Though an inclusive-language statement of faith had been brought to General Assembly a few years before, it had caused a tense debate, and there was little stomach for that again. But I was ready to take an opportunity to contribute to the reshaping of the language of worship. I was used to working in a congregation that was committed to being 'inclusive' in all sorts of ways and I had learned to use all the resources of a worship leader to name, I hoped honestly and prophetically, the new kind of community that we were imagining, hoping for and creating week by week. This work had been painstaking and part of a long-term commitment to a particular community. It depended on the personal trust that I and the congregation had for each other. I believed that because I tried to be a faithful pastor and to love them, they gave me the authority to lead worship in ways that they would not have given to a stranger. They entrusted me with the task of minister, as one who is a faithful witness to the tradition, while renaming it for a new kind of community. I had the privilege to preside at communion within a pilgrim community, of whom I was a long-term member and minister, and that patient commitment was, I think, the source of the authority I had so that I could be creative, radical even. It was a risk, of course, transferring this to the writing of a public text, to be shared in communities where I was unknown, and where the words would be spoken (and needed to be spoken) by others. But the public text could not have been written without the experience of a particular community.

I used, as carefully as I could, the skills and crafts I had honed in all the churches I had served. I made, as I would always want to, good use of biblical stories and images in the liturgy. I am struck, as I read it now, that it is so full of biblical images and quotations. This of course, gives it a particular and obvious source of authority, and one natural to a 'Reformed' pastor like me. But of course the allusions, references and quotations are chosen to emphasize a particular reading of the biblical text, in this case Mark's Gospel. I also referred in the order to 'the prayer of Jesus' rather than to 'the Lord's Prayer' (though I see now that a couple of uses of the word 'Lord' in reference to Jesus were still there in the prayers I had written). I used trinitarian structures and forms, and worked, as I always do, to use ways of writing about God that emphasize the relationality at the heart of God, but without using Father/Son language. I know that I deliberately avoided using any formulas that might readily be translated (by the editing committee) back into traditional words. I knew, from experience, that it might be argued that we should offer people at least the alternative of the traditional trinitarian endings or blessings, so I chose to write in a way which would just not lend itself to that kind of editing or adaptation. I wanted the service to have its own kind of voice and style and not be readily adapted to more formal or traditional styles, and yet not be so extraordinary and different that it would sound 'odd', singular and unrepeatable. I hoped to charm the editing committee with a simple form, and (if I'm honest) I hoped they would not all notice some of the more radical implications of what I had done or, if they did notice, that they would let them stand. In the event, and partly because of the need for this order to find its final form quickly, it was warmly received with very few amendments. I received a most gracious letter from one of the 'elder statesmen' of the denomination, who had seen the draft, thanking me for what I had done. It was even chosen to be the order for communion used at our General Assembly the year the book was launched. I received many appreciative comments, from a wide variety of people in our churches, mainly in relation to its simplicity, its contemporary feel and its use of oral forms. The use of inclusive language was not much commented on, partly perhaps because people would expect that from me, partly because no one could say it was the only order for communion offered, and partly, I suspect, because some people simply did not notice that part of what I was trying to do. It was the second of four orders. The order placed first in the book was, like the second, written new for the 2003 book, and confidently used traditional trinitarian language, though certainly not at every turn.

Using the order when presiding

Of course I used the order myself, both in congregations known to me and those where I was a visitor. I would never draw attention to my own authorship of the order, but of course in our tradition it would be expected that the words of the presider would either be their 'own' or be carefully chosen. As I preside myself, using these words, I recognize that they reflect my own understanding of what it means to preside. I am not *in persona Christi*, but one who leads the people in remembering the story of Christ ('remembering' here in a deep sense of making present now what has been past) and in responding to it. Many of the presider's prayers in the order include the word 'we' and emphasize that 'we' are the guests of Jesus. My preferred way of conducting a communion service is to gather the people around the table in a circle and to have children and adults, elders, minister and people on the same level and in no particular order. The words spoken are noticeably scriptural among the composed phrases and the voices which speak are not only the presider's but the people's too. The words I choose and the style of gathering I create as presider are chosen to evoke an image of the Church as the people of God, in all our diversity, gathered around both the open book and the open table. It is at once a very earthly and rooted image, of wounded and joyful people gathered together, sinners and saints all. Yet there is much use too of language which draws in the company of heaven: someone once commented on the references to saints and angels. There is even an allusion in the offering prayer to one of my favourite George Herbert themes of 'heaven in ordinary'.[1]

41

Susan Durber

One thing I am often conscious of wanting to do in worship is establishing an honest sense of who we are, while also creating the possibility of imagining who we will be and could be, the company of heaven. I find myself deeply attracted by the image of the people of God as the gathered faithful (an image strongly rooted in my own tradition), but also seeing that local gathering of sainted sinners being caught up in the whole company of the Church, in heaven and on earth. As minister, I am part of that company, not the representative of Christ, but simply (and of course not simply!) the one who offers words and images, from Scripture and from myself, to define the space where that gathering may be given shape and meaning. I am very conscious that we meet with Christ as we share bread and wine together as God's people, but not at all that Christ's presence is carried in particular through me. That may have something to do with gender, but also much to do with my tradition. There is certainly a high level of continuity, as I reflect on it, between my role as presider at communion and what I do as host at parties and gatherings and community events. As I am mother (and now grandmother) at home, so too I am Martha-like at communion, the one who creates the feast at which Christ is present and speaks to others as he spoke to Mary, Lazarus and their friends (and, of course, to Martha too).

Reactions to the rite

It turned out, as I discovered later, that some people had noticed the feminist implications of the service I had written. About four years after the book was published, the United Reformed Church held a conference on worship. One of the short papers was about the use of the trinitarian formula in worship and I went along, eager to wrestle with an issue dear to me about how to speak of God in ways that are faithful to the best insights of the tradition and yet responsive to contemporary concerns. The author of the paper told us that he was going to take an example of a published service to demonstrate what he saw as a negative and dangerous tendency in some contemporary liturgies, the diversion from orthodox trinitarian language. The service he had in mind was mine (though he did not know, or had not guessed, that I had written it), and he proceeded to analyse it almost line by line, raising questions about its theology and appropriateness. He concluded that the service was both heretical and idolatrous because it neither referred to God as 'Father' nor used the traditional, and therefore relational, language of the Trinity of God as Father, Son and Holy Spirit. As I sat on the front row, I wondered how to respond. On the one hand I had to applaud him for spotting some of the radical theological moves I had hoped to make. It seems to me that you cannot preach and live the radical welcome of Jesus without questioning and subverting the patriarchal,

42

and therefore exclusive, language in which Christianity has been clothed. I did not believe that a liturgy based on the inclusive table-fellowship of Jesus, in which he welcomed women, many kinds of strangers, sinners and those cast as impure, could be phrased in the traditional language derived from the world of the male domination of women. I did not believe that a liturgy with the express purpose of welcoming children to the table could be adequately or appropriately framed in words from the 'domination system' of patriarchy. But these things were not the concern of my critic. He confessed to understanding that for some (perhaps women abused by their fathers) 'father' language was painful, but he did not think that reason enough to set it aside. He did not seem to grasp, as I would argue, that the language of patriarchy is not simply pastorally unfortunate for a few abused and sensitive women, but is the language of a dangerous and sinful system in which many human beings are radically oppressed.

I did own up to being the writer of the liturgy under scrutiny and urged that we might find less heated ways of addressing both the concerns that language about God is faithful to the best of the tradition, and that ancient oppressions are overcome. But I was left very disturbed by the whole encounter. I recognized that, though the order of communion that I had written had been mostly well received, issues of language about God, and in particular at the communion table, still evoke deep passion. Just as it matters profoundly to me that the faith is carried in new forms of language, so it matters profoundly to others that traditional forms are kept, repeated and remembered. It was striking how, on that day, it was evident that very important things were being contested and fought for. Clearly my 'opponent' was deeply concerned that the denomination was letting go of the orthodox faith and that the presence of a service like mine in a semi-official 'place' was a potent sign of this. But in a church like ours, the 'contest' will not be fought on the floor of General Assembly, but as people choose which liturgies to use Sunday by Sunday in local churches.

I reflected on the central words of the communion service, Jesus' plea that we should remember him. What is it that we should remember? In the service I had prepared, the key memories were not about his being the eternal Son of a heavenly Father, but that he was the one who offered (and still offers) a radical welcome, reaching even to those despised by others. I had wanted to place in our memories Jesus' welcome of children, of women, even of his own enemies. And such memories demand to be carried in new forms of language.

Conclusion

As, now, I reread the service I wrote, it seems hardly radical at all. It seems strange indeed that it should have been condemned with such heavyweight words like heresy and idolatry. But perhaps it was always naïve of me to think that a communion service in a semi-official denominational service would not come under such close scrutiny and excite such opposition. Churches bring their most rigorous discipline to the fellowship of the table (who presides? who receives?). How could I not have thought that a suspicion of heresy at the table would not have caused trouble? I would contend, though, that the words I wrote are faithful to the gospel. My intention was never to break with tradition, but to be part of its renewal and reform. If otherwise, I would hardly have been writing for a denominational service book at all. My goal was to give the people of God words to say around the table that would carry echoes of the precious memories of Jesus, that would express a welcome for all ages in the central ritual of Christianity, and that would heal some of the wounds of patriarchal exclusion in ways both radical and faithful. Sometimes I have been present at services where the order has been used and I hope that God will accept the offering of my work, forgive its failings, and receive the prayers of the people, young and old, women and men.

The order of service

Here are some extracts from the service:[2] the prayer of praise, the invitation to the table, the thanksgiving prayer, and the blessing and sending out:

Prayer of praise

> Loving God,
> in the company of all your people
> we come to you,
> and your presence is joy to us.
> We come here
> on this first day of the week
> to meet with you and with each other
> and to listen for your word for each one.
> We are ready to break bread and to drink wine,
> to remember again the stories of our faith,
> and to be changed by being here with you.
> As we worship
> in the company of angels,
> surrounded by the saints,
> and embraced by your love,
> let us give ourselves openly and freely,
> as you give yourself to us,
> in tenderness and love.
> Loving God, Lord Jesus, Holy Spirit,

we worship you,
the one holy and eternal God.

The Invitation

Jesus was often a guest.
He shared many meals with his friends,
and they long remembered his words at the table.
Though some disapproved of the company he kept,
Jesus ate and drank with all kinds of people
and showed everyone the love of God.
Wherever people met together
Jesus was glad to be welcomed and to be fed.
Today, we are the guests of Jesus.
He welcomes us,
whoever we are and whatever we bring,
and he will feed us at his table.
Old or young, rich or poor, joyful or in sorrow,
Jesus invites us
to share bread and wine with him,
to remember the story of his life and death,
and to celebrate his presence with us today.
On the night before he died,
Jesus shared a meal with twelve of his disciples
in an upstairs room in Jerusalem.
The Gospel writer tells us what happened that night . . .

The Thanksgiving

God is with us!
God is with us!
We give thanks and praise to God!
We give thanks and praise to God!
Loving God,
the world you made is beautiful
and full of wonder.
You made us, with all your creatures,
and you love all that you have made.
You gave us the words of your prophets,
the stories of your people through the generations,
and the gathered wisdom of many years.
You gave us Jesus, your Son,
to be born and to grow up
in difficult times when there was little peace.
He embraced people with your love
and told stories to change us all.
He healed those in pain
and brought to life those who had lost hope.

He made friends with anyone who would listen
and loved even his enemies.
For these things, he suffered.
For these things, he died.
And he was raised from death and lives with you forever.
You give us your Holy Spirit,
to teach and to strengthen us,
to remind us of Jesus Christ,
and to make us one in him.
For all these gifts we thank you,
and we join with all your people
on earth and in heaven,
in joyful praise:
Hosanna!
Hosanna!
Blessed is the one who comes in the name of the Lord!
Blessed is the one who comes in the name of the Lord!
Hosanna in the highest heaven!
Hosanna in the highest heaven! (Mark 11.9b, 10b)
We praise you that we are here today,
around the table of Jesus.
We have heard the good news of your love;
the cross is the sign of your arms
stretched out in love for us
and the empty tomb declares your love
stronger than death.
Christ has died!
Christ has died!
Christ is risen!
Christ is risen!
Christ will come again!
Christ will come again!
Send your Holy Spirit
upon this bread and wine,
and upon your people,
that Christ may be with us,
and we may be made ready to live for you
and to do what you ask of us,
today, and every day to come.
We make this prayer
through Jesus Christ,
in the power of the Holy Spirit,
in the love of the Creator,
one God,
to whom be glory and praise forever. Amen.

Sending out and Blessing

Jesus said,
'Go home to your friends,
and tell them how much the Lord has done for you,
and what mercy he has shown you.' (Mark 5.19)

The blessing of God be upon you,
the One who loves you,
the Christ who calls you,
the Spirit who makes you holy,
today and always.
Amen.

Notes

1 George Herbert, 'Prayer'.
2 Extracts from the order for communion are produced by permission of The United Reformed Church – and the copyright is held by the URC.

Thoughts from the exiled edges

MARY GREY

Introduction

When this theme was first proposed, I have to confess that it not only failed to excite, but positively put me off. Fine, I thought, for those denominations with a developing history of the ordination of women, a process of historical struggle with a positive outcome. These are churches which have now been ordaining women as priests for more than a decade, in the case of the Church of England, while other traditions in the UK have ordained women to leadership roles since early in the twentieth century (see pp. 67–77). We have seen the wonderful gifts women have brought to ordained ministry and marvelled at the way they have contributed to changes in prayer, symbolism and preaching, as well as the way in which authority and power have been differently confronted. (I do not pretend that 'everything in the garden is rosy', nor that women have not continued to experience prejudice and hostility, but here my focus is on the positive developments.) Yet, concurrently, in the Roman Catholic Church we still experience an ongoing history of blockage around the issue. So I will explore some consequences of this blockage and some of its roots, and whether there are some crumbs of comfort and hope in the present scene. I should warn that, though I am often accused of being an optimist in situations of oppression, this is not an attempt to create false happy endings!

Blockage to the ordained ministry

An obvious consequence to the official situation has been the slow haem-orrhaging of women (and men) away from the Catholic Church, frequently followed by priestly ordination in other Christian churches. This is insuffi-ciently noted and mourned. Some of course have left the Christian Church completely: Charles Davis, a respected Roman Catholic theologian, was a noted example of this in the sixties: it was not the ordination issue that catapulted his departure, but the way the papal encyclical *Humanae Vitae* had been produced and promulgated.[1] The effects on those of us who stay are often depressing and disempowering: we have lost those whom we hold dear, often looked to as role models, and our own situation seems even more hopeless, even if we feel, out of deep loyalty to the church, that the way forward is to remain and struggle within its structures.

But a more important question is what this history of blockage has meant to the psyche of Roman Catholic women – and men – affected by these issues. Reactions vary from anger, bitterness and bewilderment, as the case against ordained ministry for women is shown to be empty of cogent theological content, to disenchantment with the systems of authority and governance in the church, to ostrich-like ignoring of the issue, or to stead-fast attempts to keep open the question and make theological education for ministry possible for women in preparation for such a day when ordination becomes possible. Many initiatives like the latter are keeping hope alive.

There are also deep-rooted spiritual issues. Beverly Lanzetta has alerted us to the effects of centuries of rejection on women's souls. Who has paid much attention to the consequences of centuries of powerlessness, inequality, misogyny, marginalization and violence on the female psyche, she asks. She has called this 'the oppression of women's soul' and names this spiritual oppression as the foundation of all women's other oppressions.[2] From where will come healing and reconciliation? Who has ever addressed this issue of spiritual oppression and desolation? Lanzetta stresses the need for a contem-plative wisdom to address these profound psychic wounds:

> Women's spiritual oppression, because it injures the site of a person's greatest holiness, sensitivity, and mutuality – their relationship with God – is frequently an unnamed, forbidden territory. The possession of women's ability to be rela-tional, receptive and vulnerable – to reflect an outpouring of Divine Intimacy – is a form of spiritual violence maintained through complex relationships of blame and shame.[3]

Developments in feminist theology and spirituality have been attempting to address this centuries-old desolation in positive ways.

Thirdly, I – like countless others – can trace the effects of this blockage and spiritual oppression on my own development and that of members of my family. Our generation of women were conditioned to experience both shame and fear at stepping into the church's sanctuary: we were taught that this was not 'women's place', and that the only time we could be legitimately there was on our wedding day! Even now I find I have to take a deep breath when asked to go into the sanctuary to read, or – extremely rarely – to preach (*but never to preside*). I still feel fearful that I will not be welcomed, that I may even be told to leave.[4] Yet I can address large audiences in lecture theatres without such qualms. Nerves on these occasions derive from worry-ing about the quality of the lecture content, not usually because of being considered to be the wrong gender. In academic circles women are now usually judged in the same way as their male counterparts. I have a poignant memory of my own mother, when asked – without warning – to preside over a prize-giving at a boys' summer camp, when we were on holiday on Holy Island (Lindisfarne). Stricken with nerves (yet she was a teacher – although at that moment on leave), she grabbed my small sister (aged 2) and holding on to her, was able to preside with dignity. I recall it as a sign of what it means to have no real tradition of presiding to draw on.

The barrier to the ordination of women is something to be lived with every day,[5] the pain of exclusion forming part of the spiritual desolation described above. This pain is heightened at times like the present when the Catholic Church has embarked on a 'Year of Priests': yet another campaign reinforcing women's sense of exclusion, especially as it continues – insensitively – to be put in the context of 'falling numbers of priests', a calamity for which many know there is an obvious solution. The pain is also heightened when women are mocked, on the pretext that the campaign is simply about 'women seizing power' and being unwilling to accept their supposed 'rightful place' in the church.

With the overwhelming sense of this pathway being blocked come negative consequences: blockage affects identity and brings loss of self-esteem – my own and that of countless others. There is a sense of spiritual homelessness and a loss of nurture – Rosemary Radford Ruether has referred to this as a 'eucharistic famine',[6] arising from a narrowed experience of liturgy, a clericalized, elite ordained ministry, situated as it is within a hierarchical church. Because of this impoverishment, many have chosen to put their energies outside the context of church, or at least outside the context of liturgical leadership, and have sought other pathways.

Nurturing hope – alternative pathways

A first pathway that some Roman Catholic women of great courage have pursued is to seek to authenticate their own call to ordained ministry. One group is the well-publicized ordination on a boat on the Danube in 2002.[7] These pioneering women are referred to as 'The Danube Seven'. This event was swiftly followed by excommunication from Rome even though, technically speaking, the ordinations are reckoned as valid. Dramatic consequences ensued: nine further women sought ordination in the Roman Catholic Church on 25 July 2005, in the international waters at the mouth of the St Lawrence Seaway (these are known as the St Lawrence Nine). Two other women Catholic theologians, Christine Mayr-Lumetzberger of Austria, and Gisela Forster of Germany, now bishops, came to the St Lawrence to ordain these women. Other ordinations have followed, and now, as WOW (Women's Ordination Worldwide) attests, there are increasing numbers of women being ordained and practising ministry especially in the United States. Even if the Vatican will always regard such ordinations and ministries as illegal, the fact that increasing numbers are quietly practising in such a way may indicate that change will eventually be inevitable. My own chosen way is to struggle with others for change within the structures.

A second group of women, following the Ignatian admonition to 'go where the energy is good', have ceased to struggle on this front (many think the structures are diseased and a wholesale change is more important than ordaining women), and put all their efforts into work for justice and peace in a variety of ways. This could be within a range of aid agencies, both faith-based and secular. In some, like Cafod, Trocaire, Progressio and Misereor,[8] there have been opportunities to develop a prophetic spirituality, composing and leading creative liturgies. Slowly but surely a tradition has been growing where women have been given opportunities for leadership and presidency of liturgy, and a steady confidence is being built up.

Other areas where this is taking place include teaching, spiritual direction and in religious congregations of sisters. Lay women act as school and hospital chaplains, conduct retreats and lead a variety of informal religious services, both in official religious settings as well as in the home, in a natural setting – and a variety of other spaces.

A personal story

In my own case, I have long since given up the struggle for ordination for myself, yet continue to support efforts for other women, as well as working with renewal movements within the church. I would like to put on record my deep gratitude to other Christian churches who have extended to me the hospitality of the pulpit, inviting me to preach at Eucharists and Evensong services. I have been made welcome in Anglican cathedrals, in Methodist, Baptist, United Reformed churches and by the Church of Scotland. Though I have no direct experience of presiding over a complete service, except on one occasion,[9] the nearest I have come to this is directing retreats, both in the Catholic and Anglican churches. These occasions I have experienced as a deep affirmation of ministry. On one occasion I was invited to give the pre-ordination retreat for 50 Church of England women deacons in the diocese of Lichfield. This was in 1994, the occasion of the ordination of the first women in the Church of England. It was a great privilege. A high moment came when, the day before the ordination, there arose a need to devise a means of leaving behind the pain and bitterness of many years of struggle. I created a ritual where – amid readings and prayers – we passed around a bunch of grapes. Each woman ate the grape but kept the seed, and planted it in a large bowl of earth, symbolic of burying the bitterness so as to be free to move forward. After the liturgy two of us climbed the hill behind the retreat centre and flung the bowl of earth and seeds to the four winds. Maybe somewhere in Shropshire a vineyard has sprung up from these seeds, to begin a story of new growth? What this story exemplifies is the way women's leadership in liturgy draws freely on new symbols and new symbolic action.

Another example of symbolic action was during a retreat for a group from Pax Christi. The closing liturgy, in Advent, was to centre on the Isaiah reading of the holy mountain (Isaiah 25). I suggested that we actually built the mountain – from chairs covered in bed sheets and greenery. From somewhere a toy lion and lamb appeared. But what happened could not have been predicted. Participants felt that they should prepare to go to the holy mountain (the context was the Sunday Eucharist). Some wanted to leave their credit cards behind. One lady cast off a fur coat! We all took off our shoes. There was a tangible sense of awe as we made a penitential journey to the mountain. At some point – after communion – there was an overwhelming sense of joy and no one wanted to leave the mountain and go to lunch. The point here is not that my own experience has been so different from that of others, but that enabling the liturgical leadership of women has frequently opened a sluice gate for a flood of new imagery, symbols and symbolic action. In numerous informal groups on the edges, women – and sometimes men – have begun to experience a new nurturing through these experimental liturgies that have affirmed their whole beings, body, soul and spirit. We have learnt to follow the inspiration of creation in a wider sense, and to experience the dynamic presence of God in liturgies celebrated in meadow, forest, by sea and river. A second important focus is justice and the attempt to bring justice-making into the heart of the liturgy is proving a great strength. Thirdly, there is a holistic focus, as we have tried to bring silence and contemplation back into liturgy, thus counteracting its overwordiness.

Is there another way of presiding?

But all these innovative styles of leadership of alternative liturgies and discovering leadership in other areas do not strictly answer the question implied by 'presiding like a woman?' Since, as I have been explaining, I have no direct experience, all I can offer are clues, hopes and dreams.

The first clue comes from the style of presidency I observe in the secular, political world of women like Mary Robinson and Mary McAleese, successive Presidents of Ireland. Both embody a remarkably different kind of politics and style of engagement in the way they show concerns for justice and reconciliation. They are able to connect the personal and the political and to use spiritual strengths to further their political visions. Mary Robinson (when in office) made a powerful use of symbol. In her Dublin Castle Inauguration speech (1990) she invoked the symbolism of the fifth province of Ireland, which does not actually exist geographically, but which she wanted to be a symbol of United Ireland. (This was at the height of 'The Troubles'.) It was to be an empty space, but open to all. In the same speech she famously declared that a light would always

burn through the night in her home for the people of the Irish Diaspora –
especially those who had had to leave because of the famine in the nineteenth
century.

My second clue comes directly from Christian tradition, namely that of
abbesses of monastic communities up till the Reformation, who frequently
presided over double monasteries of both women and men. Such presidency included governance but also liturgical presidency. In England
our most famous example is St Hilda of Whitby, who not only presided
over a double monastery at Whitby – she became its Abbess in 657 – but
was responsible for convening the Synod of Whitby in 664, in order to
settle the dispute between the Celtic and Roman Churches over the date
of Easter. We know something of the quality of her leadership from Bede.
He tells us that the original ideals of monasticism were maintained strictly
in Hilda's abbey. All property and goods were held in common; Christian
virtues were exercised, especially peace and charity. Everyone had to study
the Bible and do good works. Bede describes Hilda as a woman of great
energy, a skilled administrator and teacher with such a reputation for wisdom
that kings and princes sought her advice. The link with a creative mode of
authority is revealed through the story of Caedmon, the cowherd at the
monastery, who was inspired in a dream to sing verses in praise of God.
Hilda recognized his gift and encouraged him to develop it. She ordered
her scholars to teach Caedmon sacred history and doctrine, which Bede
tells us, Caedmon would turn into beautiful verse after a night of thought.
Although Hilda must have had a strong character she inspired affection.
Bede relates that all who knew her called her mother because of her out-
standing devotion and grace.[10]

Although, as I said, this form of exercising authority ended with the
Reformation, there is still one strand to call on (my third clue): this is
the theme of *sedes sapientiae*, 'The Seat or Throne of Wisdom' – an icon of
Mary, Mother of God in majesty or authority. When Mary is depicted
in *sedes sapientiae* icons and sculptural representations, she is seated on a
throne, with the Christ-child on her lap. This type of Madonna-image
appeared in a wide range of sculptural and, later, painted images, illumin-
ated manuscripts, Romanesque frescoes and mosaics in western Europe,
especially around 1200. For my theme it is a valuable clue as to Mary's
authority: she is enthroned in a teaching position, manifesting wisdom
and authority.[11] Mary as the Throne of Wisdom is a trope of Peter Damiani
or Guibert de Nogent, based on their typological interpretation of the
passage in the Books of Kings that describes the throne of Solomon
(1 Kings 10.18–20).[12] It is a type of presidency that draws on the Sophia/
hokhmah/wisdom traditions, where wisdom is symbolized as female. It is
an important source to draw on for what is distinctive about the presidency
of women.

Conclusion: a mystical hope

What can realistically be hoped for now, in a situation where, as I explained, instead of a fluid movement forward, there is blockage, a ban on discussion, and a great frustration about the general situation of women in the church? This frustration has to be placed within the wider context of growing conservative tendencies (as indicated by the increasing popularity of the Tridentine Mass and the ordination of conservative seminarians) and the analogous situation of married men, also refused as candidates for the priesthood (even though former Anglican priests who are married have been received into the Catholic Church and its priesthood). 'Presiding as a woman', through ordained priesthood, it must be admitted, will not solve all the problems of a hierarchical, elitist, centralized church with an absolutist style of governance. That is the heart of the matter. So, dreaming of the presidency of women has to be placed in the wider context of transformations needed at the deepest level.

And are we already embarked on this task? Whenever we are inspired by what the Church could become, whenever we experience a sense of 'Yes! That's what it means to be church!' – can we act on these intuitions, use whatever power we have and join the painful, messy and creative process of bringing to birth a community that heralds the dawning divine reign? I imagine us, Catholic women today (with our brothers who share this dream), in communion with Mary, Mary of Magdala, Hilda, Hildegard, Teresa, Catherine of Siena, Mary Ward, Dorothy Day, Joan Chittister and a cloud of witnesses proclaiming the good news in many contemporary contexts.

How many simple, sharing meals have we enjoyed, as we pondered new meanings of the sacred texts? *Presidency can be a shared ministry of mutuality* as we call forth the wisdom of each other. In presiding over the table, hospitality is offered, care and attention given to the ethical sources of food, to the life situations of the guests. *Presidency is expressed in terms of attention to detail.* In attending to the particularity of every day, something is disclosed of God's presence. When we preside over the classroom or the lecture hall, we give attention to the midwifing of ideas. *The presider is midwife* to this birthing process, and does not own the baby at the birth. This is a presidency that hears into speech, especially the inarticulate, the invisible, the excluded. In discussion, in dialogue – especially in an interfaith context – *we are midwives of the truth*, and blaze a trail of inhabiting another's truth.

My hope is that, even from the exiled edges, in the diverse contexts where we can already be exercising authority, leadership or presidency, barriers are broken down (especially of sacred and secular, of lay and ordained), the world of sacramentality will blossom in new contexts, and the way be prepared for new experiences of being church, where care, compassion and inclusivity become our beacon lights.

Notes

1 *Humanae Vitae* (1964) was produced by Pope Paul VI and still represents the Catholic Church's official teaching on birth control. Yet the Pope had previously set up a commission to investigate the issue: a majority report had advocated change in the ruling, but this was completely ignored in the published encyclical.

2 Lanzetta, B., *Radical Wisdom: A Feminist Mystical Theology* (Minneapolis, MN: Fortress Press, 2005), p. 68.

3 Lanzetta, *Radical Wisdom*, p. 70.

4 This fear derives from a childhood experience, when, in the days of the Latin Mass, because no male altar server was present, I was asked by the priest to answer all the Latin responses – but from the body of the church, not the altar, as I was prohibited from entering.

5 There are close analogies with the barrier to ordination of married men.

6 A theme in Ruether, R. R., *Women-Church* (San Francisco, HarperCollins, 1985).

7 See the website of WOW, Women's Ordination Worldwide, at <www.womensordination.org>.

8 Catholic Fund for Overseas Development, the official overseas aid agency of the Catholic Church: <www.cafod.org.uk>. Trocaire is Cafod's Irish counterpart: <www.trocaire.org>. In Scotland it is Sciaf: <www.sciaf.org.uk>. Progressio was formerly the Catholic Institute for International Relations (CIIR): see <www.progressio.org.uk>, and Misereor is similar to Cafod, based in Germany: <www.misereor.org>.

9 I prefer to remain silent about this occasion.

10 See McClure, J. and Collins, R. (eds), *Bede's Ecclesiastical History of the English People* (New York: Oxford University Press, 1999), p. 213.

11 Sometimes St Anne is similarly portrayed, with the child Mary at her knee. This is a popular trope in Brittany, where St Anne is an important figure and patron.

12 This was much used in Early Flemish painting in works like the *Lucca Madonna* by Jan van Eyck.

Power, pain or paralysis: Victorian women negotiating their presiding in public work

VAL WEBB

Better have pain than paralysis! A hundred struggle and drown in the breakers. One discovers the new world. But rather, ten times rather, die in the surf, heralding the way to that new world, than stand idly on the shore.

Florence Nightingale, *Cassandra*[1]

Introduction

Talk of 'presiding' and 'liturgy' assumes presiding at public worship, yet this arena, for most of Christian history, has been closed to women, except in rare situations, and is still closed or restricted in some churches. Therefore, 'presiding like a woman' must *also* consider how women presiding might have happened for the centuries prior to their formal admission into this arena. I will consider as a vignette Britain's Victorian era which produced such far-reaching reform and expansion of knowledge, highlighting a few women who struggled to find their voice and work despite societal norms.

According to dictionaries, 'presiding' means 'to possess, exercise a position of authority, act as chairperson or president, control or regulate as chief officer, be in the leading place, exercise superintendence or watch over'. Such definitions relate to the public sphere from which Victorian women were generally excluded. Theirs was the private sphere, untouched by trade and worldly sin, where they were worshipped as the 'household nun' or 'angel of the home'.[2] To accompany this imagery, women were seen as fragile, pure and inferior, 'housekeepers' of husbands' souls yet unable to match his mind or abilities. As the popular Victorian marriage manual *The Women of England: Their Social Duties and Domestic Habits* said:

> In her intercourse with man, it is impossible but that woman should feel her own inferiority, and it is right that it should be so ... she does not meet him on equal terms. Her part is to make sacrifices in order that his enjoyment may be enhanced.[3]

Yet women did not preside in their 'natural' sphere, the home, either. The husband was master of the house. A mother had no rights to her children until 1839 when she gained rights to children up to age seven. Before 1857, a wife could not divorce her husband. Women had no rights to property until the 1870s. Such inequities were argued on a natural hierarchal order of male superiority and strength and female inferiority and frailty. Victorian artists painted women reclining listlessly or leaning on one another and writers followed suit, exalting female invalidism. In his book *Woman* in the mid 1800s, Jules Michelet wrote:

> More fragile than a child, woman absolutely requires that we love her for herself alone, that we guard her carefully, that we be every moment sensible that in urging her too far we are sure of nothing. Our angel, though smiling, and blooming with life, often touches the earth with but the tip of one wing; the other would already waft her elsewhere.[4]

As for the natural order of these 'Priestesses of Humanity in the family circle', as they were sometimes known, Auguste Comte of Positivism fame wrote, 'women should shrink from any participation in power as in its very nature degrading.'[5] Such 'natural' sensitivities did not, however, include working-class women who slaved long hours in factories and upper-class homes – a *physical* proof of class differences.

Much Victorian literature about women includes the words 'women's work' and 'women's duty', bringing us to another word under consideration – 'liturgy'. While current understandings pertain to public worship in Christian churches, its origins are quite different. The Greek *leitourgia* (Latin, *liturgia*) meant 'public work or duty' (*leitos*, public; *ergon*, work). According to *Webster's New Universal Unabridged Dictionary*, liturgy was in ancient Athens

> a form of personal service which the wealthier citizens were obliged to discharge to the state at their own expense, when called upon. Such services sometimes consisted of the defrayal of the expenses of festivals, dramatic performances, equipment of ships in case of war, etc.[6]

Other dictionaries note derivatives such as *leitourgos*, public servant and *leos* (a dialectal variant of *laos*), people; thus liturgy is the public work of the *laos*, the people.

The word was used in the New Testament for gatherings of early Christians. Acts 13.2 says in different translations, 'While they were worshipping the Lord and fasting' (NRSV), 'While they were engaged in the liturgy of the Lord' (NAB) and 'As they ministered to the Lord, and fasted' (KJV). Thus *leitourgia* became their 'public function or service done' in response to God. It is interesting to note the rest of the passage – 'the Holy Spirit said, "Set apart for me Barnabas and Saul for the *work* [my italics] to which I have called them"' (NRSV). In time, 'liturgy' became restricted to *forms* – the words used in the service (note our use of 'service' to describe *worship*), especially administration of the sacraments.[7] This loss of the wider meaning of 'public work' brings to mind Jesus selecting 'love God and your neighbour' as the greatest commandment, to which the scribe replied, 'You are right, teacher . . . this is much more important than *all whole burnt offerings and sacrifices* [my italics]' – the 'temple work' of that day (cf. Mark 12.28–33).

Recovering traditions of presiding

This long preamble is not to downplay church liturgical practice but to recover, as a feminist approach, women and their 'work' prior to, and apart from, women's contemporary ability to preside over church liturgy. I discuss a few Victorian women who negotiated public perceptions and ecclesial exclusions – generalizations fail as women's different circumstances called for different action. Octavia Hill, Josephine Butler, Elizabeth Blackwell, Charlotte Brontë, Mary Clarke, George Eliot, Emmeline Pankhurst, Elizabeth Fry, Elizabeth Gaskell, Harriet Martineau, Dr James Barry,[8] to name a few, used their differing social status, persuasive ability, negotiating skills, determination and intelligence to find their place of power, authority and work within the Victorian male-constructed society.

Queen Victoria

Queen Victoria (1819–1901) was *born* into her presiding 'work' over empire *and* church, giving her name to an amazingly creative and influential era. Only child of Edward, Duke of Kent and Mary Louisa Victoria of Saxe-Coburg-Gotha, Victoria was raised in London in a sheltered environment by her mother and governess.[9] At eighteen, she succeeded her uncle William IV to the ultimate presiding position, monarch of the United Kingdom of Great Britain and Ireland, and later Empress of India. Victoria initially depended heavily on Prime Minister Lord Melbourne but would soon show her own determination when challenged. On marrying her first cousin Albert of Saxe-Coburg-Gotha in 1840, she deemed her life fulfilled and was happy to relegate much of her presiding power to Albert, giving him great influence in the court. He in turn shaped her and her reign, encouraging her to claim her role in public affairs by attending to dispatches and advising ministers.

When Albert died in 1861, Victoria went into deep mourning, absenting herself from the public for years until persuaded this was affecting the monarchy's popularity. During the conservative reign of Prime Minister Benjamin Disraeli, Victoria found both support and affinity in him. As head of the Church of England, she walked a middle path between High and Low Church. She rejected the extravagant lifestyle of some of her predecessors, having more conservative and domesticated views learned from Albert. Rather than overtly *shaping* the era which carries her name, 'Her longevity and moral steadiness during a time of rapid transformation had helped to unify the nation, the empire, and the age.'[10] Victoria did not support women's suffrage, perhaps because she already had supreme power as a woman through accident of birth. When the movement gained momentum with John Stuart Mill's advocacy in Parliament and his 1869 book *The Subjection of Women*, Victoria, according to Sir Theodore Martin, was in a 'royal rage' because she believed the male–female hierarchy was part of the biblical order of things:

> The Queen is most anxious to enlist everyone who can speak or write in checking this mad, wicked folly of 'Women's Rights', with all its attendant horrors, on which her poor feeble sex is bent, forgetting every sense of womanly feeling and propriety ... It is a subject which makes the Queen so furious that she cannot contain herself. God created men and women differently – then let them remain each in their own position ... Woman would become the most hateful, heartless, and disgusting of human beings were she allowed to unsex herself; and where would be the protection which man was intended to give the weaker sex?[11]

Florence Nightingale

Florence Nightingale (1820–1910) did not support women's suffrage either, not because she believed the biblical male–female order, but because she knew the vote would not be given to all women for years and did not consider a few token votes for upper-class women as curing women's problems. When John Stuart Mill sought her support, she refused, listing more pressing women's needs – rights to their children, education, property, money, paid employment for single women, divorce. She wanted these to occupy the few hours of parliamentary attention afforded women's issues. She also knew that male headship, argued from Scripture, was engrained in British society, and thus that a *theological* battle would have to be fought before gains could be made. She was right – reforms giving women the right to their children, property and a divorce were in place long before all women received the vote.[12]

Our earthly immortality depends on people remembering us. How well this is done determines whether we become famous, infamous or forgotten. In Florence's case,[13] her biographers made her famous, but not for the full scope of her 'public work'. Although Sir Edward Cook's 1913 biography contained this information, later biographies concentrated only on her 'nursing'. Yet Florence's 'work' went far beyond this as we shall see, including the writing of an 800-page manuscript *Suggestions for Thought to the Searchers after Truth among the Artisans of England* on a new religion for England's poor. From her experiences with local villagers and common soldiers, she knew that many working-class people, displaced by the Industrial Revolution and ignored by the Church, were without any religion, though seeking one, while others simply retreated behind bankrupt doctrines. Poverty is spoken of two ways in Scripture – a few passages about poverty as a consequence of laziness or ineptitude (Proverbs 13.23; 20.13), but most about a *class* of people kept poor by the rich and powerful against whom the prophets railed. Despite similarities between the biblical scenario and Victorian England, the Church selected the first option coupled with the Calvinistic work ethic, claiming poverty as God's design or their own folly. Florence realized the poor needed both physical *and* theological liberation – hence her new religion positing the divine Spirit in *everyone*, rich and poor, encouraging *all* towards health and happiness.

Florence's complete writings on many topics – the concept of God, Universal Law, God's will and human will, sin and evil, family life, spiritual life, life after death, reincarnation – are currently being published in sixteen volumes, an impressive list when women were not permitted to go to university.[14] At the age of seventy, Florence summed up her life: 'When very many years ago I planned a future, my one idea was not organizing a hospital but organizing a religion.'[15] As I argue in *Florence Nightingale: The Making of a Radical Theologian*, Florence was a God-intoxicated woman for whom reform was not a goal but the consequence of her religious vocation – she cannot be understood outside this parameter. After several divine calls to God's 'work' which she struggled to answer despite family opposition and lack of opportunity outside a religious order, she established an order of one, herself, grounded on her inner mystical experiences and expressed in action for the oppressed, whether village poor, daughters trapped in family drawing rooms, or Crimean soldiers. She celebrated her 'jubilee', not from the beginning of her work, but from her first call.

Florence was the younger daughter of William and Fanny Nightingale of Unitarian and social reform stock, part of England's 'upper ten thousand', the social, political and economic ruling class.[16] Cambridge-educated William (WEN for short) taught the brilliant Florence Greek, Latin, German, French, Italian, history, grammar, composition and philosophy. He introduced her to local government, political leaders and politics, civic duty, social issues and the plight of the poor. The Victorian class system was held in place with the belief that God ordained people to their 'place', rich or poor, ruler or slave; thus boundaries should not be violated. WEN's 'duty' as a land-owner was to oversee his estate, legislate local politics, care for his workers, but not seek their equality. Reform challenges were suspect as anti-English *and* anti-church. Florence and her sister accompanied their mother on her dutiful charity visits to tenant families but Florence was overwhelmed with this inadequacy: 'To visit them in a carriage and to give them money is so little like following Christ, who made Himself like his brethren.'[17]

Like Queen Victoria, she was born into privilege but, unlike Victoria, that privilege denied her the opportunity to preside over the 'public work' she felt called to do. Upper-class women were different from 'working class' – they did not *work*! Florence's family could not understand why she wanted to leave this life to work with the poor, so her story, until she was thirty, is a rollercoaster of hopes constantly dashed by family. She wrote:

> Why, oh my God, cannot I be satisfied with the life which satisfies so many people? ... why am I starving, desperate, diseased upon it? ... My God, what am I to do? Teach me, tell me. I cannot go on any longer waiting till my situation should change.[18]

Given the family opposition to Catholic orders which Florence tried to join, a Protestant institution at Kaiserswerth, Germany, that trained women to work with the poor became her goal and she *did* get her chance briefly to train there. What she had in mind was revolutionary – an order without vows where single women of all classes trained for a salaried profession of caring for the poor. More years and several suitors went by. Finally, at thirty-three, Florence was given a yearly allowance by her father to become voluntary superintendent of a London 'Home for Distressed Governesses'. From there, she was asked to lead a group of women 'nurses' to the Crimean War and she entered history.

There is no doubt that Florence saw herself as having a religious vocation – her 'public work or duty'. At thirty, around the age Christ began his mission, she vowed 'No more childish things, no more vain things, no more love, no more marriage. Now Lord, let me only think of Thy will.'[19] She made a retreat with the Sacred Heart Sisters, learning the spiritual exercises and disciplines she followed through life with their Mother Superior, her spiritual director. She kept the seventh of every month, the day of her first call, for prayer and study. She refused a good marriage, knowing that it would hinder doing whatever God wanted. After Crimea, her plans for an order of trained women were replaced by the more urgent call to army medical reform, and she worked day and night for several years on an Army Royal Commission. She then addressed army health in colonial India and the plight of Indian peasants, drafted the British delegation's proposal to the Geneva Convention, advised on Aboriginal health in Australia and that of the Maori population in New Zealand, introduced nurses into workhouses and health educators into villages, set up a midwifery training course, worked through parliamentarians for women's legal rights, supported work among prostitutes, worked on Poor Law reform, advised on medical services for the American Civil War and Franco-Prussian War, wrote copiously on nurse training and poor reform, planned a book on medieval mystics, edited Oxford theologian Benjamin Jowett's translations of Plato from Greek – all from the bed to which she retired almost completely at age thirty-eight! Many biographers have analysed her invalidism – chronic illness, post-traumatic stress, psychological problems, and protection from family – but I argue it was a monastic lifestyle to enable her public work. For Florence, all of life was spiritual, whether caring for the sick, experimenting with science or reforming parliament. She wrote towards the end of her life:

> Live your life while you have it. Life is a splendid gift. There is nothing small in it ... But to live your life, you must discipline it. You must not fritter it away ... but make your thoughts, your words, your acts all work to the sacred end, and that end is not self but God.[20]

Catherine Booth

As co-founder of the Salvation Army with husband William, Catherine Booth (1829–1890) *did* preside within Christian worship. Catherine was raised in Ashbourne, Derbyshire by a mother who was 'a model of Victorian piety, a pillar of the local Methodist church and queen of her home, who taught her only daughter the rudiments of education and the *duties* of middle-class Victorian womanhood'.[21] Catherine was destined to think beyond these womanly confines. A teenage illness provided some years of inaction during which she read the Bible and Christian authors insatiably, concluding that women should preach and be in ministry along with men. When she met William Booth, a preacher with the Methodist New Connexion, she shared these ideas with him, to which she received a lukewarm response:

> I would not stop a woman preaching on any account. I would not encourage one to begin ... I would not stay *you* if I had the power to do so. Although *I should not like it.* I am for the world's salvation; I will quarrel with no means that promises help.[22]

Long considered the superior intellect of the two, Catherine wasted no time after their 1855 marriage to speak at children's meetings – it was unheard of for women to speak at adult meetings. Her conviction of women's right to preach grew and, when a local clergyman published a pamphlet attacking as unscriptural the preaching of Mrs Palmer, an American evangelist's wife, Catherine sent him a clearly argued letter which William encouraged her to expand and publish. In this pamphlet, *Female Ministry; or Women's Right to Preach the Gospel*, Catherine systematically demolished common Victorian objections against women preaching. The 'public exercises' of women as 'unnatural and unfeminine' is the mistake of confusing nature with custom:

> Making allowance for the novelty of the thing, we cannot discover anything either unnatural or immodest in a Christian woman, becoming[ly?] attired, appearing on a platform or in a pulpit. By *nature*, she seems fitted to grace either ... Before such a sphere is pronounced to be unnatural, it must be proved either that woman has not the *ability* to teach or to preach, or that the possession and exercise of this ability unnaturalizes her in other respects.[23]

Why should women be confined to the domestic sphere when men are not confined to their biblical assignment – tilling the ground and dressing it? As for the fear that women in public positions will be 'rendered unfeminine by the indulgence of ambition or vanity', why should women be charged with ambition for using their talents for God but not men? To those who say female ministry is forbidden in the Bible, Catherine declared the opposite true and competently analysed all the verses used to argue against women's ministry. She also highlighted women apostles around Paul and women in *both* Testaments who preached, prophesied and received God's Spirit, including women at Pentecost.

> Thank God the day is dawning with respect to this subject. Women are studying and investigating for themselves. They are claiming to be recognized as responsible beings, answerable to God for their *convictions of duty* [my italics]; and, urged by the Divine Spirit they are overstepping those unscriptural barriers which the Church has so long reared against its performance.[24]

To those arguing that women preaching is unnecessary because there is plenty of 'work' for them in the private sphere, Catherine noted that Jesus did not express horror at women in public roles – the Samaritan woman proclaiming him to her town; women who followed him to his public crucifixion; and the woman anointing Jesus, leading him to say, 'what she has done will be told in remembrance of her' (Matthew 26.13, NRSV). 'If she have the necessary gifts,' Catherine said, 'and feels herself called by the Spirit to preach, there is not a single word in the whole book of God to restrain her, but many, very many, to urge and encourage her.'[25] Why else would so many women, devoted handmaidens of the divine, feel constrained by the Holy Spirit to ministry; and what of the multitudes saved and edified by the public ministry of many women whom Catherine lists?

> We fear it will be found, in the great day of account, that a mistaken and unjustifiable application of the passage, 'Let your women keep silent in the Churches', has resulted in more loss to the Church, evil to the world, and dishonour to God, than any of the errors we have already referred to.[26]

When Catherine wrote this, she had not yet preached from the pulpit. On Whitsunday in 1860, she surprised William by leaving her pew and indicating her wish to speak – her public 'work' had started. Had she been a poor preacher, the story of women in the Salvation Army might be different, but this was not the case. As her son Bramwell wrote:

> She reminded me again and again of counsel pleading with judge and jury for the life of the prisoner. The fixed attention of the court, the mastery of facts, the absolute self-forgetfulness of the advocate, the ebb and flow of feeling, the hush during the vital passages, all were there.[27]

Their joint ministry would take them to London's slums. William's father had died when he was fourteen and William's job as a pawnbroker's apprentice to support his family gave him a passion for the poor and suffering. Thus began The Christian Mission, later the Salvation Army. Catherine became known as 'army mother' to William's 'general' title. She often spoke to the wealthy to raise funds for the 'work' and led her own campaigns while raising nine children. Because of her insight, the Order and Regulations for the organization, drafted by William, included:

> A woman shall have the right to an equal share with men in the work of publishing salvation. A woman may hold any position of power and authority within the Army. A woman is not to be kept back from any position of power or influence on account of her sex. Women must be treated as equal with men in all intellectual and social relationships of life.[28]

Conclusion

Three women, three different ways of negotiating the 'public work and duty' for God over which they presided in Victorian England. It is significant that two are commemorated in the Church of England's Liturgical Calendar – Florence Nightingale, Social Reformer, on 13 August; and William and Catherine Booth, Founders of the Salvation Army, on 20 August. At a time when women presiding within *ecclesial* halls was fraught with opposition, exclusion and pain, each woman epitomized the broader meaning of *leitourgia* as 'public duty or work' for the common good of the *leos* (*laos*), people. This recovered concept of liturgy counters inward-looking absorption *within* halls of ritual or places of 'burnt offerings and sacrifices'. It reminds us that our 'liturgy' as people of God includes the public sphere of our world to which we are called, working for the good of all as our gift to the whole. In Florence's words, 'I have always felt I could live 1,000 lives to prove to [God] how inestimable the blessing I think it to be called.' [29]

Notes

1 Stark, M. (ed.), *Florence Nightingale's Cassandra* (New York: Feminist Press, 1979), p. 29.

2 See, for example, <http://www.victorianweb.org/authors/dickens/ge/rose3.html>.

3 Quoted in Moore, K., *Victorian Wives* (London: Allison and Busby, 1985), p. 205.

4 Dijkstra, B., *Idols of Perversity: Fantasies of Feminine Evil in Fin-de-siècle Culture* (Oxford: Oxford University Press, 1986), p. 26.

5 Comte, A., *System of Positive Polity, or Treatise on Sociology, Instituting the Religion of Humanity* (1851–54); quoted in Dijkstra, *Idols of Perversity*, p. 19.

6 'Liturgy', in McKechnie, L. (ed.), *Webster's New Universal Unabridged Dictionary, Second Deluxe Edition* (New York: New World Dictionaries/Simon and Schuster, 1979), p. 1058.

7 M'Clintock J. and Strong, J. (eds), *Cyclopaedia of Biblical, Theological and Ecclesiastical Literature, Vol V* (New York: Harper & Brothers Publishers, 1894), p. 456.

8 Dr James Barry's (1792–1865) method of presiding in his chosen profession of medicine was the most dramatic and risky. This brilliant medical student became

a military doctor practising in South Africa, the Mediterranean, the Caribbean and Canada, rising to the rank of Inspector General in charge of military hospitals. He also worked tirelessly to improve conditions for free and enslaved women, lepers and the indigent. On his deathbed, it was discovered for the first time that 'he' was a woman. See Holmes, R., *Scanty Particulars: The Scandalous Life and Astonishing Secret of Queen Victoria's Most Eminent Military Doctor* (New York: Random House, 2002).

9 Her father died when she was eight months old.

10 Corey, M. and Ochoa, G., *The Encyclopedia of the Victorian World: A Reader's Companion to the People, Places, Events and Everyday Life of the Victorian Era* (New York: Henry Holt and Company, 1996), p. 471.

11 Quoted in Webb, V., *Florence Nightingale: The Making of a Radical Theologian* (St Louis, MO: Chalice Press, 2002), p. 115.

12 Some women received the vote in 1888, though only in local or county elections, and without the right to stand for office themselves; women over thirty gained the full vote in 1918; and women over twenty-one in 1928.

13 Some argue that calling a woman by her first name rather than her surname demeans women if men are called by their surnames. However, I use women's first names in empathy for, and affinity with them and their work, as a woman. To avoid any criticism, I will deal similarly with the men to which I refer.

14 McDonald, L. (ed.), *The Collected Works of Florence Nightingale*, 16 vols (Ontario: Wilfred Laurier University Press, 2001). Florence's writings in the British Library alone form one of their largest personal collections.

15 Quoted in Webb, *Florence Nightingale*, p. 298.

16 Florence's grandfather, William Smith, proposed the 1813 Unitarian Toleration Act that removed Unitarian beliefs from the criminal list and also campaigned for the 1828 Test Act repeal allowing Nonconformists into Parliament. Although Florence was raised Church of England, the Unitarian influence shows through her theology.

17 Quoted in Webb, *Florence Nightingale*, p. 26.

18 Nightingale, F., *Ever Yours, Florence Nightingale – Selected Letters*, ed. Martha Vicinus and Bea Nergaard (Cambridge, MA: Harvard University Press, 1989), pp. 46–8.

19 Quoted in Webb, *Florence Nightingale*, p. 73.

20 Cook, E. T., *The Life of Florence Nightingale*, 2 vols (New York: Macmillan, 1943), Vol. 2, p. 434.

21 Parkin, C., 'Pioneer in Female Ministry', *Christian History* 26 (1990), pp. 10–13, at p. 11.

22 Parkin, 'Pioneer', p. 11.

23 Booth, C., *Female Ministry: or Woman's Right to Preach the Gospel* (New York: The Salvation Army Supplies Printing and Publishing Department, 1975), p. 5.

24 Booth, *Female Ministry*, p. 13.

25 Booth, *Female Ministry*, p. 14.

26 Booth, *Female Ministry*, p. 20.

27 Parkin, 'Pioneer', p. 13.

28 Parkin, 'Pioneer', p. 13.

29 Sullivan, M. C. (ed.), *The Friendship of Florence Nightingale and Mary Clare Moore* (Philadelphia, PA: University of Pennsylvania Press, 1999), p. 183.

A history of the presidency of women: snapshots from the movement for women's ordination in America, Britain and Australia

JULIA PITMAN

The history of women's ordination is relevant to any discussion of how women preside over congregations and church life in contemporary societies.[1] The issue of the similarity or difference of the ministry of women from that of men is not new. Evidence of the tension between women reflecting male practice and providing an alternative is apparent from the start of the modern movement for women's ordination in America in the 1850s and is still with us today. This 150-year history shows that women have sought both to transcend gender and also to provide a ministry that would be complementary to that of men in order to expose as wrong the definition of ministry as exclusively male. Women ministers sought to perform this function in areas such as preaching, presiding over congregations and church life more broadly, pastoral care and administration of the sacraments, which in Reformed and evangelical ecclesiology are baptism and the Lord's Supper or Eucharist. This chapter will explore how women addressed opposition to presiding at the sacraments in particular and the continuing relevance of this critique for the Roman Catholic Church, for the Orthodox Churches and for some branches of Protestantism.

In the 1850s as much as today, women's ordination was symbolic of the access of women to leadership in all areas of church life and the presentation of an alternative form of ministry. The first woman ordained in America was Antoinette L. Brown (1825–1921), in South Butler Congregational Church, New York, in 1853.[2] The women's conference at Seneca Falls (1848) supported the overthrow of the male 'monopoly of the pulpit' and over the years other ordinations followed in decentralized and theologically liberal denominations such as Universalist (1863), Christian (1867) and Unitarian (1871).[3] As members of Reformed and evangelical churches in a society without an established church, the first generations of women ministers justified the right to preach but they were also forced to address the question of the administration of the sacraments. Central to this history of advocacy on their own behalf was a critique of the doctrine of *in persona Christi*, the notion that only men could preside at the Lord's Supper, as well as the argument for an alternative contribution from women to ministry based on their capacity for maternity and their roles as wives and mothers.[4]

While this critique of male presidency at the Eucharist would start in the USA, it would be developed fully by women in Britain after the ordination of Constance Coltman (1889–1969) in English Congregationalism in 1917 and the appointment of Maude Royden (1876–1956), a member of the Church of England, to the position of Assistant Minister to Dr Fort Newton at the City Temple.[5] Closely related to the women's suffrage movement, the British movement for women's ordination emerged from within church suffrage societies started before the First World War.[6] These societies advocated spiritual militancy largely in opposition to the violent tactics used by suffragists who sought support for their cause from Church and State alike by setting fire to buildings and attacking letter boxes. In Britain, therefore, the movement for women's ordination was firmly embedded in the wider desire for equality for women. The first women ministers, lay preachers and pastors saw the need for the churches to appeal to woman suffragists who found little place in what they saw as thoroughly male-dominated institutions.

On both sides of the Atlantic, proponents of women's ordination provided a searching critique of the refusal to allow women to preside over congregations and the consequences for church life. Through a systematic reading of Scripture, the priority of Scripture over tradition and the critique of the notion of Christ as icon, women exposed the definition of ministry as exclusively male as idolatrous. They sought to address bias towards the experience of men in prayers of intercession and sermon illustrations. They tried to reform sacraments and pastoral services such as baptism, marriage and funerals. Women in the UK in particular sought to address opposition to women presiding at the Eucharist and to provide an alternative basis for such presidency. They sought nothing less than a new doctrine of God, Christology, call to discipleship, account of church history, and approach to pastoral care and to social justice campaigns that included the perspectives of women and children. Whether in Britain or America, presiding like a woman meant both transcending and emphasizing the difference of women from men in order to show that the definition of ministry as exclusively male should not be normative for the churches.

The United States

Antoinette Brown justified the right of women to preach from a careful exegesis of Scripture. From within a theological college and relying on modern biblical criticism, she focused her critique on Paul's injunction that women should not speak in church. Brown relativized the command that women be silent as culturally appropriate to the early Church but not to the churches of mid-nineteenth-century USA. Once in ministry, she was also forced to address opposition to women presiding at the sacraments. Having occupied the lay pastorate of South Butler Congregational Church for nine months, she wrote to her friend and woman's rights campaigner Lucy Stone (1818–93), that those who had become prepared to accept a woman preaching did not yet support her conducting the Lord's Supper.[7]

When Brown was ordained on 15 September 1853, Dr Harriot Hunt (1805–75), one of the first women medical doctors in the USA, argued for women's ordination on the basis of historical precedent, the special ministry of women, the transcendence of gender and Reformed ecclesiology. She argued that Brown's delivery of the benediction at her ordination service, the custom for ordinands in Congregationalism, invoked images of women in the Bible such as Anna, Phoebe, Priscilla, and the women at the tomb who 'proclaimed the glad tidings of the resurrection'.[8] Second, Hunt argued that a woman's special religious nature, particularly her biological capacity for maternity, fitted her particularly for ministry: 'there was something grand and elevating in the idea of a female presiding over a congregation, and breaking to them the bread of life.'[9] Third, she argued for the transcendence of gender in her use of Isaiah 49.15 where God's love is depicted as stronger than that of a mother who may in weakness forget her child. Finally, she argued that for Reformed churches, the practice of men 'performing *every* spiritual service, even to the dispensing of the sacraments' amounted not to the good ordering of the church, but to its '*disorder*'.[10]

In their apologetic for women's ministry and in their own practice of it, women ministers would combine both the transcendence of gender and an emphasis on it. While Antoinette Brown's ministry was short-lived, her successors would sustain their pastorates by transcending gender and by better personal and theological compatibility with their congregations.[11] Olympia Brown (1835–1926), ordained in the Northern Universalist Association in 1863, and Anna Howard Shaw (1847–1919), ordained in the Methodist Protestant Church in 1880, found that courage, risk-taking and judicious use of the threat of resignation could be required in the face of pettiness, unreasonableness and domineering attitudes. Shaw confronted conflict in her congregation head-on. She even refused to marry a couple because the bride wanted to vow to 'obey' her husband.[12] Olympia Brown critiqued what she saw as an unnecessary focus on the gender of Christ and the twelve disciples that was used to preserve a definition of ministry that was exclusively male. Contemporary churches did not require their ministers and church members to be Jewish, fishermen, tax-collectors or men – simply to search for the truth and to be 'filled with the Holy Spirit'.[13]

Women ministers also provided their own particular emphasis on pastoral care and reform of sacraments and pastoral services. Unitarian and Universalist women clergy working in churches on the expanding Western frontier sought to make the home sacred and to make the church a home where their people were cared for all week through services and programmes.[14] Women ministers conducted 'home christenings', modified baptism, marriage and funeral services, and gave priority to pastoral visiting when many male ministers were neglecting it. Instead of promoting a gospel of hell, judgement and damnation, they proclaimed a religion of love, personal responsibility and justice, where God could be imagined as a mother as much as a father, or a loving parent instead of a judge.

The United Kingdom

In Britain, the relationship of the nonconformist churches to the established Church of England meant that the context in which women's ordination emerged was very different. In fact, by contrast with America and in the light of the first women ordained in the Church of England in 1994, the history of the ordination of women in the UK has been relatively hidden from public consciousness.[15] By the First World War, the question of women's ordination had become a real issue for the Church of England and the Free Churches. Women had been ordained in Unitarianism from 1904, in Congregationalism from 1917 and were accepted into lay pastorates in Baptist Churches from 1918 and as ordained ministers from 1925. In Scotland, the question of the ministry of women would inform church union debates and the composition of the reunion of the Church of Scotland in 1929, with the United Free Church staying out of the union for reasons that included commitment to the ordination of women.[16]

The war had created opportunities for women to preach in the Free Churches and the National Mission of Repentance and Hope in 1916 had raised the issue of women preaching in the Church of England. A. Maude Royden became particularly famous in 1921 after the Bishop of London prevented her from conducting the Three Hours Service on Good Friday because it was '*especially sacred*'.[17] Women had already begun to discuss the inclusion of women in church government and ordination within church suffrage societies started before the war.[18] Spurred on by the Woman's Social and Political Union, suffragists targeted the churches as well as state and private institutions to enlist the churches' support for suffrage from the pulpit and in intercessory prayer. When their requests were not granted, women torched over fifty church buildings, boycotted local churches, staged dramatic walkouts of services, and interrupted services with questions, prayers and shouts of 'votes for women'.

The first women ministers, lay preachers and pastors responded to suffrage agitation in their worship services and advocacy work. The Revd Gertrude von Petzold (1876–1952), suffragist and first woman Unitarian pastor in

Britain, sought to add Emily Wilding Davison, who had thrown herself in front of the horses at Epsom racetrack on Derby Day (4 June 1913), to the tradition of Christian martyrs.[19] M. Ballard Dawson, suffragist and Methodist lay preacher in Swanage, argued for women's ordination if services were to have any meaning for women: 'Only on rare occasions does one hear a prayer, full of real understanding, offered in any place of worship for women whose burdens are almost too heavy to bear.'[20] While a few male ministers included women suffragists in their prayers, Hatty Baker, suffragist and author who shared a number of lay pastorates of Congregational churches with men, prayed for suffragists consistently, especially those imprisoned for suffrage.[21] Baker provided a systematic apologetic for women's ordination based on historical precedent, the special qualities of women and the humanity rather than the masculinity of Christ. She testified that suffragists longed for 'a church presided over by a woman minister'.[22] For Baker, 'a woman-pastor praying at the bedsides of sick and dying women, or at the incoming of new life into the world', was 'unsurpassable'.[23]

Constance Coltman, the first woman ordained in English and Welsh Congregationalism, was the first Reformed woman minister to critique the idea of ceremonial uncleanness that underpinned opposition to women presiding at the sacraments. The daughter of wealthy Scottish Presbyterians, Constance Todd had read History at Somerville College, Oxford, before starting theology at Mansfield College in 1913.[24] She was ordained on 17 September 1917 to Darby Street Mission, a mission of King's Weigh House, in a joint pastorate with her fiancé Claude Coltman. Claude focused on preaching and chairing meetings, while Constance applied herself to pastoral care, baptism, weddings and suffrage services. She offered pastoral care to those who would not seek it from a man, revised the marriage service, and became an advocate for women's ordination in the church and women's movement.[25]

Technically, Reformed theology did not accept the doctrine of *in persona Christi*, that the administration of the sacraments had to reflect literally the image of Christ presiding at the Lord's Supper, but among lay people this view could be powerful.[26] Coltman's apologetic for women presiding at the sacraments was informed by the debate on reunion between the Church of England and the Free Churches, and the decisions of Lambeth Conferences in relation to the ordination of women. She saw the debate on the place of women within the Anglican Church as the 'strategic centre of the struggle' between Protestantism and Roman Catholicism.[27] Coltman was also influenced by a catholic movement within nonconformity: the minister at King's Weigh House was Dr W. E. Orchard, the leader of the Society of Free Catholics who would eventually become a Roman Catholic. Coltman argued for women confessors and the church press reported the Coltmans' assistance to Orchard at Holy Communion in King's Weigh House and the presentation to them at their ordination service of a Bible and a chalice.[28] With Maude Royden, Coltman promoted the idea of women combining marriage, motherhood and ministry.

In response to the refusal of the Lambeth Conference in 1920 to allow deaconesses to administer the sacraments, Constance Coltman argued:'Whence comes this widespread shrinking among men and women alike from a woman having aught to do with the Blessed Sacrament?'[29] For Coltman the incarnation should abolish any sense of 'curse' on a woman's body. She argued that after the fourth century women were excluded from priestly roles and that the idea of ceremonial uncleanness was introduced at the Reformation.[30] In her advocacy of women's ordination in the State Church of Sweden she would argue that the experience of newly confirmed children who had received Holy Communion from women ministers would be more powerful 'than any argument'.[31] She invested women's presidency at the Eucharist with positive significance, reflecting the image of the incarnation through the body of Mary and the maternal functions of women who were claiming

> the privilege and duty of exercising the ministry not only of the Word but also of the Sacraments. Through Mary the Word became Incarnate, and from a woman's body was wrought the flesh and blood that hung on Calvary. What more fitting than that by the hand of a woman the Body and Blood of Our Lord should ever and again be given to His people? Christ has re-deemed the whole sphere of sex, and women no longer shrink from the pangs of motherhood as from the onslaught of demons, but they may joyfully accept their privilege of filling up the measure of the travail of the creative love of God. What more fitting than that the child who is the fruit of that travail should be welcomed by the hand of a woman into the Church of Christ?[32]

Maude Royden would develop this critique of ceremonial uncleanness even further, but she would not live to see the advent of women's ordination in the Church of England. Royden's biographer, Sheila Fletcher, argues that hers was a story of a 'fading, if not a failing of vocation'.[33] An intelligent, passionate and dramatic Oxford scholar, Royden combined a love of High Church ritual, Reformed preaching and an evangelical passion for the saving of souls with commitment to the ecumenical movement. Having occupied a seat in the pew for forty years, as a lay pastor she sought to combat clericalism in all its forms.[34] Despite two pastorates at the City Temple (1917–1920) and her own ecumenical venture, the Guildhouse (1920–1937), Royden would focus more and more on preaching and her work for peace, which would take her away from her pastorates on tours of the UK, the United States and, in 1928, around the world.

Royden's critique of the doctrine of *in persona Christi* arose from her understanding of priesthood and her approach to worship. She sought to transcend gender – she argued that lay people would only concentrate on a minister if they too forgot gender.[35] She also saw motherhood as a metaphor for ministry.[36] She introduced new methods into her services to encourage lay participation such as discussion after the sermon, interaction during the offering, and encouragement to learn music with the Guildhouse organist and quartet.[37] From the pulpit, Royden offered her own feminist theological perspective on the doctrine of God, humanity and social justice issues, arguing for a new reading of Genesis of humanity made in the image of God and against vices such as regulated prostitution in France.[38] At the City Temple, she started a clinic for women seeking pastoral care.[39] Often counselling grief-stricken young women whose loved ones had been killed in the Great War, she asked them to sublimate their sexuality in community service.

Royden did not administer the Eucharist lest it expose her to discipline from the Church of England.[40] Within Anglicanism, she was ostracized and ridiculed for baptizing children and offering forgiveness to penitents, but she appealed to the decisions of past church courts to defend her right to baptize children as a lay person.[41] Her baptism and marriage services were modifications of the Grey Book suggestions for the revision of the Book of Common Prayer (1928). In her baptism service, she rejected the opening paragraph of the received version that expressed baptism as an antidote to original sin, stressing instead the child as a gift from God and the responsibility of the parents before God in raising it.[42]

Royden defined ceremonial uncleanness as theologically sanctioned and ritualized revulsion against the natural functions of maternity: menstruation, conception and childbirth, which was most fully expressed in the Roman Catholic Church where women were excluded from the sanctuary, from washing communion linen, and from speaking in consecrated buildings.[43] She was appalled that the controversy during the National Mission was related to a woman speaking in a consecrated building rather than an ordinary one. Royden argued that this attitude and set of practices arose from the Church's failure to address the question of sex and, in particular, from the doctrine of the virgin birth, which, she believed, was entirely possible by natural means. She therefore rejected the purification of women after childbirth in the Jewish, Roman Catholic and Anglican 'churching' rites, and sought instead to invest motherhood with positive significance as was often found in the world of politics and nonconformist religion.

Royden's thought informed that of Christian women in Britain and around the world through the Guildhouse and the Society for the Ministry of Women (1929).[44] Of over three hundred members on the Overseas Roll of the Guildhouse, the greatest number of subscribers was from America, Australia and New Zealand.[45] The thought of the first woman ordained in the British Commonwealth, Winifred Kiek (1884–1975) in South Australian

Congregationalism, was thoroughly indebted to Royden.[46] An English migrant originally from Manchester who had been raised as a Quaker, Kiek gained experience as a preacher in the Brotherhood Movement in Yorkshire, and followed her husband to Australia in 1920 for him to assume the position of Principal of Parkin College, Adelaide.[47] In 1926, having been awarded the Bachelor of Divinity from the Melbourne College of Divinity in 1923, Kiek was called to the vacant pastorate of Colonel Light Gardens and was ordained on 13 June 1927. During Royden's world tour in 1928, Kiek presided at a service in Stow Memorial Congregational Church in which Royden preached.[48]

Through Kiek's work in two pastorates and her co-ordination of the Australian response to the World Council of Churches' Inquiry into the Status of Women in the late 1940s and early 1950s, Royden's insight 'that there is something in the very nature of woman that desecrates a holy place' remained pertinent.[49] Kiek believed that such ideas need not be a 'curse', rather 'there is motherhood in God' indeed, 'joy in the creation of a soul maternal'.[50] The issue of ceremonial uncleanness would continue to play a powerful role in opposition to women's leadership and ordination into the 1980s and 1990s, when the first women Moderators were elected in the Uniting Church in Australia (inaugurated 1977) and women were ordained in most dioceses of the Anglican Church.[51] Dr Jill Tabart, the first woman President of the Uniting Church, was elected in 1991 amid a wave of feminist enthusiasm. She noted soberly, however, that the 'time of genuine ... equality' was not 'yet here'.[52]

In Reformed and evangelical traditions in nineteenth-century USA and Edwardian Britain, women gained access to roles as Christian ministers and lay pastors that allowed them to preside over congregations and to convey an ideal of ministry that both transcended gender and allowed for gender difference. Women sought to reform services, and to write sermons and prayers that reflected a renewed vision of theology, of the motherhood as well as the fatherhood of God, of the discipleship and experience of women as well as men, and of a new world order that recognized gender equality and difference. In the USA, the position of the Reformed churches in a society without an established church meant that Antoinette Brown, Olympia Brown and Anna Howard Shaw focused on the priority of Scripture over tradition in their defence of the right to preach, but they were also forced to address the doctrine of *in persona Christi*. In Britain, where there was a much stronger movement for women's ordination within the Church of England that influenced the Free Churches, Constance Coltman and Maude Royden would provide a thorough critique of opposition to women presiding at the sacraments that was based in the idea of ceremonial uncleanness. Coltman and Royden's new basis for such presidency transcended gender and infused womanhood, particularly motherhood, with positive value. In the construction of their arguments British women could be as essentialist about women's bodies as the arguments they sought to counteract, but they played a considerable role in exposing as wrong the assumption of a definition of ministry that was exclusively male and, in doing so, they started to erode the trenchant opposition to women in ministry. Their efforts would be appropriated around the world in places such as Australia, and remain unfinished. The final overthrow of theologically sanctioned opposition to the very nature of women's bodies may be a long road, but it remains a vitally important task of the Church of today, of tomorrow and into the future.

Notes

1 The research for this chapter was assisted by the award of a Travelling Research Fellowship from the Australian Academy of the Humanities.

2 Cazden, E., *Antoinette Brown Blackwell: A Biography* (Old Westbury, NY: Feminist Press, 1983).

3 Zink-Sawyer, B., *From Preachers to Suffragists: Woman's Rights and Religious Conviction in the Lives of Three Nineteenth Century American Clergywomen* (Louisville, KY: Westminster John Knox Press, 2003), p. 18; Chaves, M., *Ordaining Women: Culture and Conflict in Religious Organizations* (Cambridge, MA: Harvard University Press, 1997); Wessinger, C. (ed.), *Religious Institutions and Women's Leadership: New Roles Inside the Mainstream* (Columbia, SC: University of South Carolina Press, 1996), pp. 352–3.

4 The critique of *in persona Christi* has a longer history in the modern period than Frances Young allows. See her 'Hermeneutical Questions: The Ordination of Women in the Light of Biblical and Patristic Typology', in Jones, I., Wootton, J. and Thorpe, K. (eds), *Women and Ordination in the Christian Churches: International Perspectives* (London: Continuum, 2008), pp. 21–39.

5 Kaye, E., 'A Turning-point in the Ministry of Women: The Ordination of the First Woman to the Christian Ministry in England in September 1917', in Sheils, W. J. and Wood, D. (eds), *Studies in Church History* 27 (Oxford: Blackwell, 1990), pp. 505–12; Fletcher, S., *Maude Royden: A Life* (Oxford: Blackwell, 1989), pp. 156–84.

6 deVries, J. R., 'Transforming the Pulpit: Preaching and Prophecy in the British Women's Suffrage Movement', in Mayne Kienzle, B., and Walker, P. J. (eds), *Women Preachers and Prophets Through Two Millennia of Christianity* (Berkeley, CA: University of California Press, 1998), pp. 318–33; Inkpin, J., 'Combatting the "Sin of Self-Sacrifice": Christian Feminism in the Women's Suffrage Struggle: (1903–1918)', unpublished PhD thesis, University of Durham, 1996.

7 Cazden, *Antoinette Brown Blackwell*, p. 78.

8 Hunt, H. K., *Glances and Glimpses* (Boston, MA: John P. Jewett, 1856), p. 306.

9 Hunt, *Glances and Glimpses*, pp. 304–5.

10 Hunt, *Glances and Glimpses*, p. 203, emphasis in original.

11 Zink-Sawyer, *From Preachers to Suffragists*, pp. 123–69.

12 *New York Times*, 15 June 1914, p. 1.

13 Quoted in Zink-Sawyer, *From Preachers to Suffragists*, p. 92.

14 Grant Tucker, C., *Prophetic Sisterhood: Liberal Women Ministers of the Frontier, 1880–1930* (Boston, MA: Beacon Press, 1990).

15 Kaye, E., Lees, J. and Thorpe K. (eds), *Daughters of Dissent* (London: United Reformed Church, 2004), p. viii.

16 Orr MacDonald, L. A., *A Unique and Glorious Mission: Women and Presbyterianism in Scotland, 1830–1930* (Edinburgh: John Donald, 2000), p. 210.

17 Fletcher, *Maude Royden*, pp. 185–7, 194–5, emphasis in original p. 195.

18 These included the Church League for Woman Suffrage in 1909, the Free Church League for Woman Suffrage in 1911, and the Scottish Churches' League for Woman Suffrage in 1912; see deVries, 'Transforming the Pulpit'; Inkpin, 'Combatting the "Sin of Self Sacrifice"', pp. 1, 383; MacDonald, *Unique and Glorious Mission*, pp. 294–326.

19 Gilley, K., 'Gertrude von Petzold – The Pioneer Woman Minister', *Transactions of the Unitarian Historical Society* 21.3 (1997), pp. 157–72; *Suffragette*, 20 June 1913, p. 602.

20 *Vote*, 16 August 1918, p. 355.

21 For suffragists' interjections and male ministers' prayers for suffragists see *Suffragette*, 14 November 1913–20 March 1914; For Baker's prayers see *Suffragette*, 28 November 1913, p. 148; 5 December 1913, p. 173; 27 March 1914, p. 546.

22 *Suffragette*, 19 December 1913, p. 225.

23 Baker, H., *Women in the Ministry* (London: C. W. Daniel, 1911), pp. 52–3.

24 Kaye, E., 'Constance Coltman – A Forgotten Pioneer', *Journal of the United Reformed Church History Society* 4.2 (1988), pp. 134–46.

25 *The Coming Day*, February–March 1918, p. 15; *Vote*, 17 August 1923, p. 259; 3 March 1922, p. 66.

26 Forsyth, P. T., *Christian World*, 23 August 1917, p. 4.

27 *Woman Citizen* (New York), 14 January 1922, pp. 11, 22.

28 *Christian Commonwealth*, 4 July 1917; *Coming Day*, October 1917, p. 80.

29 *Free Catholic*, October 1920, p. 162.

30 *Vote*, 3 March 1922, p. 66.

31 *Christian World*, 18 August 1960.

32 Coltman, C. M., 'Post-Reformation: The Free Churches', in Royden, A. M. (ed.), *The Church and Woman* (London: James Clarke, 1924), pp. 134–5.

33 Fletcher, *Maude Royden*, p. 4.

34 Royden to Dick Sheppard, 4 October 1920, MS 3747 f.51, Sheppard Papers, Lambeth Palace Library, London.

35 *Guildhouse Monthly*, June 1928, p. 189; Royden, M., *Sex and Commonsense* (London: Hurst and Blackett, 1922), p. 163.

36 Royden, A. M., *The Lambeth Conference and the Ministrations of Women* (London: League of the Church Militant, 1920), p. 4.

37 Fletcher, *Maude Royden*, pp. 212–13.

38 Royden, *Sex and Commonsense*, p. 27; Fletcher, *Maude Royden*, p. 175.

39 Fletcher, *Maude Royden*, p. 174.

40 Joseph Fort Newton, 'A. Maude Royden', *The Christian Century*, 12 May 1921, pp. 9–11.

41 See *Sunday Circle*, 15 December 1917, 7AMR/1/58 folder 1 of 2; Royden to the Editor, *The Challenge*, n.d., 7AMR/1/69, Royden Papers, Women's Library, London.

42 See the marked copy of *A New Prayer Book* (1923), pp. 144–50, 157, 7AMR/2/36, the Baptism 7AMR/2/06 and Marriage Services 7AMR/2/07, Royden Papers.

43 Royden, *The Church and Woman*, pp. 207–11; *Church Militant*, April 1921, p. 30 quoted in Fletcher, *Maude Royden*, pp. 198–200; see also pp. 151–3.

44 Kaye et al., *Daughters of Dissent*, p. 72. See, for example, the testimonials of Margaret Hardy and Kathleen Hendry.

45 Overseas Roll of the Fellowship Guild, 1929–1931, 7AMR/1/05, Royden Papers.

46 Julia Pitman, 'Prophets and Priests: Congregational Women in Australia, 1919–1977' (unpublished PhD thesis, University of Adelaide, 2005); Knauerhase, M., *Winifred: The Story of Winifred Kiek, the first woman to be ordained to the Christian ministry in Australia, 1884–1975* (Adelaide: Lutheran Publishing House, 1978); *Australian Dictionary of Biography*, vol. 9, pp. 587–8. Winifred Kiek is listed among the saints in the 'Calendar of Other Commemorations' in *Uniting in Worship 2*, but is best remembered by members of Australian Church Women (founded 1963) for the scholarship that bears her name. Robert Gribben, 'Saints Under the Southern Cross: The Uniting Church in Australia', in Burns, S., and Monro, A. (eds), *Christian Worship in Australia: Inculturating the Liturgical Tradition* (Strathfield: St Paul's Publications, 2009), pp. 91–105.

47 Kiek, W., Ordination Statement, p. 4, PRG 225/1, Kiek Papers, State Library of South Australia, Adelaide.

48 *Adelaide Register*, 2 July 1928.

49 Kiek, W., *We of One House* (Sydney: Australian Council for the World Council of Churches, 1952), p. 22.

50 Kiek, *We of One House*, pp. 51–2.

51 Drake, N., and Whitlam, F., 'Freda Whitlam', in Wood Ellem, E. (ed.), *Church Made Whole: National Conference on Women in the Uniting Church in Australia 1990* (Melbourne: David Lovell Publishing, 1990), pp. 272–4; Porter, M., *Women in the Church: The Great Ordination Debate in Australia* (Harmondsworth: Penguin, 1989), p. 6 and Porter, M., *The New Puritans: The Rise in Fundamentalism in the Anglican Church* (Melbourne: Melbourne University Press, 2006), p. 94.

52 *Weekend Australian*, 20–21 July 1991, p. 3.

Unequivocal affirmation of the saving significance of 'difference'

ANN LOADES

Introduction

In the last century and in some parts of the world there have been significant shifts in what we now may refer to as 'gender' relationships, indicating by 'gender' the relationship of the 'feminine' to the 'masculine' and vice versa, and this in turn to the biological sex differences between males and females. Neither gender nor sex are uncontentious as categories, since how one becomes one or the other or a mix of both in a given society or culture may be a complicated matter, though sexual difference in itself may on average be clear in many cases. That said, being a person whose genitals are interior rather than exterior to one's main body structure can hardly count as decisive without reference to any other consideration when considering a person's potential or actual maturity, gifts or achievements. Controversy almost inevitably arises, however, when habits of expectation about being 'feminine' or 'masculine' shift, and shift markedly, as social and economic structures, educational opportunity, life expectancy, health, threats to one's life-group, location, privileges, the values associated with one's race, and mobility may alter those habits piecemeal and in unpredictable ways. The grace of a hitherto unsuspected vocation or ambition may in one context or another discomfit those who had never thought of such possibilities either for themselves or for anyone they know. It can be difficult to accept and to act on the realization that patterns of expectation and habit which have suited human beings in their interactions no longer do so and need renegotiation, not least with regard to such central concerns as the care of the very young, and of the vulnerable of whatever age. Particularly difficult to negotiate may be the disturbances arising from within rather than from without a particular tradition and when the arguments that arise can be shown to put in question the human dignity of each person. Where that seems to be the case, and it would appear that gifts to a whole community are neither appropriately valued nor shared, that talent is being ignored or undeveloped on wholly inappropriate grounds, such as being 'female' rather than 'male', then much honest rethinking is required. Timidity, unacknowledged fear, or rage and resentment that someone has the possibility to be or to do something denied to oneself in the past or present, may be

77

deeply damaging to all concerned in the process. And distress at someone's undertaking a role unquestioningly thought to be the preserve of one particular group or one sex rather than the other can take subtle forms, including what may seem at first to be no more troublesome than sheer indifference – which may of course deprive a movement for change of much-needed energy, commitment and far-sightedness.

Habits can die hard …

So far as the Church of England and the Anglican Communion and many other post-Reformation churches were concerned until about a century ago, it would have been difficult for a woman herself to suppose that she had a vocation to ordination, though some women had rediscovered the possibilities of life in a religious order or order of deaconesses and were tackling all sorts of social work, freed from the constraints of family expectations of what to some seemed to be of a profoundly boring range of options. The devaluation of women as intrinsically inferior to men (depending on what has been made of such texts as 1 Corinthians 11 and 1 Timothy 2.12 by theologians down the ages) was expressed in social and economic conditions, though these inevitably affected the lives of most men too, depending on social class. Many women were overwhelmingly preoccupied with sheer survival of multiple childbearing and rearing in actual or near destitution, in backbreaking work on the land or in factories or 'sweatshops', managing households which were still economic units, living in atrocious conditions, and with few opportunities for the education which might open up other possibilities for them. In the nineteenth century in the UK as elsewhere legislation had made it possible for married women to keep some of the financial resources which had accrued to them after their marriage, not least the money they themselves earned, which had done something to reduce the preference of some of the better educated for the single state, but without the vote and a significant voice in public life, women remained vulnerable in all too many ways. Even some of the most competent might still be diffident about taking the minutes of a committee meeting – let alone chairing it – or daring to join the few prepared to speak from a platform in public. There were of course some admirable examples to be followed, not least in their development of such political skills as could be used to change public opinion, such as writing petitions, taking part in marches and parades, organizing rallies, and, like it or not, drawing on the support of those men who had the sense to see that changes were needed at every level of society, and that these would benefit men as well as the women who were campaigning for them. Then as now, there were many demanding social causes which required the energies of women to tackle. It was during the twentieth century that some of the needed changes were put into effect.

Reconsidering religious tradition

The upheaval of terrible wars, which stretched far beyond Europe with appalling casualties and economic devastation, contributed to massive upheavals of all kinds, with fundamental questions inevitably asked about whether things had to be the way they were. If women could have access to education and to a measure of economic independence, could vote and even stand for election to a legislature, could even qualify in medicine and the law, to mention only two obvious 'professional' areas of expertise where the bastions of male privilege had had to fall, and given the degree of support they gave to their religious traditions, there was no very convincing reply to the question as to why they could not act as churchwardens, serve on parish councils, collect financial offerings, read lessons, write intercessions, and even preach – despite what ecclesiastical tradition had made of the supposed significance of women's bodily difference from males. On the one hand women enjoyed a certain equality with men in that they could be baptized, confirmed, forgiven, be ministers of sacramental exchange with a male in marriage, receive communion, chrism, or a blessing, and like any other person they could baptize someone in extreme circumstances. On the other hand, it had long been supposed that they would never themselves be able to confirm someone, pronounce forgiveness in the name of a merciful deity, celebrate communion, chrismate or bless someone, though they could have considerable responsibility for the transmission of religious traditions in the lives of their groups of kin. They had no say in gatherings of ecclesiastics, though of course neither did lay males. The difficulties all clustered round what seemed to be a matter of divinely authorized sanction, as it were, which was that although males as males could in principle avail themselves of all sorts of opportunities and adventures as these presented themselves, women as women could do nothing of the kind.

Those wanting biblical support for this position might turn to Charles Gore's *St Paul's Epistle to the Ephesians: A Practical Exposition* of 1905,[1] and in particular Gore's comments on Ephesians 5 and 6, which appear amazingly unedifying to at least some readers in the twenty-first century, though undoubtedly expressing what some still suppose to be defensible in the name of Christian tradition. It is clear that for Gore and for those who would still support his perspective, women are necessarily subordinate because inferior to men, whatever might be urged in favour of their 'spiritual' equality. It is still the view of some that women should in no circumstances be in a position of authority over men, such as teaching in mixed classes, running a school or a government department, certainly not teaching theology or holding any kind of office in a church, including chairing a board of social responsibility or whatever, simply by virtue of their biological sexual differentiation from males. The implications for domestic life are obvious, and arguably grim. And careful exegesis of other parts of Scripture has to be undertaken to put this kind of material from Ephesians in its place as not finally authoritative, given other theological convictions, for example, the significance of baptism for the affirmation of the full human dignity of all human persons, male and female alike. From this of course nothing inevitably follows one way or another unless weight is given to the significance of the grace of possible vocations to various forms of ministry, to be appropriately considered and valued in an ecclesial group. It does not seem rational to argue that a woman's vocation cannot be taken seriously simply because she is female, with the implication that she must be thoroughly deluded in some way to suppose that she has some such vocation, or that it needs redirection.

Given that religious traditions are vehicles of stability as well as, in some circumstances, of radical change, it is understandable that in such circumstances as the upheavals of the first part of the twentieth century the comfort of the familiar and traditional might well seem to be worth valuing and defending. And it has to be remembered that until well on into the second half of the twentieth century research in the history of women as distinct from men, outside as well as within the churches, simply had not been done or was not widely available. It took time to establish, in respect of the origins of Christianity in particular, that women had played significant roles in early Christian communities, founding and providing hospitality for churches visited by Paul and others, that they were 'ordained' to the diaconate and exercised authority in various communities well into the second millennium – depending of course on what might be meant in different contexts by 'ordination'. In any case, 'ordination' to a variety of roles seems to have been characteristic in respect of a wider range of responsibilities for women and men alike than we might now suppose to require religious authorization.[2] Unsurprisingly, when the question of the ordination of women in the Church was raised after the Second World War (and it had been raised in a variety of ways well before that) some warhorse-style arguments were to be rehearsed.

A classic example

C. S. Lewis had become a convert and stalwart member of the Church of England as he found his footing in English academic life, one of the exceptionally privileged few males to have secured a university-level education, in a university – Oxford – which after the First World War admitted women to degrees. The UK was as a whole a very long way behind, for example, the USA in the educational opportunities open to women, and in such universities as existed they remained in the minority. There was no problem in seeing (or not seeing) women undertaking menial jobs, or in taking the place of men unavailable for filling traditional occupations, but working alongside women as professional equals remained a novel experience for most men. And immediately after the Second World War it was understandable that those who could would want to re-found families, which in the circumstances of the time would almost inevitably mean that many women would manage household and family, rather than battle with the commercial or professional world. Poor women had no option but to juggle multiple commitments. Circumstances alter cases, however, and it became known that the Bishop of Hong Kong had in 1944 ordained Florence Tim-Oi Li to serve Christians in China, otherwise bereft of ordained ministry with all that it entailed. In 1948 the Bishops of the Lambeth Conference condemned their fellow bishop's action, at which point Tim-Oi ceased to exercise her ministry until 1970, by which time views on the matter had shifted significantly elsewhere in the Anglican Communion. C. S. Lewis in 1948 published a reaction to the proposal that women should in fact be ordained in a lamentable essay, 'Priestesses in the Church', with the very title making it clear that 'priest' was not a gender-inclusive term. Republished several times in collections of his essays, it is also to be found in Louis Bouyer's *Woman in the Church* with an epilogue by Hans Urs von Balthasar,[3] as an interesting item in ecumenical exchange in favour of the defence of a preconceived position.

Whatever the merits of some of Lewis's writings, he sometimes found it very difficult indeed to take on board perfectly fair criticism of values rightly defended in themselves if not in one application or another. Such, arguably, helps to illuminate his problem with 'priestesses', though he was by no means blind to the failings of 'masculine' males, aware as he was of their capacity for self-interested and devious behaviour, of their violence, cruelty and capacity for intimidation. He wrote as a veteran of the First World War as well as a close observer of the course of the Second World War from his Oxford college. There was abundant evidence all around him, as well as in his own haunting memories, of the damage done to several generations of young men, not least those that were recovering from their wounds if not from their traumas as they began or resumed their university degree courses or found themselves teaching again. Lewis understood what it was to be 'masculine' in a Christlike way, in having the strength and intelligence integrated with emotion to be self-sacrificing and self-giving, and when he criticized members of his own sex for not being 'masculine' enough he was urging his understanding of Christlikeness upon them. This was to render his position, and the position of those who think like him, problematic in that the 'feminine' obverse of this was supposed to be 'receptivity', the receptivity of all human persons to such divine initiative, when it was clear enough that self-sacrifice and self-giving were being urged as 'feminine' virtues, in addition to self-effacement, for example. It is far from self-evident that females should be deemed to be exclusively 'feminine', that is, 'creaturely/receptive' and males exclusively 'Christlike' in self-giving and initiative-taking, except as part and parcel of gendered patterns which consistently render the female/'feminine' as inferior to the male/masculine, but this underlies Lewis's convictions when he discusses 'priestesses'. Given his skills as a novelist and as a broadcaster as well as a letter-writer, he had ample opportunity to recommend his view as normatively Christian without self-criticism or a serious attempt at re-evaluation.

In his 1948 essay, therefore, Lewis thought that ordaining women would cut us off from the Christian past – which one might of course think would have much to recommend it in a church which had committed itself to 'reformation' centuries earlier. He did not consider the view that the ordination of women could well be regarded as the fruition and enrichment of ministry in direct continuity with the past, nor that it remains a strange view of divine grace to suppose that it (so to speak) does not 'take' in the case of a female, irrespective of any other consideration, given her capacity to receive grace and blessing otherwise. Lewis also thought that the ordination of women would widen the differences between the Church of England and other churches, but again, that depends on one's ecclesiastical conversation partners.

Given that the Roman Catholic Church does not recognize the validity of the orders of Church of England or Anglican clergy in any case, and that there were and are many other ecclesial groups to consider, it remains far from clear why this matter was thought to be so central rather than, for example, Petrine primacy, papal infallibility, transubstantiation, the dogma of the Immaculate Conception, and compulsory celibacy for all clergy. Commitment to most of these, assuming it could be sustained, could and would snarl up relationships with other ecclesial groups, whereas the ministry of women as 'ordained' has become a matter on which they might unite, and that for very good theological reasons.

In any case, Lewis was treading a knife-edge in his discussion, seeing that he claimed to have every respect for those who thought some women to be sincere, pious, sensible, well able to preach, sort problems out, able to be tactful and sympathetic and give good pastoral advice, visit parishioners, able to learn theology – something of a concession in UK universities until after the Second World War admittedly, though other avenues for theological study had been opening for many years, not least under the aegis of the Archbishops of Canterbury. In other words, it was only too evident that women could do things once thought only to be possible or proper for men, despite the many attempts there had been to block them – in 'middle-class' professions at least. Lewis did not consider the sense in which 'ordination' was a matter of joining a profession, and in any case depended to some degree on the social standing of the clergy, which itself was to shift. Lewis was far from uncritical of those he knew at close quarters, as well as having much sympathy for those so badly financed that they were not far from starving. Lewis's conclusion could well have been that it was essential to maintain the integrity of pastoral ministry and the ministry of word and sacrament, and that if women were undertaking one they should be undertaking the other. Alternatively, if this were not to be the case, since they were acting in 'masculine' roles, they should have been excluded from them.

Lewis's most significant problem lay with the issue of 'representation', however, the matter of the representation of humanity to God and God to humanity. In common with many others he was familiar only with eastward-facing celebrations of Holy Communion, but also inevitably with the conduct of Matins and Evensong where again the matter of representation would have to be considered. He found no objection to a woman representing humanity to God – indeed, given that the 'feminine' symbolized 'receptivity' this might well be thought to be particularly appropriate. He found a difficulty, however, in the divine being represented to a congregation when a woman faced an assembled congregation. Here Lewis surely failed to grasp the full implications of his discomfort. We can spare him the crudity of the Archbishops' Commission of 1936 which had most foolishly suggested that there would be a lowering of the 'tone' of Christian worship if a woman were conducting it because of the way men would be likely to look at her (presumably implying as a 'sexed' person) whereas women were unlikely so to regard ordained males.[4] The grounds on which the Commission made this astonishing claim about women is unclear, quite apart from the way males might regard males, or for that matter, women regard women – clearly beyond the imaginative horizon of the Archbishops' Commission members, or beyond their capabilities to address in print. It is perfectly possible to learn to discipline one's imagination and desires in most contexts, and worship is one such context. Lewis knew perfectly well that the Eucharist would be valid even if the priest were in a state of mortal sin, but the implication of what he said was that it would be invalid simply by virtue of a woman's sexual difference from a male, clear once she turned round, irrespective of the 'masculine' gender she would embody in preaching and celebrating.

Lewis did not explain himself at this point, and so leaves us uninformed as to the problem of how a woman's presence could be so problematic if clothed in cassock, surplice and scarf (and academic hood), or alb and chasuble, since only hands and face would be visible, minus 'Adam's apple' and the need to shave, admittedly, and with a different pitch of voice, probably most evident if a liturgy were to be 'sung'. Could Lewis really have supposed that such visible and audible differences could make a nonsense of the 'representation' of the divine, if any human person may so 'represent' God, since it could hardly be argued that no one could literally look like a first-century Galilean rabbi? And in any case, on one view, Christ's 'presence' was deemed to be sought as it were in the consecrated elements, or one could suppose oneself to be related to the glorified Christ in faith. The visual appearance of the priest was now being made an issue, with unacknowledged implications for the understanding of the eucharistic rite.[5]

All in all, Lewis put in jeopardy the principle that the priest existed to minister to the grace of God and Christ's self-giving, and in turn Christ's redemption of the whole of humanity. It was then, and it remains now, a question as to how this could be rendered meaningless were a priest female. As Lewis said, he wanted the 'salute' to be given to the 'uniform', not the wearer, claiming that only one 'wearing the masculine uniform' can between now and the parousia represent the divine to the Church, but since he construes the 'masculine' as he does, it would seem appropriate to argue that a female can wear such a 'masculine' uniform – it is not a matter of biological sex. The 'uniform' (whether construed as 'masculine' or 'feminine' in all their variability) is the authority given to an ordained person by the Church, and signified in various ways, as, for example, in the garb for conducting a service. And in respect of another 'ordained' office, Lewis knew this perfectly well, for in appreciation of Queen Elizabeth II's coronation he wrote that she represented humanity called by God to be God's vice-regent and high priest on earth, which seems to be a clear case of saluting the 'uniform' rather than the 'wearer' as it were, irrespective of the biological sex of the one crowned.[6]

Into the future

Lewis was of course right to perceive that the very language of theology and devotion would change if women could represent the 'divine' to humanity as well as vice versa. We can agree with him that bowdlerization of (for example) the major Christian creeds or the Prayer that Jesus taught need not be an option, and indeed find very good reasons for the Incarnation of God having taken a male form, in terms of 'the humility of a non-gendered God'.[7] It may be possible also to continue with the gendered language of the relationship between Christ and the Church as Bridegroom and Bride, the latter being understood as a 'collective' metaphor. But there are also very good reasons to amplify the range of language used of God in both worship and devotion in order precisely to make it clear that God remains mysterious beyond our comprehension, yet inviting response in humanly inclusive ways. The female/feminine can as adequately and inadequately 'say' God in as full and in as limited a way as the male/masculine, each correcting the other, and reminding us that when we speak of God we stammer, we say 'yes' and 'no'.[8]

Moving beyond Lewis, we could further constructively argue from the presence of Mary the Mother of Jesus at Pentecost (Acts 1.14) that there are implications here for the evangelistic and ordained ministry of women if such implications exist for men, since the proclamation of Christ's resurrection is the responsibility of those whose vocation it is to be placed in the apostolic succession, irrespective of biological sexual differentiation. It is also certainly necessary to reconstrue Mary's response to God at the 'Annunciation' in terms of generosity, courage and delight, rooted in her discipleship throughout her life, no matter what the difficulties and experiences of anguish her commitment to God was to entail. This also has consequences for the understanding of her 'Assumption', given that this means that her 'bodiliness' remains held to the centre of divine and sacred life. Since Christ became and remains through God's recreative grace incarnate 'from the Holy Spirit and the Virgin Mary' and his humanity is that through which our own salvation is mediated, there is arguably an implication that she remains central and not peripheral to the human hope for blessing and transformation of human life. As Tina Beattie has proposed, picking up a phrase of Irenaeus in referring to Mary as 'Eve's advocate', Mary as it were 'voices' Eve in the Magnificat, bearing Eve in her own person, each implying the other.[9] She does not exist as a counterpart to a disobedient Eve (that is, all other women) but rather Eve's 'mothering' of all living, graced by God, finds in Mary a new embodiment, who speaks with Eve and for her. Eve/Mary must then be presented and re-presented in the living presence of women in the worship of the Church. The Church positively requires women's bodily presence in its lived expression of redemption, as unequivocal affirmation of the saving significance of 'difference', and the enlargement of symbolic imagination as human persons re-explore their relationships to one another and to God. Given that reflection on eucharistic liturgy may provide a way forward for the way in which we rethink the implications of baptism for Christian living, this is above all an important time to be appreciating the graces of the female/feminine as well as the male/masculine in the ordained ministry of the Church.[10]

Notes

1 Gore, C., *St Paul's Epistle to the Ephesians: A Practical Exposition* (Whitefish, MT: Kessinger Publishing, 2008).

2 See Macy, G., *The Hidden History of Women's Ordination: Female Clergy in the Medieval West* (Oxford: Oxford University Press, 2008).

3 Bouyer, L., *Woman in the Church* (Ft. Collins, CO: Ignatius Press, 1979).

4 Furlong, M. (ed.), *Feminine in the Church* (London: SPCK, 1984), p. 2.

5 MacKinnon, D. M., 'The *Icon Christ* and Eucharistic Theology', *Theology* 95 (1992), pp. 109–13 was later to tackle these points when the 'visual' appearance of the priest became increasingly important in a wholly novel way as the movement for the ordination of women gained momentum.

6 Kilby, C. S. (ed.), *C. S. Lewis: Letters to an American Lady* (London: Hodder & Stoughton, 1969), p. 18.

7 Storkey, E., 'The Significance of Mary for Feminist Theology', in Wright, D. F. (ed.), *Chosen by God: Mary in Evangelical Perspective* (London: Marshall Pickering, 1989), p. 198.

8 Johnson, E. A., *She Who Is: The Mystery of God in Feminist Theological Discourse* (New York: Crossroad, 1993).

9 Beattie, T., *God's Mother, Eve's Advocate: A Marian Narrative of Women's Salvation* (London: Continuum, 2000).

10 Hauerwas, S. and Wells, S. (eds), *The Blackwell Companion to Christian Ethics* (Oxford: Blackwell, 2004).

Worshipping as a woman

VERONICA BRADY

Introduction

According to the *Macquarie Dictionary*, to preside means 'to occupy the place of authority or control, as in an assembly; act as chairman or president or to exercise superintendence or control'.[1] On the surface, at least in our culture, by and large this is not the place in which one would expect to find many women. In the past especially, this kind of authority has largely been reserved for men: women's place was in the home. In wider society recently this has changed. But the churches generally often tend (for reasons both good and bad) to be less open to change so that as far as they are concerned 'presiding like a woman' can be a problematic, even challenging, topic. This is especially true for the Roman Catholic Church to which I belong, perhaps because the issue raises a central issue, the nature of the assembly we call 'church'.

As far as I am concerned, the answer to this question is particularly challenging since the church to which I belong and into which I was born is generally seen as even more patriarchal than most others. As a woman and also as a 'religious' my position is especially anomalous, somewhere in between the official clergy – which is exclusively and, we are told, irrevocably male – and the laity. In fact we are lay people, but the institutional habit of mind means that many ordinary Catholics see us as semi-clerical, somehow set apart from lay people in general though on a lower level in the hierarchy than priests. At the same time there are advantages in this situation, since the outsider often sees more of the game than those more fully involved and is able to escape many of the constraints imposed by the official system.

In my case I should also add that I am a member of a community of women which was founded by a remarkable seventeenth-century English woman, Mary Ward, a feminist before her time, who was called to found a community of women who would neither be enclosed nor ruled by the local bishop but, like the Jesuits, would be free to serve the Church as a whole and go wherever they were needed. Not surprisingly, this met strenuous official opposition and for a time she was imprisoned by the Inquisition, so that compromises had to be made if the community was to survive. But the dream continued and is being carried on today in various ways, though much still remains to be done. For that reason, however, I am especially grateful for the opportunity to contribute to the present discussion.

Given that history and the situation in which many Roman Catholic women find ourselves, it seems best to conduct my argument on two levels: first, what I see as the present reality in our church today, and second, what it might, and in my opinion, should be. Not that there is anything unusual in this state of suspension between 'is' and 'ought'. It has always been the essential situation of Christians as 'people of the Way' who are committed to 'realities at present unseen' and yet to be fully realized. We are tightrope walkers, if you like, negotiating a rope suspended over the gap between worlds, keeping our balance by fixing our eyes on the horizon ahead, aware that others have made their way before us on the long journey through history and that others will continue to do so in the future long after we are gone. In the meantime we must play our part in that journey towards a community in which there 'is no longer Jew or Greek, there is no longer slave or free, there is no longer male or female, for all . . . are one in Christ' (Galatians 3.28).

The transforming work of God in this world

To begin, then, with the horizon, with what this goal might be and, in its own mysterious way, already is. But before doing this we need to reflect on the meaning of the key word, 'preside', since it bears heavily on the goal, the nature of the community to which we belong but also the one we have in mind, which is not ultimately of human making but created by the grace of God which has called each of us to it – even if for many, if not most of us Roman Catholics, that calling has come to us indirectly by way of our parents.

But this, I suggest, underlines the communal nature of our calling and illuminates the nature of the task it imposes, to carry on the transforming work of God in this world and celebrate God's presence in this world in prayer and worship. In the Catholic tradition the centre and climax of this celebration is the Eucharist, the action in which the community comes together to recall the life, death and resurrection of Christ and anticipate his final victory. But this work continues also in the other sacraments of initiation, healing and forgiveness which hallow the stages and occasions of our lives, keeping alive the connection between time and eternity.

So it is a community which enables us to rejoice in a presence and power beyond ourselves which also manifests itself here and now in the people and physical realities around us, especially in moments of grace in which, as Judith Wright puts it in her poem of that name, the presence of God slants 'a sudden laser through common day',[2] bringing a sense of reality to challenge the common sense of a culture which is preoccupied with material possessions and power. But this does not mean that the Christian community exists in a negative relationship to that culture. Rather it points to the possibilities grace provides within it which are enriching and ennobling, humanistic in the best sense of that word.

In one of the last letters he wrote from prison before he was executed for his opposition to Nazism, Dietrich Bonhoeffer, for example, expressed his belief in what he called this 'polyphony' of a life of faith:

> What I mean is that God wants us to love him eternally with our whole hearts – not in such a way as to injure or weaken our earthly love, but to provide a kind of *cantus firmus* to which the other melodies of life provide the counterpoint. One of these contrapuntal themes . . . is earthly affection.[3]

Grace and nature are not at odds in this view but confirm and support one another, and love, as one hymn puts it, becomes 'the fulfilling of the law', linking our lives to one another and drawing us into the work of creation as a whole, asking us not to exploit the world but to care for it and, as Rainer Maria Rilke says, to name and praise it,

> . . . to say: House
> Bridge. Fountain. Gate. Jug. Fruit Tree. Window.
> At most: Pillar. Tower . . . but to *say*, you understand,
> O to *say*, with an intensity the things themselves never
> Hoped to achieve.[4]

Merely 'poetic' as this may seem, the environmental crisis facing us today suggests that in fact it is very practical since, as Rilke goes on, it is becoming increasingly clear that all the world around us, so fleeting, seems to need us, to strangely concern us,[5] not just because it sustains us physically, so that in damaging it we damage ourselves, but also because it manifests and can thus intensify our awareness of the ongoing creative workings of God in which we are called to share. As Jesuit poet Gerard Manley Hopkins put it in 'Pied Beauty', a poem praising

> All things counter, original, spare, strange;
> Whatever is fickle, freckled (who knows how?)
> With swift, slow; sweet, sour; adazzle, dim;
> He fathers-forth whose beauty is past change:
> Praise him.[6]

We are called also to love and serve our fellow human beings since

> . . . Christ plays in ten thousand places,
> Lovely in limbs, and lovely in eyes not his,
> To the Father through the features of men's faces.[7]

Rethinking meanings of feminine and masculine

All this may seem a long way from the question at issue, what it means to 'preside like a woman'. But as we have said, it is important to be clear about the nature of the community involved and thus of the appropriate kind of leadership or, better, stewardship, required. My next point is that the community I have been describing can be seen as 'feminine' – a term which I will define – and that therefore it is difficult, if not impossible, to justify the exclusion of women from roles of leadership in it. Not that men should be excluded. That would be to repeat the misunderstanding implicit in the idea that it should be limited only to men. Instead I suggest that we need to rethink the meaning of 'feminine' and 'masculine' and accept that this meaning is existential rather than biological.

Here I am drawing on the thinking of French philosopher Helene Cixous. In her view, 'feminine' and 'masculine' are not, as they are usually seen, fixed and determinate conditions, a matter of biology, but have to do with different ways of being in the world which are available to people of either sex, though it is true that cultural conditioning tends to encourage women to be 'feminine' and men 'masculine'. Cixous' point, however, is that, as Jung argued, in each of us there exist 'masculine' and 'feminine' possibilities. As she describes it, 'masculine', which she calls the 'Economy of the Proper', is preoccupied with externals like property, propriety and power and with dominating what is other-than-self in order to direct it to ends which it regards as important. So it exists at the centre of a closed circle around self, a circle of sameness which guarantees its security and power. This, I suggest, is the 'one-sided masculinity . . . [and] linear narrowness of thought' described by Judith Wright which she believed was leading us 'nowhere but to a world scarcely worth living in'.[8] But it also describes what Karl Rahner calls the 'ecclesial consciousness of a militant kind' which is 'tempted to make [this] ecclesiality the most specific and central thing about Christianity in an indiscriminate way'.[9] It can also be traced back to the beginnings of 'Christendom' as Kierkegaard defined it in the Constantinian alliance or even at times identification between Church and State.

What Cixous calls the 'feminine', the 'Economy of the Gift', offers a different model, however. In it the self is no longer preoccupied with domination and control but is open to others and to the Other, prepared to give to and receive from them. As she says, 'if there is a "propriety of woman" it is paradoxically the capacity to depropriate unselfishly, world without end.'[10] Identity is not fixed and monolithic but open and dynamic since the 'feminine' 'dares and wishes to know from within', listening for 'the resonance of fore-language . . . the language of 1,000 tongues which knows neither enclosure or death'.[11] 'Her unconscious is worldwide', so that she embraces creation as a whole and wishes to celebrate it, not alone but with others with whom she shares and from whom she draws strength – and in this way, the kind of church I have been describing can be seen as 'feminine'.

But the 'feminine' also has theological consequences. Its habit of mind would not envisage a God 'out there' reigning over us from afar like a celestial monarch and exerting authority of a more or less military kind, being more attuned to the 'God with us' described by Eberhard Jungel: a God 'whose being is in coming', who 'goes on ways to himself' through this world, even when they seem to lead to places which are not God.[12] It follows also that human relationships are open and communal rather than individualistic, and authority a matter of listening, sharing and service rather than domination. According to Cixous, however, this is something which the 'masculine' fears since it tends to imagine that to receive anything from another would render the self vulnerable and threaten its authority, which depends on superior power. Instead, wanting 'to break the circuit of an exchange that could have no end', it must refuse or return any gift as a threat to its independence, its desire 'to be nobody's child, to owe no one a thing'[13] and to impose its own certainties unchallenged.

In many respects, then, official Roman Catholicism today can be seen as 'masculine' in this sense, with its hierarchical structure, emphasis on rational understanding and dogmatic certainty (even in areas as complex as moral behaviour) and firm belief that men and women are biologically defined and therefore essentially different. To revert to Karl Rahner's critique of 'militant eccclesiality', it tends to downplay 'Christian realities like the Sermon on the Mount and freedom of spirit'. But he sees this as an aberration, arguing that the Christian community centres on a faith and love which entrusts itself 'to the darkness of existence and into the incomprehensibility of God in trust and in the company of Jesus Christ, the crucified and risen one'[14] – a community which exists in the 'feminine' mode, as Cixous defines it.

There is a great deal at stake here theologically since the distinction, to draw on one made by Edith Wyschogrod, is ultimately between an idea of God who is more or less a 'conceptual anchor' – Pascal's 'God of the Philosophers' – and one who is a 'living force' interrupting and challenging our human preconceptions, whose voice, to quote Judith Wright, 'is not our own/ and yet its tone's deeper than intimate', an 'implacable awaited voice' which 'asks of us all we feared, yet longed, to say'.[15] Responding to this voice, as Wyschogrod says, is 'less like grasping an argument and more like understanding a musical theme'. This returns us to the idea of a community of prayer and worship since, as she goes on to point out, the listener must first 'have some notion of music and of how people respond to it before the theme can be grasped'.[16] The Christian community is, or ought to be, a listening community and those who preside over it should also listen to the community and be in tune with it.

Renewed understanding of church as the *laos*

So it is beginning to emerge what presiding like a woman might mean, at least if my definition of the nature of the community involved is accepted.

But this is not to say that it is a purely spiritual community. Roman Catholicism, like Anglicanism, also puts more emphasis on the Church as a visible social institution than does Protestantism, whose emphasis falls more heavily on the individual's relationship with God. One reason for this may be because grace and nature are more at ease with one another in the former tradition than in the latter, though historical and cultural reasons have something to do with it. As Rahner explains the Catholic position, if 'religion does not just concern some particular sector of human existence but concerns the whole of human existence in its relationship to the all-encompassing God',[17] then it involves and blesses the institutional nature of the believing community.

True, this institution is also pneumatic, the creation of the 'living force', the mystery of a God who goes on ways to godself through this world and desires to carry us with God to realize the promise made in Jesus of a community in which distinctions between Jew and gentile, slave and free citizen, male and female, are swept away and we are all one in Christ. So the refusal by the church to which I belong to ordain women who believe they are called to priestly leadership because they are not men seems to me theologically incomprehensible. I would also argue that this has its effects on the nature of leadership in our community.

While it may be, as we have been arguing, that 'masculine' and 'feminine' properly understood are not biological but existential categories, nevertheless in the nature of things a priestly caste made up exclusively of celibate males tends to preside in 'masculine' ways, putting an emphasis on rational order, organization and control. That is not to say, of course, that women would necessarily act differently in this context. What we need is a renewed understanding that the Church is essentially, as the Second Vatican Council put it, 'the People of God', called and empowered in the Spirit to praise God and let a liberating power into this world, serving one another and all of creation in faith, hope and love. Properly to preside over this community is to be open to 'the language of 1,000 tongues', the 'voice which is not their own'. The Spirit of God and the true centre of the community is here, in the worship and prayer which gives rise to love and service of others.

Such worship and prayer have, of course, always gone on in the Church in the mystical tradition which has included so many remarkable women like Hildegard of Bingen, Julian of Norwich, Teresa of Avila and, in recent times, Thérèse of Lisieux and Edith Stein. But it has often been suspect and largely separated from the conception of leadership as 'presiding' which has been seen in more or less bureaucratic terms. But that is to neglect the central mystery, 'the still point of the turning world', both a new world and the old made explicit, understood,[18] the life of prayer and worship.

Conclusion

Let me conclude by making the point that to be Christian is to be utopian since the society we are seeking to build lies elsewhere. But in another sense it is already present as we celebrate our faith in it. But this faith also imposes the obligation to keep believing in it and working to bring it about by changing the ways things are now. If, as Karl Barth said, God can be compared to a river flowing through this world, we need to remember that rivers have a habit of changing course. We may be sitting on the banks of a river which has flowed elsewhere. One way of avoiding this danger may be to learn to 'preside like a woman', to let go our preconceptions and certainties and follow the river as it flows onwards to 'make all things new'.

Notes

1 See <http://www.macquariedictionary.com.au>.
2 Wright, J., *Collected Poems 1942–1985* (Sydney: Angus and Robertson, 1994), p. 331.
3 Bethge, E. (ed.), *Dietrich Bonhoeffer: Letters and Papers from Prison* (New York: Simon & Schuster Touchstone Book, 1997), p. 303.
4 Mack, M. et al. (eds), *Maria Rainer Rilke: The Duinese Elegies, Ninth Elegy* (New York: W. W. Norton, 1965), p. 1302.
5 Mack, *Duinese Elegies*, p. 1302.
6 Gardner, W. H. (ed.), *Gerard Manley Hopkins: Poems* (London: Oxford University Press, 1948), p. 74.
7 Gardner, *Hopkins*, p. 94.
8 Brady, V., *South of My Days: A Biography of Judith Wright* (Sydney: Angus and Robertson, 1994), p. 121.
9 Rahner, K., *Foundations of Christian Faith: An Introduction to the Idea of Christianity* (New York: Crossroad, 1985), p. 324.
10 Cixous, 'The Laugh of Medusa', *Signs* 1.4 (1976), pp. 875–93, at pp. 888–9.
11 Cixous, 'The Laugh of Medusa'.
12 Jungel, E., *God as the Mystery of the World* (Grand Rapids, MI: Eerdmans, 1983), p. 159.
13 Cixous, 'The Laugh of Medusa'.
14 Rahner, *Foundations*, p. 324.
15 Wright, *Collected Poems*, p. 210.
16 Wyschgorod, E., *Saints and Postmodernism* (Chicago, IL: Chicago University Press, 1990), p. 47.
17 Rahner, *Foundations*, p. 323.
18 Eliot, T. S., *Four Quartets* (London: Faber and Faber, 1954), p. 9.

Why is that priest singing in a woman's voice?

LUCY WINKETT

When women sing, no one can pretend they are men. A human voice, its timbre, resonance, pitch and cadence, is a deeply implanted expression of our identity and self-understanding. The visitor to a busy cathedral in London asked the question that forms the title of this chapter when he happened to see a woman at the altar presiding at the midday Eucharist. His question betrays his visceral assumption that 'priest' and 'woman's voice' are somehow mutually exclusive and it's an assumption that shaped some of the first reactions ranging from puzzlement to aggression that greeted the first generation of ordained women. As a metaphor too, 'finding a voice' has been a powerful way to express movements of liberation as women, historically excluded from the structure of church hierarchy, have often used this image to describe a growing freedom to define and describe humanity's relationship with God. Women sing different notes from men. They have the same names but they are generally an octave higher. The notes are distinctive, in a register that adult men do not sing (apart from trained counter-tenors). The tone and timbre of women's voices are distinctive in song too: not just the pitch but the sound itself. In antiquity, the ritual singing of women has expressed the joy and lament of communities: our scriptural foremothers were the singers of their generations. Biblical accounts of rejoicing and lamenting in the Hebrew Scriptures give us pictures of Miriam at the Red Sea leading her people in song, and the women of Jerusalem welcoming King David back from battle, Deborah the judge singing in victory (Judges 5) and Jephthah's daughter first rejoicing and then instigating an annual lament among the women of Israel (Judges 11). In the New Testament, the lament of the women of Jerusalem at Jesus' crucifixion, the weeping of the widows at Tabitha's raising by Peter, give women the role of the ritual singer, expressing the joy and grief of their people.

Imaginative writers have given us Mary's lullaby to her child in Bethlehem, the most famous of which is probably the Coventry Carol of the sixteenth century and the song of all songs is given to Mary in her Magnificat, after the tradition of Hannah. This song, repeated as a canticle in churches and cathedrals across the world at Vespers and Evensong, is a song of revolution, of liberation, of a new world order. Jesus would repeat this vision in the song of the prophet Isaiah when he unrolled the scroll in Nazareth to proclaim the year of the Lord's favour. We often meditate on and learn from Jesus' relationship with his Father in heaven but, in his song of liberation, it's clear he was his mother's son too.

There is a close association in the musical expression of the Western Church between the unbroken voices of boys and the voices of women. The notes are the same but the sounds are not. The pre-pubescent sound of a boy singing praise to God is special and particular, and as it matures and approaches the inevitable change into adult depth, it acquires a 'bloom', a kind of 'flowering' that is achingly beautiful. It speaks of innocence, hope, youth, and has for adults, a tone of lost childhood, and even regret. It moves many to tears and is an iconic musical sound for Christians in the West. The castrati tradition in the Roman Church attempted to prolong this male expression of innocence, and the last castrato died as recently as 1922 (Alessandro Moreschi, born 1858).

Although they sing the same notes in the same register, women have not received such adulation in the history of music in Christian worship. Still today, church musicians are often squeamish about hearing a distinctive femininity in music. The professional early music groups that sing mass settings by Byrd, Tallis, Vittoria and so on, will often require their women members to sing with the 'purity' of a pre-pubescent boy. Alongside the musical arguments about the complex polyphony that requires a simple tone, there is an anxiety expressed about too mature a sound not being 'appropriate' for such music. There is a stronger reaction among churchgoers when, say, a pregnant woman sings in church. When pregnant women preside or sing, the congregation has to acknowledge the visible unavoidable presence of sexuality within the liturgy. The truth is, whoever the man or the woman who reads the lesson or preaches the sermon, it is possible never to remember that they are sexual beings themselves. This makes pregnant women a new icon of the presiding singing woman.

The place and presence of music itself within Christian worship has a deeply conflicted history within Western Christian worship. Even though today we would celebrate music as a language of the human spirit, in antiquity music itself was personified as female and as such a dangerous if evocative embellishment of plain scriptural text. Early Christian theologians, including Augustine, had warned against the power of music to evoke an emotional response, thought to be distracting and inappropriate in worship of God. It is a striking and consistent strand of teaching, from him and others, such as John Chrysostom and Gregory of Nanzianzus. For the twelfth-century reformers of chant, such as Bernard of Clairvaux, music is itself dangerous especially when performed in an 'effeminate' way as he exorted his monks in his sermon on the Song of Songs.[1]

As one contemporary commentator has put it,

From a feminist perspective, it would seem that music and women provoke almost interchangeable attitudes and responses from church authorities. Keeping women in their place becomes analogous to keeping music in its proper place – subservient (to a text) and virtuously pure (free from the stain of dissonance); ideally, both must be chaste love-objects who inspire disembodied union with God.[2]

Epstein further comments on the 'double jeopardy' of women actually making music themselves. Early Christian bishops explicitly applied Paul's exhortation that women should be silent in church to music-making, even exclusion from communal singing: 'Women are ordered not to speak in church, not even softly, nor may they sing along or take part in the responses, but they should only be silent and pray to God.'[3]

Women priests who sing the Eucharistic Prayer emerge from underneath the weight of this centuries-old double jeopardy. Free Church ministers may sing and lead their congregations in hymns and spiritual songs but rarely if ever do women ministers sing at the altar. It is therefore one of the distinctive implications of the ordination of women in the Church of England that women's presidential voice has been heard in ancient eucharistic chant.

What women sound like in public has been a matter for comment for as long as women have preached or read the Bible out loud. Commentators in the early 1990s, both before and after the vote in General Synod, worried that women wouldn't be heard in the historic buildings in which they were required to minister. More than once, the cliché of a 'squeaky voice' was dug out to add colour to the argument that women were simply not suited to this authoritative role within a church community. As traced over time in the archive footage of both the Queen and Margaret Thatcher, women have found that in public situations, the lower their voice the better and the more acceptable and authoritative it is deemed to be by those listening. In the twenty-first century, most 'satnav' electronic voices are a low woman's voice – not so much maternal as slightly seductive, but ultimately safe. The majority of public recorded announcements, including the speaking clock, are spoken in a similarly authoritative female voice.

Singing is a skill rather like drawing or running. It is something that often people feel inadequate about – we can either do it or we can't – and the apocryphal story of being thrown out of the school choir is one that many adults repeat as their own. If I were given a pencil and paper and asked to draw a picture, I would most likely draw a childlike house with a tree and a path. It's the first thing that comes into my head because I haven't spent time developing my drawing skill or my visual imagination to the extent that I might be able to produce a good picture, even if I were copying it. My artistic imagination and level of ability has stalled aged about ten. It is the same with singing. Many women (more than men, because of the smooth transition vocally through female puberty – that is, women's voices don't 'break' in such a dramatic way) sing just as they did when they were a child. It is early days, but one of the liturgical tasks before ordained women is clear: to take our own singing voices seriously enough so that we learn to sing, not as a child, a young girl or a pre-pubescent boy – but as the mature women we are. This doesn't necessarily mean developing a pejoratively described matronly 'wobble', but it does mean taking time to discover the amazing resonances that God has given us in our bodies, discovering the depth to which we can breathe, and the muscles that support that breath as it flows through us. Our bodies are truly amazing and singing is a full-body experience when we learn to breathe and sing as we were created to do. It is this distinctively female voice that calls the Church into the future by embodying and remembering at the altar the new creation that the Eucharist makes possible.

Singing women are familiar on a stage or in a club, but the movement of women from assistant to president means that in churches where they sing, women will sing alone the Eucharistic Prayer for the first time in Christian history. Women now chant in the Levite tradition and as such can be said to be inheritors of the Melchizedek tradition in a new way. There is a physical as well as a symbolic movement from the side to the centre. Together with my female colleagues at one of the most public places of worship in the world, I have sung the Eucharist in front of thousands of people from every continent over the past twelve years. In my experience, the reaction of most men and women when they hear a woman sing the Eucharist for the first time is a measure of shock, a little puzzlement, but followed swiftly by a feeling that their experience is somehow a moment of annunciation. Something new has been declared: they have heard a sound that heralds change and in itself embodies difference. Especially for women, but also for men, it has many times provoked tears of recognition and joy.

One of the greatest privileges of my life so far as a musician and a priest has been to sing the Eucharist as set by the Roman Catholic composer James MacMillan. His Mass sets not only the choir parts of Kyrie, Sanctus, Benedictus and Agnus but sets the Eucharistic Prayer itself, composed to be sung by the priest accompanied by the organ. Of course, the notes are written in bass clef for a man, but to sing them an octave higher brings new colours into the text. It means that the priest's voice is placed in a different place within the accompanying chord of the organ; the priest's tone is higher within the chord that surrounds her rather than in the middle of the chord. MacMillan's setting creates a pattern of notes reminiscent of the astonishingly innovative composer Hildegard of Bingen. At a time when the twelfth-century church authorities were silencing her sisters, she was writing extraordinarily original chants and melodies in praise of God. The intervals, that is, the leaps between notes, were unusually daring. And in her mini oratorio written for 18 women, the character of Mary is required to sing a huge range of 14 notes – giving the mother of God musical audacity, and obliging the singer to be courageous and free.

One of the distinctive intervals used by Hildegard is the perfect fifth (the interval at the beginning of the 'Last Post' on Remembrance Sunday). MacMillan uses this interval at the heart of the prayer, in setting Christ's words 'do this in remembrance of me'. In the echoes of Hildegard's courage and originality, I heard again Christ's proclamation of a new creation made possible by this sacrifice offered for a broken world. MacMillan's exceptional music gives a new layer of meaning to this sacrifice as we hear the echoes of a woman's chant across a thousand years.

The shapes of our chant have their roots not only in the singing of women and men over a thousand or fifteen hundred years, but in the Temple at Jerusalem. The Gregorian chant that gives shape to our Eucharistic Prayers has patterns and shapes as it rises and falls that find their origin in Jewish song. In early Christian liturgy, Gregorian chant takes over 75 per cent of its texts from Scripture, mostly from the Psalms. The Roman Catholic Czech scholar László Dobszay has shown that the patterns, for example, of the ancient Christian canticle the Exultet, traditionally sung on Easter Eve, find their roots musically in Jewish Temple chant as do the variations of the Kyrie. The cadences and patterns of the Eucharistic Prayers have not been borrowed note for note but there are distinct forms and types of pattern in Mediterranean culture that provide us with more than an echo of our Temple roots.

As women have sung a traumatized child to sleep, and have sung a protest against a violent regime; as women have sung songs of delight at the sight of their beloved and led the community in lament for those killed in war: so women are called now to sing praise to the Creator and lament for God's wounded creation, as God's song of redemption is heard in the presence of holy wisdom and the renewing call of Christ. Women carry with them a hermeneutic of remembrance. When they sing, women carry the memory of ancient voices – the storytelling, folk songs that remind us of the sacrifices and tragedies of our past.

Freedom from literalism

When women sing at the altar, we in the congregation are freed from literalism. We are released from our persistent tendency towards religious reductionism. When women sing, we are freed from remembering only the upper room and the institution of this commandment so often obeyed. We are freed to join in the eschatological hopeful future-already-here of the worship of heaven.

If a man's singing evokes images of the incarnate Jesus of Nazareth, does a woman singing re-emphasize the renewal of creation, the eternal strangeness of a resurrected Saviour freed from earthly definition? It's important not to suggest that women's presidency is of itself somehow better or even qualitatively different: these are God's sacraments made holy only and wholly by the activity of God. But it is in the ontological difference from Jesus of Nazareth that women priests can signal the new creation. Women's chant, in its very difference from the incarnate Jesus, reveals afresh the resurrected Christ and the saviour freed from the human limitations that we inevitably place on our imaginations, as we shut our eyes and try to see the Galilean preacher. We are freed from any attempt to mimic Jesus as an impressionist would. In this profound way, we are not called to have the same voice as Christ but we are called to find our own voice and to join in the redemption song he is singing. Following Jesus is not attempting to be Jesus. Following Jesus is knowing that we are fully ourselves.

If liturgy rehearses the just and mutual relationships we find in the banquet of heavenly worship, then a woman's voice may call us to this not only as powerfully as a man, but in a distinctive and enlivening way. New possibilities are opened up in our faithful imagination. Holy Wisdom, that enigmatic feminine presence at the creation of the world, the figure of the woman who stands at the crossroads and calls for justice (Proverbs 8), the one who, with the angels 'holds all things together', the one who gathers and binds, the one who embodies harmony, balance, co-operation, interdependence and creativity. It is in her voice that we call for the grain once scattered on the hillside to be reunited in bread.

What should priests sound like? Holy Wisdom heralding a new creation made possible in Christ. In the words of the prophet Joel (chapter 1), priests are themselves lamenters – like farmers who have lost their harvest and also like young women who have lost their husbands. Priests are those who know the passion and poignancy of widowhood: the loss of hope, of a known future. What is a priest supposed to sound like? Like those who know the song of a grieving woman.

Jesus taught his disciples (John 16.20–22) that while the world rejoiced they would mourn. The analogy he uses is that of a woman whose pain is unbearable during childbirth but who forgets the anguish when the child is born, in the light of the new life that is before her. Jesus' teaching about lament is that it is a necessary part of life in the world, but it is not for ever. It is more analogous to birth pain: strong, but with a sense that it will be given meaning by something new. In this way, the Eucharistic Prayer is giving expression to the birth pangs of a new age inaugurated in the sacrament. When women sing at the altar, there is a new recognition of the feminine resonances in the divine voice. She who sings at the altar embodies the searching woman of Luke's Gospel – as Jesus described God, searching for her people – calling and not being satisfied until they are found. She is the one who rejoices with all the angels over the lost one she has found and her delight is heard in heaven and echoed on earth (Luke 15.8–10).

In the words of Emily Dickinson's mystical poem, it is in brokenness that the song finds its expression. If we 'split the Lark' of women's experience, we will find the music buried deep inside their history of silenced singing.[4] Much of it has been made at a high cost to the writers and performers, in the tradition of the blood of St Cecilia, the patron saint of musicians – the 'scarlet experiment' of which Emily Dickinson speaks. To borrow Dickinson's imagery, in the new life that Christ brings, the flood will gush and gush as the life blood poured out in the Eucharist flows out in what might be termed the liquid music of the chant, moving, creative, all-enveloping and free.

High in the dome of St Paul's Cathedral in London stands a series of inspirational ecumenical statements. The statues of the Eastern Doctors of the Church face west and the Western Doctors face east. Jerome is there, as are Augustine and Aquinas. It is under this exchange of glances that women now sing the ancient chant as the Fathers look across at each other and down onto this new world. It is under this same dome, built to imitate the dome of the skies in Genesis, that creation is renewed when bread is broken and wine poured out for the life of the world. Women preside here and find themselves guarding space, fiercely sometimes in such a public marketplace. Although the architecture impresses, and the marble statues of colonial generals populate the sacred geometry of Wren's masterpiece, the woman priest sings in celebration in the presence not so much of the sculpted stone of a mere three hundred years, but of the fossils in the Portland stone that remind her she is surrounded by memories of the last Ice Age. She celebrates the ancient wisdom of Scripture and the possibility of a new creation as she presides, arms outstretched with palms open and undefended. In a modern virtual age, to continue to gather physically to sing together, to tune our ears to the harmonies of heaven, to listen for the songs of the angels, requires a rediscovery of our connection to the earth and our co-dependence on it. It is for church communities to cultivate this wisdom, this binding, this mutuality that finds expression in the wisdom tradition in the voice of a woman.

The contemporary choreographer Mark Morris has written of an over-whelming experience he had of music which illuminates this point from a secular perspective. He attended a recital by the world-famous English mezzo-soprano Janet Baker.

> It was the . . . thing that Janet Baker was telling me as she sang one night many years later at Carnegie Hall. Standing in recital, singing song after song in ravishing voice, in languages I didn't understand, I knew her only essential message could be translated as: I love you, I love you, I love you.[5]

This is a secular description of a theological truth: that music communicates across cultures and languages the mystery of love. It is a truth that underpins the whole of the Hebrew canon and the whole of the gospel. Even when the languages are not translatable, even when the chant seems inexplicable or impenetrable, women sing at the altar, in the tradition of enigmatic wisdom, to bind, to hold together and to participate in the new and renewing song of the angels. As we hear her voice raised on behalf of her people in praise and grief and joy, we will hear the echo of the eternal conversation between God and humanity: I love you I love you I love you.

Notes

1 Walton, R. (ed.), *Bernard of Clairvaux on the Song of Songs,* Vol. 3 (Kalamazoo, MI: Cistercian Publications, 1979), pp. 9–10.
2 Epstein, H., *Melting the Venusberg: A Feminist Theology of Music* (London: Continuum, 2004), p. 57.
3 *Didascalia* c. 375, quoted in Quasten, J., *Music and Worship in Pagan and Christian Antiquity* (Washington, DC: National Association of Pastoral Musicians, 1973).
4 See <http://famouspoetsandpoems.com/poets/emily_dickinson/poems/7240>.
5 Flash Flashback, 8–25: I Love You, I Love You, I Love You, in Morris, M., *Fact and Mystery* © Mark Morris, 1998. These remarks, originally delivered to the Midwest Arts Conference in Cleveland in September 1998, were first and exclusively published by the *Dance Insider*, with permission from the Mark Morris Dance Group, in December 1998.

Being and becoming: how the woman presider enriches our sacred symbols

ALI GREEN

A collision of meanings

My friend Jude attends a church whose incumbent does not accept the ordination of women. Jude has never, in her own church, seen a woman at the altar or in the pulpit, nor received communion from a woman. But some years ago she did attend a church service at which I and three other women were priested. 'When I took communion there', she recalls, 'I was given a piece of bread by a woman. I was standing, not kneeling. As she put the bread into my hands our faces were level. We smiled at each other. The smile did it. It was a simple act of sharing, of joyful giving, woman to woman,' something that was markedly different from her usual experience. Jude felt surprise and joy, and discovered that, despite the many excellent qualities of her own parish priest and congregation, there was something lacking in what she called the 'all-pervading male hierarchy' of her home church.

In the Anglican Communion (and elsewhere) the Eucharist is the central rite which proclaims the Christian story, the narrative of faith that is learnt, upheld and passed on by the faith community. It uses natural symbols rooted in daily life, such as water, bread, wine and light, to draw us into the realm of the sacred and to call us to further commitment and action. Through our response to these symbols we reinterpret the example and work of Jesus, deepen our relationship with God and touch on ultimate realities that give life meaning and inspire our discipleship and ministry.

The presiding priest, in representing both the Church and God, plays a key role in articulating the relationship between the community and its sacred things. Priestly actions and words at the altar come from the shared life of the community, yet point beyond it towards the numinous, inviting worshippers to enter into the realm of the sacred. Some symbols used in worship – processions and candles, coloured vestments and incense, priestly gestures and choreographed movements – are more characteristic of what we might call the analogical imagination of the catholic tradition. The Reformed churches put greater emphasis on the Word through teaching and interpreting Scripture than on elaborate ritual and ornament; but there remains a high degree of symbolism attached to the narrative of faith and to the traditions of worship, however they are practised.

At the service Jude attended, she was aware of a metaphorical collision between the tradition and customs of her own parish and those of a wider community of gathered believers. It challenged her to reinterpret the potent and deep-seated symbolism carried by the priest, especially when presiding. In the Anglican Church in Britain, the United States, Canada, New Zealand, Australia, Japan, South India, Uganda and other countries, there has been a recent and significant change, in that those who preside at the Eucharist now include women. And a woman bears a whole range of symbolic meanings and associations that are different from those carried by a man. So the female priest causes a collision because there appears to be a disjunction between symbols associated with our image of God and the sacred and those associated with women.

When we enter church to worship, we often think in terms of leaving our worldly concerns at the door and trying to concentrate on 'higher' things – the spiritual, the numinous, the transcendent – and symbols, in the form of icons, incense, music, the words of Scripture and liturgy and the movements and gestures of the priest, all aid that tuning-in process. But when the presider is a woman, we encounter another set of symbols that may seem at odds with sacred ritual. Women have, throughout recorded history, been associated in male-dominated cultures with the material as opposed to the spiritual, with body rather than mind, with the led rather than the leader. Historically the Church's male hierarchical elite reinforced the notion that women are closer to nature, more prone to sin and less rational than men. Women have been seen as inferior to men, less able to image the divine, in need of control and requiring to be kept away from holy spaces and objects such as the sanctuary and the chalice. Elizabeth Johnson argues that there has been a 'pervasive exclusion of women from the realm of public symbol formation and decision making, and women's consequent, strongly enforced subordination to the imagination and needs of a world designed chiefly by men'.[1]

Prevailing patriarchal cultures have viewed women largely in terms of their sex and their relationship to men. In fact men's preoccupation with women's bodiliness and sexuality figures highly in arguments against women's ordination. In 1936 the Archbishop's Commission on the priesthood of women noted:

> The ministration of women will tend to produce a lowering of the spiritual tone of Christian worship ... it would be impossible for the male members to be present at a service at which a woman ministered without becoming unduly conscious of her sex.[2]

We might nowadays wonder at the own goal scored here (apparently without irony) by men of a previous generation professing such a lack of control over their minds and bodies; but similar arguments are still current today, and they expose the seeming contradiction in symbolic associations around priesthood and sex, bodiliness and the sacred. If women have always more readily symbolized the earthly and material, then how can a woman symbolically represent the utterly transcendent divine? How can the feminine, traditionally seen as inferior to the masculine, symbolize the Father, Son and Holy Spirit? How can women, historically regarded as inferior and subordinate to men, and fit more for the domestic than the public sphere, take positions of leadership in worship?

Sexual difference: a third way

Since we are rational creatures, this collision of symbolic associations causes us enough discomfort to look for a resolution. Those who find the collision irreconcilable respond by rejecting the validity of women's priesthood. In this case, as Tina Beattie argues, the female body remains as 'always a sign of sacramental exclusion, never of sacramental inclusion'.[3] An alternative response is to ignore the differences and assume that there is nothing distinctive about female priesthood or presidency. But this contradicts the age-old recognition that there *are* differences in what women and men signify, which is why women have for so long been excluded from sacred roles and practices. To ignore sexual difference in this way is not the sacramental exclusion of outright rejection; but it amounts to sexual forgetfulness. In order to preside with truth and integrity the priest must act through the whole, embodied self. As Robert Hovda remarks about priesthood, 'it is the whole person, the real person, the true person, the full and complete person who functions.'[4]

A third option is not to reject or ignore sexual difference but to work with it in a way that pays sacramental attentiveness to gender by recognizing and honouring the feminine aspects of God and God in the feminine. There is much of our faith story, and the way it is expressed liturgically, that has remained under-explored because sexual difference has been overlooked. The exclusion of women from sacred rituals, roles and spaces has led to women being left without symbolic representation as full and equal members of the Body of Christ. The excluding nature of sacred ritual has been a problem for men too: where the masculine is taken as normative and more closely imaging God, and female experience is devalued, then men can feel destined to appropriate public and sacred space, to take leadership roles and to guard jealously their positions of power. They then feel threatened when this assumed masculine destiny is invaded by 'others' – those who have been excluded, for instance by their sex, race or sexual orientation.

Women's experiences and narratives are different from men's, and there is difference in the symbolism associated with each sex. When we pay attention to sexual difference we can discover further meanings within the rich symbolism of eucharistic worship and of other areas of religious experience. In this way, ancient symbols and narratives of our faith can continue to offer new meanings which mould our discipleship: that transforming purpose is what our worship is about. When we first become attuned to looking for the feminine, we may notice a paucity of references in our story of faith: Scripture tends to focus on male figures and to portray God in male terms; commentaries have historically been written by men from a male perspective. We have to search harder to unravel the thread of female experience. The same is true of traditional liturgy, developed and enacted by male clergy. Reading between the lines of Scripture, doctrine and liturgy we become aware of the value and significance of the feminine where at first we notice only absence. When we are free to acknowledge and affirm sexual difference, then we are freed to inhabit our own gendered and unique identity as equally loved and valuable people all formed in the divine image.

Coming to terms with the female body

The woman priest makes evident the sacramental significance of the female body and its distinct functions and experience. She invites us to acknowledge and reflect on the likeness to the divine in the feminine as well as in the masculine, and so to uncover unfamiliar territory in our religious imagination. The symbolism borne by the woman priest includes that of the maternal body and its functions (this remains true whether or not the priest is herself a mother: the symbolism applies to the female body in general). And here we find a particularly strong collision of signifiers. The uterus, for example, has been variously celebrated as the vehicle for life and for God's incarnation, and denounced as a source of temptation and sin. Tertullian (born in the second century AD) rather ambiguously taught that women should be honoured for their reproductive function but were also responsible for marring men's potential to image the divine.[5] Some of our most insulting language refers to female genitalia, and according to science writer Natalie Angier, many people – even medical practitioners – regard the vagina as 'dirty'.[6]

As with female reproductive organs, menstruation has been regarded with suspicion, fear, anxiety and ignorance, and so subject to widespread social taboos. Pliny the Elder, the Roman naturalist and contemporary of Jesus, wrote of the contaminating effects of menstrual blood, and his ideas influenced attitudes for centuries. Kate Summerscale's book *The Suspicions of Mr Whicher*,[7] about a notorious murder case in England in the 1860s, mentions a bloody nightgown which featured as a possible piece of evidence. Taboo, stigma and embarrassment surrounding menstrual blood hampered the gathering of witness statements and added to the difficulties in identifying the murderer. Social discomfort and revulsion around the menses still exist today. Adolescent girls may welcome their first period as a sign of womanhood, but they know that there is a sense of embarrassment and shame about this natural process. Iris Marion Young argues that this ambivalence keeps menstruation 'in the closet' so that, given our received ideas about what is clean and proper, 'it is difficult for me not to experience my being as defiled and out of control'.[8] Across a range of religions, women do not take part in religious ceremonies during parts of their menstrual cycle. The Orthodox Christian Information Center website[9] instructs that a woman must avoid holy communion during her menses, on the ground of cleanliness of mind and body, and asks: 'what woman would actually want to commune during her period?'

The association of women's bloodshed and procreative powers with impurity, defilement and shame is central to women's age-old exclusion from sacred ritual, particularly sacrifice. Through the history of patriarchal culture, virtually any sacrifice involving blood has been conducted exclusively by men. From a sociological point of view, rituals of sacrifice – including the Eucharist – have been interpreted as maintaining father–son lines of descent (in the Church through the Apostolic succession of an all-male priesthood) which transcend mortality by looking to an afterlife. In this way, according to Nancy Jay, the Eucharist becomes 'a ritual instrument for establishing and maintaining an enduring male-dominated social order'.[10]

Building on Jay's work and drawing on the field of developmental psychology, William Beers has written about the ritual violence he sees in the practice of sacrifice (including the Eucharist) performed by men, and the way he believes men use it to identify with each other, to gain self-affirmation and self-validation, and to separate themselves from women. Underlying this, he argues, is a deep-seated male desire for control over the power of the mother figure and for the subordination of women: 'man envies woman and seeks to confiscate her power'.[11] Beers concedes that the male function of sacrifice makes it psychologically just about impossible for female priests to preside at the Eucharist.[12] He is anxious, however, not to imply that women are solely the victims of male narcissistic rage, and so he wants the task of working out the nature and role of women to be left to women: 'I have a hard enough time figuring out who I am; I would rather struggle with who women tell me they are than tell them who I think they are.'[13]

With that encouragement, how can we interpret that maternal symbolism carried by the female priest? How can it be reconciled with – and even enhance – the traditional symbolism borne by the Eucharist? And in answer to Beers, if sacrifice is psychologically about men confiscating woman's power, then can a woman validly preside at the Eucharist?

The maternal domain

Along with the uterus and menstruation, childbirth has been subject to taboos across many cultures, and is similarly weighted with symbolic possibilities. Central to the symbol and narrative of the Eucharist is the understanding that Jesus Christ shed his blood in order to redeem humankind, free us from evil and restore our relationship with God. Jesus gave himself to bring life to all people; in pregnancy and childbirth, the mother gives her body, her labour and blood in order to bear new life. When the priest representing Christ at the altar is a woman, her own embodied presence reinforces the symbolic link between the self-giving of the mother to birth and nurture her child and the self-giving of Christ in redeeming humankind. All Christians are called to help others to be born again into faith, as Jesus taught (John 3), and priests share this midwife's role. The woman presider brings to the table her flesh-and-blood, female body, with all its human strengths and weaknesses, and all that it has symbolized for good or ill. In doing this, she physically and symbolically affirms sexual difference, and opens up the possibility of finding and cherishing the feminine in the sacred and the sacred in woman.

As well as being childbearers, women are also oftentimes the carers and homemakers who look after the very young and old and put food on the table. Essentially, the Eucharist is a meal of companionship where everyone is invited to the table, and where the priest, representing Christ, feeds the guests. The woman presider offers a reminder of this very concrete and humble connection: the transcendent, unsearchable God, through the incarnation, becomes known to us in the basic staples of life. My friend Jude, recalling the ordination service, remarked: 'I felt a much more "earthly" connection, somehow, in receiving communion from this female priest. This was both woman as Christ's representative, in other words separate from me, but also woman as communicator (there was real communication in that smile) freely giving of precious food, and therefore very close to Jesus sharing bread with that crowd of people.'

The woman presider readily embodies the connection made by the incarnation between the sacred and the everyday, because she is inhabiting what has historically been the mother's domain: not only giving birth and nurturing, but teaching the young, preparing food, laying the table, feeding the family, clearing up, caring for the sick and frail. These are all highly appropriate symbolic associations to make in the context of the Eucharist and the presiding priest. Together they express a sense of hospitality around the table that affirms the notion of inclusiveness, a warm welcome for all without exception. During an all-age eucharistic service I once told a story which I illustrated by collecting vegetables from various members of the congregation who had been primed and were ready to hand these over (the

message was about sharing what we have, in this case to feed the hungry).
One parishioner mentioned after the service that she found it incongruous
for me to be leading a service in a fine chasuble and simultaneously to
wander about with a shopping basket full of vegetables. I agree with her
that there must initially have been some collision of symbolic meanings, but
surely there could hardly be any more appropriate metaphor for ministry,
especially for a female priest, than a basket of humble garden produce to
be transformed into a feast to satisfy the hungry. Margaret Harvey notes
that after the first Eucharist following her priesting, parishioners gathered
around to talk to her. 'We didn't think it would be different – but it was!'
they said. 'What was different?' 'Now we understand what you've been
saying. It isn't your meal – it's ours!'[14]

Up to now, women have largely been associated starkly either with asexual-
ity – the saintly virgin – or with sexual sin – whore, adulteress, temptress. Now,
with the woman at the altar, we have a figure who affirms that the female
body, with all its associations of sexuality, fecundity and procreative power,
is a symbolic locus for the spiritual and the sacred, and can represent the
point of mediation between all people and the divine. As Beattie argues,

> When a woman speaks as a sacramental presence in her own body, she sets in
> motion a new relationship between language and the body, reminding us that
> living symbols have a volatile and transgressive capacity to shatter the limits of
> meaning and to usher in new visions of grace.[15]

A new understanding of self-sacrifice

The Eucharistic Prayer recalls the self-surrendering of Christ on the cross
for our sake. The notion of self-sacrifice is one that requires attention to
sexual difference. The Church has traditionally offered women a particular
ideal of subservience and subordination that has not applied to men. 'Good'
women have been taught to adopt a sort of self-denial and non-assertiveness,
usually for the sake of men, to suppress their own desire and will and to
find fulfilment primarily in motherhood and domesticity. One result is that
many women experience poor self-worth and an underdeveloped sense of
identity other than in relation to family. When women do assert themselves
outside traditional spheres they are regarded as somehow 'unfeminine'.
A man speaking his mind is 'assertive' or 'authoritative'; a woman is 'shrill',
'wilful' or 'strident'. We have to ask whether the prevailing feminine ideal
has more to do with the assumptions and desires of male-dominated culture
than with the Christian belief that all people are formed equally in the
image of God, and called to develop their God-given talents to their full
potential.

The female presider, I believe, is emblematic of the notion of self-sacrifice,
but she invites an interpretation rather different from the traditional one

that has long hampered women's self-fulfilment. As with her male colleagues, she has necessarily responded to a call from God and undergone a rigorous process of selection and training; she endeavours to live her own life in imitation of Christ. So self-sacrifice is part of her discipleship. At the same time, she has taken on the discipline and dignity of the priestly office, with its own recognized identity and authority. So she offers a model not of passive subservience or self-abnegation for its own sake, but a conscious, mature and measured profession of obedience and discipline. This is a form of self-sacrifice that is constructive and empowering for other women and edifying for the whole Church. In recognizing and nurturing her own God-given gifts, she encourages other women to come to maturity and to find their voice as full and equal members of the Church.

All these symbolic meanings borne by the woman priest – symbols associated with birthing and nurturing, with hospitality and empowering self-sacrifice – overcome Beers' diffidence about the psychological validity of the female presider. Women priests do not negate ancient 'male' symbolic meanings and traditions, but they do add other meanings and associations that are appropriate to women, and that can enrich the religious experience of both women and men alike. Hence a priesthood of both sexes more truly images both God and the Church.

Enhancing sacred symbols

The symbolic meanings borne by a female presider in no way deny or ignore other more male-related symbols. Christ's sacrifice is of course intimately involved with death, violence, sin and punishment. But it is also about suffering to bring forth new life, about nurturing and feeding others, about loving relationships that allow individuals, families and communities to grow and to flourish. The maternal symbolism embodied in the female priest is appropriate not only to women but to men also, since every living person is conceived and nurtured in the womb and is born of a woman. Our maternal origin should not be veiled or dismissed in our worship, but rather affirmed, because our bodies are the very places where we meet with and encounter God's presence. This recognition of the importance of the body is a recurring theme in current theological thought. Grace Jantzen, for example, has developed her theology on the basis that 'persons are created and affirmed by God as embodied human beings, not as souls imprisoned in an alien body from which they yearn to escape'.[16]

By honouring sexual difference we can encourage and inspire others who, in their quest to find a sense of identity, self-worth and purpose, have felt excluded by their own culture, both within the Church and in wider society. In a book about menstruation, Penelope Shuttle and Peter Redgrove comment:

There is no reason why Everywoman should not consciously inhabit the kingdom of her body, from which she has been exiled by male certitudes which are called 'objective' but which are often rather the turning-away from unexpected powers and abilities.[17]

In representing all people before God, the woman priest offers a symbol of those powers and abilities that women hold but that have been ignored or suppressed by the Church and by wider culture. Female presiders may not have much opportunity for liturgical innovation. Since many Anglican women clergy are non-stipendiary curates rather than incumbents, they may have little say in the development of the text or choreography of eucharistic worship. But despite any such restrictions, their very presence remains, and that in itself carries with it the challenge to interpret anew the symbol and narrative of our religion.

One sex alone can never fully represent all of humanity or the symbolic meanings carried by each sex that reveal something about the nature of God. Where women and men preside together, they offer a wholeness in symbolic possibilities for our image of God, for ourselves in the image of God, and for the way we relate to God and to each other. When we worship together, sharing sacred symbols in full partnership, we become a truer reflection of the sacred and a truer pattern of the equal, mutually loving relationship that we are called to live out as God's children.

Notes

1 Johnson, E. A., *She Who Is: The Mystery of God in Feminist Theological Discourse* (New York: Crossroad, 1993), p. 4.
2 Cited in Furlong, M., *A Dangerous Delight: Women and Power in the Church* (London: SPCK, 1991), p. 41.
3 Beattie, T., 'Vision and Vulnerability: The Significance of Sacramentality and the Woman Priest for Feminist Theology', in Watson, N. K. and Burns, S. (eds), *Exchanges of Grace: Essays in Honour of Ann Loades* (London: SCM Press, 2008), pp. 235–49, at p. 240.
4 Hovda, R. V., *Strong, Loving and Wise: Presiding in Liturgy* (Collegeville, MN: Liturgical Press, 1986), p. 57.
5 Tertullian, 'On Female Dress', Book 1.1, in *The Writings of Tertullian*, Vol. 1, Ante-Nicene Christian Library 11, trans. Holmes, P. (Edinburgh: T&T Clark, 1869).
6 Angier, N., *Woman: An Intimate Geography* (London: Virago, 1999), p. 52.
7 Summerscale, K., *The Suspicions of Mr Whicher* (London: Bloomsbury, 2008).
8 Young, I. M., *On Female Body Experience: 'Throwing Like a Girl' and Other Essays* (New York: Oxford University Press, 2005), p. 109.
9 <www.orthodoxinfo.com>.
10 Jay, N., *Throughout Your Generations Forever: Sacrifice, Religion and Paternity* (Chicago, IL: University of Chicago Press, 1992), p. 304.
11 Beers, W., *Women and Sacrifice: Male Narcissism and the Psychology of Religion* (Detroit, MI: Wayne State University Press, 1992), p. 178.

12 Beers, *Women and Sacrifice*, p. 167.

13 Beers, *Women and Sacrifice*, p. 187.

14 Harvey, M., 'Margaret's Story', in Harvey, M. and Stallard, M., *Stories along the Way: Stories from Women Called to Ordained Ministry in the Church in Wales* (Cardiff: Church in Wales, 2007).

15 Beattie, 'Vision and Vulnerability', p. 240.

16 Jantzen, G. M., *God's World, God's Body* (London: Darton, Longman and Todd, 1984), p. 6.

17 Shuttle, P. and Redgrove, P., *The Wise Wound* (London: Marion Boyars, 1999), pp. 24–5.

In this moment of utter vulnerability: tracing gender in presiding

ANDREA BIELER AND DAVID PLÜSS

Introduction

In this essay we offer a basic contemplation on how to reflect on the performative dimension of presiding while focusing on gender as something that is also performed.[1] We begin our deliberations with a scene from a workshop on liturgical presence in which the participants were delving into their embodied felt sense of particular ritual gestures such as the benediction at the end of a service.[2] Two Caucasian women, in their mid forties, both clergy, describe what their bodies know as they stand in front of a congregation opening and lifting both arms, smoothly with open palms as they are speaking extempore their words of blessing. The first woman, Heather, describes her experience as follows:

> Although I have practiced this ritual gesture for almost twenty years I still feel extremely vulnerable. The exposure of my torso – my breasts and my belly – leaves me with the fear of losing my protection. I often feel an inner resistance the moment before I offer a benediction. I do not want to expose myself this way. I sense the scars of humiliation written onto my body that I seek to protect. The more I come to terms with my discomfort the more I try to learn to see it not as a weakness or just an experience of victimization but also as a resource of body wisdom. It is in this moment of utter vulnerability that I seek to pray for, be in touch with and channel divine presence – the countenance that shines above us and gives us peace. Interestingly, it does not matter much if I wear a robe in that situation.

The exposure of vulnerability that this ritual gesture releases for Heather does not belong to her common repertoire of body language in the public square. She is aware that in her daily routines she often crosses her arms in front of her chest in order to feel comfortable. The body posture she inhabits as she blesses people pushes her beyond her comfort zone.

The other woman, Julie, ponders on her sense of embodied self as a presider when she enacts the ritual gesture of a blessing. She says:

> The benediction is one of my most favourite moments as a presider in a service. When I open my arms I often feel this increase of energy, something flows back and forth as if I could embrace the whole congregation. This increase

of energy gives me a concrete sense that my body extends beyond its visible boundaries. It is an increase of power as well. I feel that God has gifted me with the ability to embrace and care for others. I experience this as a mother but also as the priest in my congregation. This ritual posture helps me to access and step into this power as a presider: power not in the sense of domination but rather as a sense of spiritual fertility that God pours out onto us.

Gendering ritual gestures

These two women have a very different felt sense of a gesture they perform in similar ways. We suggest that – albeit with the different sensibilities displayed here – these performances have a gendered quality. In the case of Heather, we see how she experiences her body as a threatened terrain. She even speaks of scars of humiliation. Her upper body especially is vulnerable and needs protection. She also describes a momentary sense of shame at what seems like the inappropriate unveiling of her breasts in a worship service. Female breasts mean very different things in different times and cultural settings.[3] There is definitely not a single 'natural' meaning to this part of the body. Heather has learned to see her breasts as the sexualized locus of her female body. This terrain carries very ambiguous connotations.

For Julie, the ritual gesture of blessing is steeped in a deep felt sense of motherhood and of embracing others in which her experiences as an Episcopal priest and as a mother converge. Here, breasts are the symbolic terrain of nurturing; breastfeeding can establish very powerful relationships. The mother becomes the archaic symbol of relationality and dependence as sacred power.

Presiding at a worship service and performing a particular gender have both to do with the subconscious and conscious showing of something. This showing is an interactive, communicative practice in which we engage certain ways of embodied knowing of what it means to be a woman as well as a presider who offers leadership in liturgical celebrations. This ritual knowing of what it means to be a woman and a presider happens through kinaesthetic processes and is expressed through embodied metaphors. So in our example, the ritual gesture of blessing is gendered since as an embodied metaphor it is related to a certain sense of motherhood and to the female body as sexualized locus of vulnerability. These embodied metaphors become powerful as they are recognized in the interactive communication in worship, for instance, when worship participants sense that in the place in which a woman experiences her own vulnerability the divine is present as a fertile force of power in the flesh. The posture of blessing – although it might be performed by different women technically in a similar way – can invoke very different things.

Following Catherine Bell's emphasis that 'the molding of the body within a highly structured environment does not simply express inner states. Rather, it primarily acts to restructure bodies in the very doing of the acts themselves',[4] we assume that the practice of the very posture itself produces ritualized bodies onto which particular ways of knowing the divine are imprinted. So we ask: what kind of restructuring of bodies might occur in the described scenes?

In both circumstances a reordering of power is experienced: the power that might lie in the ritualized exposure of vulnerability and the power that resides in shifting qualities of nurturing and mothering. Vulnerability and nurturing are perceived as female qualities in the terrain of intimate relations. In the public arena of ritual they get visible and have the potential to reframe the experience of offering a blessing and of being blessed. In both cases we might say that the embodied metaphors of vulnerability and nurture as gestures of blessings are enveloped in gender performances. In ritual performances particular actions and sensual receptions have particular significance and are set apart from actions and receptions of daily life. These processes of setting apart are able to echo gender performance from everyday life routines. Moving with a scarred body through the streets or engaging in acts of mothering which are gendered as female activities find their traces in the embodied felt sense of the ritual gesture of a blessing. In the case of Heather and Julie we get a glimpse of how a ritual gesture might be gendered, especially if we try to reflect the felt introspection.

Yet, what is missing at this point in our contemplation is the interactive quality of the performance of their roles. Gender performance happens in interactive processes of recognition as well, in which 'I' am seen into existence as a particular gender through the gaze of another person. We also want to explore this interactive dimension of this gender performance. How is a woman seen into existence as a female presider through the interaction with her congregation? These interactive processes are entrenched in other ways of how identities are marked. We thus need to ask further: How does her perceived race and ethnicity or her age shape her gender performance? It is interesting to see that Heather and Julie, who are identified as white within the North American context, do not reflect on their 'whiteness' as part of their embodied knowing of ritual since this identity marker can remain invisible for the dominant group. The politics that are attached to their perceived skin colour do not need to be made explicit in their narratives about ritual knowing. This invisibility and the silence that comes along with it are part of the constant power negotiations that happen within and beyond ritual practices.

Gender is what is put on with anxiety and pleasure

Gender identity is performed through acts in which we might reduplicate, ignore, exaggerate or subvert certain expectations and visions of what the liturgy as well as gender identity is about. This becomes most evident when unconscious expectations are disrupted: for instance, when two gay men bring their adopted child to the baptismal font in a Lutheran church in California, the hetero-normative expectation of what family is about gets disrupted in the context of baptism. Or when a Roman Catholic worship participant watches, puzzled, a female Episcopal priest who shows her pregnant belly as she lifts the chalice during the words of institution. In this moment of bewilderment her upbringing in which she had learned to see priesthood as a male terrain gets reactivated.[5]

Performing gender identity in worship is also about the effort of authentically forming into gesture what seems natural, true and real. By 'authentic' here, we mean the effect of congruence, and a sense that something feels 'real' in its complexity.[6] In this vein we might say that we seek to authentically give a 'shape' to the body of Christ in communal acts and gestures, songs and silence.

At this point in our contemplation, though, we want to turn specifically to gender studies for the orientation of our thoughts about worship. We are struck by the helpfulness of deconstructive and de-essentializing moves in gender studies that emphasize the idea of doing, rather than being, a gender.[7] This approach is spelled out especially in the work of Judith Butler, who emphasizes:

> Gender is not passively scripted on the body and neither is it determined by nature, language, the symbolic or the overwhelming history of patriarchy. Gender is what is put on, invariably, under constraint, daily and incessantly, with anxiety and pleasure, but if this continuous act is mistaken for a natural or linguistic given, power is relinquished to expand the cultural field bodily through subversive performances of various kinds.[8]

Gender, Butler says, is what is put on with anxiety and pleasure in daily practices which are reiterated over and over again. Most of the time this happens in the realm of the unconscious, and the repetitive character of gender performances make them so powerful that they occur as natural – inscribed into our flesh, our genes, our genitals, our body language as what we are. We develop a felt sense of what it means to inhabit a female body and thus to be a woman. I rarely decide, today, in this liturgy, that I want to act as a female presider. It is rather something vague I carry with me, something that has an inner felt sense. This internal sense of being a gender is accompanied and regenerated by external acts. There is thus an external as well as an internal dimension to the performance of gender.

To reflect on this external dimension of performance, and presiding, as a gendered activity, we also want to follow Butler in her turn to theatre studies.[9] Butler asserts that ritual and theatre are *willed* performances, consisting of conscious acts of performing. The performative quality of enacting a gender, however, has a different quality from theatre, and hence she draws a distinction between performance (in theatre) and performativity (of gender). Performativity, she suggests, is not a singular 'act', but it is always a reiteration of a special model of behaviour. Even more: it is a norm or a set of norms for the behaviour which is concealed or dissimulated as a convention of which it is a repetition. Moreover, this act is not primarily theatrical; indeed it seems to be theatrical to the extent that the normative model of behaviour remains dissimulated. Its theatricality is even inevitable to a certain extent because a full disclosure of its historicity is impossible.

While we find the distinction between performativity and performance to a certain degree helpful, we also see that lines are blurred in the act of presiding. On the one hand, liturgies are indeed willed performances, which follow a particular script that presiders consciously engage. On the other hand, we see that performativity – a quality that conceals and dissimulates how gender identity is put into practice – is at work at the same time.

In bringing liturgical, gender and theatre studies into conversation, we want to begin the next stage of our reflection on presiding with attention to the mechanical dimension of theatre production. Artful theatre develops different sequences of actions by means of various 'media such as space (structure, light, materials, decoration, colour), roles, movements, voices, sounds, and music'.[10] For sure, all of these aspects could be analysed in relation to gender performances in presiding. Gendered performance of presiding might be either highlighted or hidden.

And theatre studies suggest ways to further understanding. 'Dramatizations are sensory processes deliberately produced or introduced ... and thus are *intentionally created events.*'[11] As such, they set free interactive dynamics of denotation and of presence. In a dramatization, a culture of denotation is developed through the audience's response to what is presented; they decode meanings in what is re-presented. A culture of presence is developed as the audience's experiences are touched, and so are invited to a state of self-discovery beyond the interpretive act of what is on stage. Denotation and presence are engaged in every dramatization – and in presiding as well.

The notion of presence is especially important. Speaking of the notion of performance in theatre performances, Erika Fischer-Lichte emphasizes:

> We speak of presence in performances especially in referring to the special mode of physical presence of the one presenting, but partly also in connection with atmospheres. In this sense presence means the specific projection of an actor produced by his or her mere physical presence in a space; hence it is not related to the dramatic figure (in case there is one), but emanates from the phenomenal body of the actor ... One could describe this as a kind of transfer of energy from the actor to the audience, which makes it possible for the experience to possess an unusual intensity. The audience senses the power that emanates from the actor without feeling overwhelmed by that power.[12]

116

Here, Fischer-Lichte focuses on the exchange of energy and the emergence of atmospheres in the phenomenon of presence. We want to relate this to how Michael Meyer-Blanck speaks of presence as broken authenticity: 'Presence is the authenticity broken by the awareness that something is staged ... "Presence" describes the actors' role-related, role-conscious, and yet communication-directed soul-body presence on the stage.'[13] Like Fischer-Lichte, he refers to theatre, and we want to apply their insights to presiding, in which it is pivotal to focus on the moment of intensified liturgical presence in which an energy transfer between presider and congregation takes place. We agree that this event is finally not controllable. Yet the question of how these moments of heightened presence are carried by a particular quality of gender performance can only be answered by looking at discrete liturgical events.

In liturgical celebrations a variety of people are engaged in the act of presiding.[14] They all interact bodily in the performance and must find a balance between their role and their own sense of self. So it is important to see how these roles have a gendered connotation and how that affects the worship experience of a congregation. An obvious example is when women are excluded from leading certain liturgical actions, such as presiding at the table. But besides legal regulations of ecclesiastical bodies, there is a sphere of uncodified social custom in each particular community to contend with.

We can also learn from the ways in which drama and performance theories attend to the role of the body in dramatization. In a drama, a body shows itself to other persons physically present, and this showing contains a basic form of communication that is prior to verbal and sensual culture. That is, it is mimetic:

> Mimetic action is *neither* identical repetition of something already given *nor* altogether original ... It is characterized by *having recourse* to what is known and familiar and *adapting* it to the new situation. This adaptation takes place as a *staging adequate to the situation*, or as *re-staging*. The current action is like whatever functions as a model without being identical with it.[15]

Mimetic action is always bodily action produced by the perception of the body and its surface, by habitus and gesture, and interpreted by those present within a given space. Mimetic acts happen all the time in worship: for instance, the preacher's walk to the pulpit, how she creates a space after arriving there, how she makes eye contact with the congregation before she begins with the reading of Scripture, and how she uses her voice as a means of intensifying atmospheres and emotional states. In these mimetic acts facets familiar to those present are always incorporated and at the same time modified to a degree. If the preacher leaves the pulpit and walks through the nave during the sermon, or speaks from some place in the church where she is invisible, this could be seen in some congregations as a disturbance in the order of things. A change in how bodies move in sacred space while the expected art of a liturgy is going on might change gender perceptions as well.

So far, our contemplation has sought to draw liturgical, gender and theatre studies into conversation in order to see that liturgical presiding is an embodied activity embedded in interactive acts of communication in which a particular showing of a doing and being is enacted. And now we turn to some explicitly theological considerations.

Eschatological performances and the motion of not-knowing

When we preside at the table, when we pray for the world, when we proclaim hope in the midst of suffering, and when we join in song we yearn to see glimpses of divine reign unfolding through the work of the Holy Spirit among, despite and for us. We suggest that a glimpse of God's vision might shine forth in our interactive showing, doing and amplifying out of the depth of an eschatological abyss which holds the unrealized hopes and possibilities that linger in our liturgies, waiting to be birthed. In our presiding we seek to dramatize and perform something that we usually do not experience much: there is food for all. In the drama of the liturgy, our cultivated cynicism can be challenged as a deadening posture towards the survival of the planet; a sense of empathetic listening may arise from the face of the deep. A vulnerable body becomes the site of divine blessing; nurturing becomes a public, political virtue. And performing gender unfolds in ways which move beyond hetero-normative and white stereotyping. However, these performances are always broken, fragmentary – they are eschatological. They force us to come to terms with the painful abyss, the lingering hope, and the joy that wants to unfold in the tenuous space of 'the already and not yet'. This eschatological hope for the coming of God grounds our presiding in a posture of anticipation – in which various modes of divine and human becoming are cherished and prayed for.[16]

Within this eschatological perspective we commend the cultivation of 'a motion of not-knowing', which is especially important for us as we bring contemplation on gender into conversation with intercultural insights. In our view, issues of gender performance need always to be embedded in critical intercultural perspectives. Such perspectives also encourage us to think theologically about the expression of gender identity in ways of presiding so as not to identify and essentialize. So if we take into account the various moves in which the universalized category 'woman' has been questioned – for example, through women of colour, through queer perspectives – we believe an apophatic, or unknowing, posture is most help-ful, one that does not seek to grasp what presiding like a woman should look like. Projecting imagined value systems and cosmologies, practices, habits or features of character onto a particular gender or ethnic group and their ritual performances in homogenizing ways can potentially lead to the erasure of particularity as well as of dissonance, contradictions and contesta-tions that occur in such performances. We do not want to prescribe how women ought to preside, and how this might be different from the way men do. Especially in an ecumenical perspective which takes into account the trans-national moves of a globalized Christianity, a more careful perspec-tive seems to be appropriate.[17]

To put this point constructively, we assert that presiders ought to grow in attentiveness with regard to the inherent relational and constantly shifting qualities that emerge as people worship together. This relational in-between space in which identity performances are negotiated and expressed is shaped by the fluid subject-positions each person inhabits as well as by multifaceted dimensions of formation of the self.[18] Self-formation is a complex, multi-dimensional process that has both creative and destructive potential, and it is vital to our contemplation because it can be especially intense for persons of colour. A multitude of internalized voices can produce a cacophony in which many conflicting demands of identity representation emerge all at once. The 'multiphrenic' self strives towards authenticity through fragile performances of identity that express a necessary complexity of one's self-hood. Yet as one strives in this way, one is also being constantly torn apart as one is 'othered' for one's difference.

Presiding rests on such fragile performances, and happens in contexts in which power struggles that create exclusions and acts of violence are, in fact, going on all the time. So the Roman Catholic Church still excludes women from the priesthood; a father who sexually abuses his daughter sits in the pews next to her; a feminist theologian who prays for victims of violence imagines only white bodies as she prays. A sensitivity towards multiplicity is needed, such that gender, ethnicity and other dimensions of the self resist violent dynamics.

So intercultural perspectives help us also to think theologically about gender performances in presiding. With such perspectives, we assume that we do not 'know the other' in a final, complete way. Moreover, we agree with Mayra Rivera, who points to the possibility of an apophatic theological approach that negates the possibility of a complete comprehension of God. Rather, she proposes an understanding of inter-human difference that is inexhaustible: the other can neither be imagined as 'univocal as a thing in the totality of my world, nor as equivocal as the absolutely exterior either'.[19] Hence, Rivera presents a relational understanding of transcendence that alludes also to inter-human encounters: '*Transcendence designates a relation with a reality irreducibly different from my own reality, without this difference destroying this relation and without the relation destroying the difference.'*[20]

What is true for our knowledge of God is true for our encounter with the human other. Neither an ambiguous nor an unambiguous entry into perception of subjectivity is fruitful; instead, we need to seek space for the recognition of difference and of connection at the same time. The other cannot fully be absorbed into my life-world, nor is she so distant from me that I cannot see the connections and points of contact between us. This notion of what Rivera calls 'relational transcendence' can inspire a culture of not knowing as we look at gender performances in liturgy. If we refrain from assuming too much, we might be able to recognize each other more fully in our particular singularities with which we inhabit different ritual life-worlds.

Conclusion

We draw these theological reflections to a close with a memory of a female Protestant student, Inga, from Samoa, who has taught us how the multiplicity of her gender performances unfolds in the different places of worship she inhabits. In her seminary chapel, she is part of a web of women of colour and white women in which she feels encouraged to take on leadership roles as a presider in chanting, in preaching, and in serving at the table. In this worship context she feels she can expand her repertoire of performing her gender. At the same time she feels the constraints of being exoticized, since as a *Samoan* woman she is constantly addressed as the other. In her Samoan church she experiences the opposite. She feels diminished in her space as a presider since she is not allowed to participate in particular leadership roles. At the same time she is able to move with a certain sense of comfort in her community as the congregation engages in its immigrant narratives of cultural belonging. She knows that none of these places of worship offer her the opportunity to develop herself as a presider in an authentic way. Inga captures this shifting of subject positions poignantly as she describes herself being present in different worship settings as a Samoan woman and how the different 'invocations' she receives from such different environments create constant conflict in her, which she finds hard to handle.

In the way that Inga embodies the tensions that intercultural theologies engage, we find a powerful vignette to invite contemplation in relation to how liturgical, gender and theatre studies help us to trace gender in presiding.

Notes

1 For discussion of performance theories and gender perspectives with a focus on feminist liturgies, see Enzner-Propst, B., *Frauenliturgien als Performance: Die Bedeutung*

von Corporealität in der liturgischen Praxis von Frauen (Neukirchen-Vluyn: Neukirchener Verlag, 2007).

2 The following vignettes reflect the notes Andrea Bieler took after a workshop on 'Liturgical Presiding and Presence' she offered in Berkeley, California, in 2009. Names have been changed.

3 See Miles, M., *A Complex Delight: The Secularization of the Breast 1350–1750* (Berkeley, CA: University of California Press, 2008).

4 Bell, C., *Ritual Theory, Ritual Practice* (Oxford: Oxford University Press, 1992), p. 100.

5 See further Bieler, A., 'Mimesis und Irritation in der Darstellung von Geschlecht im Ritual', in Waltz, H. and Plüss, D. (eds), *Theologie und Geschlecht: Dialoge Querbeet*, Theologie und Geschlecht, Vol. 1 (Zürich/Berlin: Lit-Verlag 2008), pp. 203–7.

6 See Plüss, D., 'Liturgische Präsenz und Geschlecht: Überlegungen zu einer performativen Geschlechtertheorie des Gottesdienstes', in Waltz and Plüss (eds), *Theologie und Geschlecht*, pp. 192–203, at p. 198.

7 See further Karle, I., *Da ist nicht mehr Mann noch Frau: Theologie Jenseits der Geschlechterdifferenz* (Gütersloh: Gütersloher Verlagshaus, 2006).

8 Butler, J., 'Performative Acts and Gender Constitution: An Essay in Phenomenology and Feminist Theory', in Conboy, K., Medina, N. and Stanbury, S. (eds), *Writing on the Body: Female Embodiment and Feminist Theory* (New York: Columbia University Press, 1997), pp. 401–18, at p. 415.

9 See Plüss, D., *Gottesdienst als Textinszenierung: Perspektiven einer performativen Ästhetik des Gottesdienstes* (Zürich: Theologischer Verlag, 2007).

10 Plüss, *Gottesdienst*, p. 92.

11 Plüss, *Gottesdienst*, pp. 92–3.

12 Fischer-Lichte, E., 'Performativität und Ereignis', in Horn, C., Umathum, S. and Warstat, W. (eds), *Performativität und Ereignis* (Tübingen: Francke, 2003), pp. 11–37, at p. 30. Fischer-Lichte asserts that the actors can practise techniques of presence, but for the audience that presence is a happening that grips them with the speed and power of lightning. In this sense presence is always an event and is ultimately uncontrollable.

13 Meyer-Blanck, M., 'Liturgische Rollen', in Schmidt-Lauber, H.-C., Meyer-Blanck, M. and Bieritz, K.-H. (eds), *Handbuch der Liturgie* (Göttingen: Vandenhoeck & Ruprecht, 2003), pp. 778–86, at p. 781. See also Friedrich, M. A., *Liturgische Körper: Der Beitrag von Schauspieltheorien und – techniken für die Pastoralästhetik* (Stuttgart: Kohlhammer, 2001).

14 The variety of ways in which presiding happens in worship is pointed at in Garrigan, S., 'The Spirituality of Presiding', *Liturgy* 22 (2007), pp. 3–8.

15 Plüss, *Gottesdienst*, p. 167.

16 See, on the question of becoming, Hutchins, C., 'Uncomforting Becomings: The Significance of Whitehead's Novelty and Butler's Subversion for the Repetitions of Lesbian Identity and the Expansion of the Future', in Armour, E. T. and Ville, S. M. S. T. (eds), *Bodily Citations: Religion and Judith Butler* (New York: Columbia University Press, 2006), pp. 120–56. For a reflection on the deconstruction of binary gender dualisms in eschatological perspective see Heβ, R., 'Es ist noch

nicht erschienen, was wir sein werden: Biblisch (de)konstruktive Anstöße zu einer entdualisierten Eschatologie der Geschlechterdifferenz', in Heß, R. and Leiner, M. (eds), *Alles in Allem: Eschatologische Anstößess,* J. C. Janowski zum 60, Geburtstag (Neukirchen: Neukirchen-Vluyn, 2005), pp. 291–323.

17 For liturgical reflections that are sensitive to postcolonial perspectives as well as gender analysis, see Burns, S., Slee, N. and Jagessar, M. M. (eds), *The Edge of God: New Liturgical Texts and Contexts in Conversation* (Peterborough: Epworth Press, 2008).

18 With regards to multiphrenia in the constitution of self, see Gergen, K. J., *The Saturated Self: Dilemmas of Identity in Contemporary Life* (New York: Basic Books, 1991).

19 Rivera, M., *The Touch of Transcendence: A Postcolonial Theology of God* (Louisville, KY: Westminster John Knox Press, 2007), p. 79.

20 Rivera, *Touch of Transcendence*, p. 82 (italics original).

'And ain't I a woman': the phronetic dramaturgy of feeding the family

ANITA MONRO

That little man in black there! He says women can't have as much rights as men, 'cause Christ wasn't a woman ... Where did your Christ come from? ... From God and a woman! Man had nothing to do with him![1]

Introduction

Sojourner Truth's defiant oration provides the title for this chapter through her confronting demand to be acknowledged as a woman despite her race and socio-economic status. Truth's demand to face the reality of her sex prompts this exploration of the reality of the confrontation which women's presidency at the Eucharist provokes.

The advent (or re-advent) of women presiding at the Eucharist explicitly disrupts the delicately balanced metaphorical role of the 'priest'/presider in the Christian meaning-making project. This disruption is clearly identified by opponents of women's presidency in their fear and rejection of it. This paper seeks to explore the disruptive nature of women's presidency and its consequences. In the process of this exploration, the disruption will be highlighted as ambiguous, that is, as holding within itself both life and death, hope and despair. This ambiguity, though messy and dangerous, is also the very stuff of incarnation which is the very heart of the Eucharist: the embodiment of God in Jesus Christ and of Christ in the people of God, the body of Christ.

Against the background of the theoretical framework of René Girard and Julia Kristeva, the appropriation of that framework by Martha Reineke, my own appropriation of the work of Julia Kristeva, and some commentary on Kristeva's work provided by Kathleen O'Grady, this paper explores the powerful duplicity of the narrated and embodied enactment of Eucharist whereby a masculine sign/symbol is reified while the sacrificial act is performed on the feminine body. In the Eucharist, Christ feeds his people as a woman feeds her children – with her own body – but the true identity of the body is masked in the masculine assumption of the meaning-making process. In Kristevan terms, in the process of enacting meaning, the masculine symbolic suppresses the feminine semiotic.

In the act of presiding at the Eucharist, then, women are placed in the ambiguous position of re-presenting the feminine re-presenting the masculine re-presenting the feminine. It is a double or quadruple bind. To preside re-enacts the suppression of the feminine. Having a woman as presider places the act of suppression in feminine hands, masking the masculine symbolic culprit, just as the feminine victim has previously been masked. Not to preside re-enacts the exclusion of the feminine, and maintains the meaning-making project in masculine hands. Exposing the femininity of the victim makes women's presidency even more fraught as it destabilizes the meaning-making project.

Yet, this paper will argue that it is precisely the ambiguity of women presiding that most accords with the phronetic dramaturgy of incarnation: the historically embodied, socially enacted, narrative subjectivity of Christ. In the phrase 'phronetic dramaturgy', I reference a wisdom Christology that draws on notions of 'practical wisdom' (*phronesis* in Greek) to understand the nature of the incarnation as embodied and enacted as well as narrated – in short, dramatic. In the problematic space of women's presidency at the Eucharist, the stark and messy reality of the drama of the incarnation is confronted.

Background presuppositions

This paper rests on a number of key premises which arise from the work of the previously identified theorists. First, human identity, meaning and subjectivity arise from an act of sacrifice and/or suppression.[2] Second, the sacrificial and/or suppressed victim is the feminine.[3] Third, the explicit introduction of the feminine into the meaning-making process exposes the nature of the victim and disrupts the meaning stasis or implicitly accepted world-view.[4] Fourth, a highly likely response to this disruption is the attempted re-establishment of the prior meaning stasis (world-view) and the reinterment or suppression of the victim.[5] Finally, despite the re-suppression, the restored (or renewed) meaning stasis will have already shifted because of the process of the confrontation.[6] Because there is insufficient space to explore each of these in turn, this paper assumes these presuppositions rather than arguing them.

As Martha Reineke observes,[7] while Girard exposes the first of the premises listed above, it is Kristeva who uncovers the femininity of the actual victim of the meaning-making process. It is also Kristeva's work which highlights the disruptive role of the feminine in the meaning-making process; and the likely response to such disruption. Kristeva's account of the development of subjectivity also confirms that it is precisely the interplay of masculine and feminine, stasis and disruption that characterizes the continuing meaning-making process – an eternal rehearsal of stasis and disruption.[8]

In connection with the Eucharist, the notion of sacrifice/suppression does not depend on the explicit theology of the Eucharist being founded in such concepts. Rather, it is the very act of Eucharist as constitutive of meaning that links it with sacrifice/suppression. Whether we wish it or not, at the heart of the Eucharist is sacrifice.

In the face of those presuppositions then, this paper seeks to explore the nuances of identity, meaning and subjectivity brought to the celebration of the Eucharist when a woman presides.

Eucharist as meaning-making event

For the Christian Church, the Eucharist is meaning-making event par excellence. It is one of the key rites of identity formation. In this rite, the relationships between God and humanity and within the Godhead are rehearsed. Participants ('the faithful') are understood to commune with God through giving thanks to the Father (first person of the Trinity), re-membering Christ (second person of the Trinity), calling upon the Holy Spirit (third person of the Trinity) to effect the communion whereby the participants' identity is subsumed/founded in the very act of communion, and consuming/participating in a symbolic meal which is understood to enact and presage the fullness of the promised relationship with God ('the kingdom').[9] In the major Christian traditions, the 'ordained' priest/presbyter/minister/elder is the one who presides at this rehearsal.

O'Grady points out that, for Kristeva, Eucharist is 'the perfect enactment of the metaphorical process', that is, of the essential process underlying all meaning-making which is simultaneously 'consummation with the maternal body' and the sublimation of the recognition of the role of the feminine.[10] While O'Grady is keen to focus on the 'consummation with the maternal body', Kristevan theory of language and subjectivity always recognizes the inherent double bind of the meaning-making process, that is, the feminine/maternal/(m)other/semiotic is intrinsic to the process but masked in its participation by the masculine/patriarchal/one/symbolic. A further aspect of the differential relation which different genders have with the meaning-making process must also be acknowledged here: the masculine subject is permitted singularity, autonomy, separation and completion; the feminine subject is generally characterized as heterogeneous, derivative, dependent and incomplete.[11]

Against this background, male priesthood/presidency may be understood in the following terms: a male subject (singular, autonomous, separate, complete) presides at a meaning-making event where participants are incorporated into a masculine identity – the body of Christ – by virtue of their communion with the divine through this rite which involves consumption of a meal (that is, penetration of participants by the masculine body).

Participants are feminine – the heterogeneous female body which needs to find a singular identity through incorporation into a masculine body. In Christian theology, the Church, the participants, is often described in feminine terms (for example Church as bride, Christ as bridegroom). The masculine penetrates the feminine in order to redeem/reconcile/liberate the feminine body.

There is a slight sleight of hand in the reversal inherent in Christ/ Church (masculine/feminine), and this reversal is the place where the ambiguity of the Eucharist is most exposed. The christic identity is masculine; although the bodiliness of the christic association in the rite is connected with the assignment of body and flesh to the feminine in the symbolic order. At the point that the body of Christ is no longer Christ's body, but the body of Christ, the Church, the gender reversal emphatically occurs, but the place of the reversal is not clear. The reversal ultimately maintains the patriarchal nature of the symbolic order, but does open up the possibility of the escape of the feminine, fleshly, carnal subordinated subjectivity which is inherently part of the exchange from which meaning arises.

Nevertheless, with male presidency the feminine is carefully kept in control. The Church is not Christ, but the body of Christ. The carnal, the fleshly, is feminine and subordinate. In the very process of meaning-making contained in the rite (or any act of meaning-making, for that matter), the feminine/maternal is suppressed in the process of creating the required meaning for participation in the symbolic order. A certain security is produced, at the expense of the concealment of the complexity of the meaning-making process and the heterogeneity of meaning itself.

The male presider is somehow understood as being somewhat separate from the messy process of meaning-making, having already attained the necessary singular, autonomous, separate and complete subjectivity required. The male presider is able to negotiate the messy transition smoothly, keeping masculine and feminine subjectivities firmly separated. The meaning-making process is understood to be in rightful hands: the appropriate product of the process – a masculine, singular, autonomous, separate, complete subject. The male presider is understood as provider of that which is required for the dependent family to feed.

So, what may be understood to happen when the gender of the presider changes?

Exploring the possibilities

Against the background of the work of Caroline Walker Bynum, Reineke offers an account of the role of medieval women mystics 'who, in saintly ascetism, deliberately abstained from all food but God's food: the eucharist'.[12]

For Reineke, these women were involved in three kinds of 'works of sacrifice': first, 'soma (the body of ascetic practice) was killed to create the sign (of a saved community)'; second, 'the symbol (a community infused with the saving power of Christ) was somatized (in a sacrificial transgression of the flesh which touched the sacred on the far side of the thetic order)'; and third, 'the power of the sacrificial economy to destroy *and* create was demonstrated as a dying mystic – both poison and antidote – sacrificially cleansed the community and secured it from threat.'[13]

In this analysis, the death of the women is the mechanism by which meaning is achieved – the sacrifice is clearly feminine. The question is raised as to the complexity of the role of the women during their lifetimes; and that question is relevant for trying to understand the dynamic of women's presidency at the Eucharist in our time.

In relation to medieval female mysticism, Reineke observes that:

> Perhaps in no other time did Western culture come so close to unveiling the truth of its origins. Perhaps in no other time were the fractures at the foundations of the sacrificial economy deeper or the possibilities for women's subversion of the Law greater than during the late medieval age.[14]

And yet, the very mechanism for subversion ensured the death of the women and the maintenance of the symbolic order; and their deaths 'secured' communal identity 'from threat'. In this context, it is not the women's deaths that must be considered, but their lives. That it was their lives that presented the most potential for disruption is confirmed by Reineke's observation (based on Bynum) of the progressive overt victimization of the women by the symbolic order as they come to be seen in terms of 'witchcraft' rather than piety:

> The late medieval age, site of the struggle to resurrect the sacrificed Mother and to retrieve her daughters from the grip of the sacrificial economy, ended in paroxysms of violence ... The mystics' stigmata became devil's marks and milk from their breasts no longer healed the sick but nursed incubi.[15]

In this context, it is clearly the living body that has the most potential for disruption, and the woman presider at the Eucharist is a living body. This 'soma' is not 'killed to create the sign' but remains alive, before, during and after the creative act. The 'somatization' of the 'symbol (a community infused with the saving power of Christ)' is embodied by a live female body. The 'sacrificial economy' with its power 'to destroy *and* create' is thwarted by this continuity of feminine life which appears to inhibit the consummation that can only be found in the death of the feminine.

Within a Kristevan framework, the power of the sacrificial economy is decisively invested in the masculine. When the production of the sacrificial economy is presided over by a male, the equilibrium of the economy is retained intact. The male priest dismantles/pours out/sacrifices the body of Christ (Eucharist) in order to secure the life/identity of the body of Christ (Church). The feminine body is consumed in order to re-create the sign of the saved community which is now identified with male subjectivity, that is, Christ. The female body of Christ, the Church, achieves completion through this identification with the masculine.

When the production of the sacrificial economy is presided over by a female, it becomes clear that the feminine cannot be killed, or at least that her death is illusory. The fragility of the economy is exposed. The female priest dismantles/pours out/sacrifices the body of Christ (Eucharist) in order to secure the life/identity of the body of Christ (Church), but the identification of the female body of the priest with the female bodiliness of the Eucharist is irresistible. The separation is unable to be maintained. The body shared is the body not yet dead. The female presider is seen to be the point where the ambiguity of the meaning-making enterprise is embodied. A continuous chain of bodies is constructed as the body of the presider slides into the body of Christ (the Eucharist), and the body of Christ (the Church). The feminine body (Church) is fed with the feminine body (Eucharist) by the feminine body (presider). The female presider is provider for the family. Christ feeds her people with her very self at her own hand.

A feminine subject, heterogeneous, derivative, dependent, incomplete, is not as easily separated from the action. A female presider exposes the role of the feminine in the production of meaning. The boundaries between presider and participant, presider and sacrificial victim, are not so easily drawn. The body of the woman (because woman and body are not so easily separated) juxtaposed with the body of Christ (the Eucharist) raises issues about its gender. The body of the woman juxtaposed against the body of Christ, the Church, blurs the boundaries between presider and participant. The bodies merge, and the illusion of singular, autonomous, separate complete subjectivity is exposed.

Again, within a Kristevan framework, this point of ambiguity, the woman's body, is also the place of *jouissance* – the product of the unresolved moment of meaning creation, the 'perpetual and oscillating process of becoming'.[16]

> As an adept balancing act between the two brinks of language and subjectivity, *jouissance* is a 'joying in the truth of self-division' – an ambivalent and risky recognition of both the subject's complicity in the use of the tools of meaning construction, and the limitations of such tools in exploring the complexity of an identity which defies them.[17]

The place of *jouissance* is the very moment of meaning-making, but it is unstable. The process of meaning-making is exposed. It is at once joyous and painful; and it prompts both celebration and fear. It is the site of 'truth', but a truth that is ambiguous, multiple and diverse.

By implicitly exposing the meaning-making process, the presidency of a woman destabilizes but does not destroy the meaning-making process. The sacrifice rehearsed is sacrifice enacted as the woman gives up her personal identity for the sake of identity with the community which in turn is identified with the Eucharist (body of Christ). A semi-stable meaning is produced, but one that is more comfortable with the inherent complexity of the meaning-making process and the messiness of the meaning produced. The theological implications of this situation will be explored further below.

Seeking confirmation

Just as Reineke observes that the responses to medieval mystics confirm their status in the meaning-making process, so too it is possible to observe the response to female presiders as indicators of their role in the meaning-making process.

When a female is given 'honorary' masculine status as presider, she is understood to stand in place of a male and participates in the meaning-making process that suppresses the feminine. The woman must masquerade in order to preside over the sacrifice of the masked victim. This honorary 'promotion' places women in an extraordinary position of compromise and contradiction. Masked as male, the woman presides at the murder of the (m)other in order to ensure the survival of the male subject. A stable subjectivity is assured at the expense of the suppression of that which is involved in its production/creation – the female presider embodying the (m)other, and by implication the place of women as women in the sacrificial economy.

When female presidency is denied or repealed, the instability of the meaning produced and the exposure of the meaning-making process is actively worked against by removing its possibility. Again, a stable subjectivity is assured at the expense of the suppression of that which is involved in its production/creation. The feminine is never allowed to be exposed. The mechanism of the sacrificial economy remains safely hidden with the concomitant probability that women themselves remain suppressed within the symbolic order.

For Kristeva, Christianity's opening to the (m)other, the feminine implicitly present within the meaning-making process, is part of its relevance:

> The nutritive opening up to the other, the full acceptance of archaic and gratifying relationship to the mother, pagan as it might be, and undoubtedly conveying paganistic connotations of a prolific and protective motherhood, is here the condition, for another opening – the opening up to symbolic relations, true outcome of the Christic journey.[18]

In this context and the context of Kristeva's understanding of Eucharist as 'the perfect enactment of the metaphorical process', the role of women as presiders is made imperative as a means of exposing the complexity of the meaning-making project, and opening up the sacrificial economy to the recognition of the feminine and the enhancement of the role of women in the symbolic order.

Theological implications

If Eucharist is 'the perfect enactment of the metaphorical process', then incarnation is its outcome, that is, the embodiment of the divine in the human; in this case, not a single human, but the body of Christ (the Church). In her analysis of the work of Hannah Arendt, Kristeva links the place of *jouissance* with the concept of *phronesis* or practical wisdom and the notion of incarnation.[19]

According to Kristeva, for Arendt, 'political action' (that is, public action) is 'an actualization – of a *who*',[20] that is, the narrated life of public action is the negotiated life of embodied subjectivity. 'Activity means life.'[21] Subjectivity is historically embodied as well as discursive or narrative. It is dramatized. The body is the agent of this vital or life process, and these bodies which act are uniquely socioculturally and historically located. For Kristeva, this type of subjectivity is the very act of incarnation itself. The subject constructed through political/public/social activity/ interaction is embodied/incarnated.[22] Kristeva explicitly connects this embodied subjectivity with the Christian story[23] and, thereby, *phronesis* with incarnation.

It may be argued that Kristeva's notion of incarnation is insufficiently theologically grounded. Her concerns are psychoanalytical, not theological. Nevertheless, there is a short step from her analytical concerns to a theological reinvigoration of her concept of incarnation. If incarnation is subjective entry into the public space, in the context of a theological interpretation of the Christian story, the entry of the Second Person of the Trinity into the created order is precisely a revelation of the very nature of God in accordance with Christian theological tradition. Similarly, in the public action of Eucharist, the incarnation is re-membered, and the Second Person of the Trinity is re-embodied this time not in a single human, but in a community, the body of Christ, the Church.

Eucharist where the meaning-making process is exposed is a rite that confronts us with the messiness of incarnation. It problematizes the subjectivity of the presider, the participants and the rite itself. This problem-atization has the potential to reinvigorate the rite through the explicit sacrifice of the feminine body (the presider and the body of Christ [the Eucharist]) for the sake of the resurrection of the feminine body (the body of Christ, the Church) as the incarnated body of Christ (both masculine and feminine).

Conclusion

This paper has sought to explore the meaning-making dynamics of the Eucharist in the context of women's presidency. It has done so against the background particularly of the work of Julia Kristeva, but also of the appropriation of that work by me and Martha Reineke. Kathleen O'Grady's commentary on Kristeva has helped to highlight the connections that Kristeva herself makes between the Eucharist and the meaning-making process. In seeking to draw out some of the theological implications of these meaning-making dynamics, the paper has highlighted the connections that Kristeva makes with the meaning-making process, Eucharist, and also incarnation. A range of background premises have been assumed in order to manage this exploration in a short paper.

Notes

1. Truth, S., 'Ain't I a Woman?' (Philadelphia, PA: Historical Documents Co., 1994). See <http://www.fordham.edu/halsall/mod/sojtruth-woman.html>.
2. Girard, R., *Violence and the Sacred* (Baltimore, ML: Johns Hopkins University, 1977); Kristeva, J., *Revolution in Poetic Language* (New York: Columbia University Press, 1984).
3. Girard, *Violence*; Kristeva, *Revolution*.
4. Kristeva, J., *The Powers of Horror: An Essay on Abjection* (New York: Columbia University Press, 1982); Reineke, M., *Sacrificed Lives: Kristeva on Women and Violence* (Bloomington, IN: University of Notre Dame Press, 1992).
5. Kristeva, *Horror*; Reineke, *Sacrificed Lives*.
6. Kristeva, *Horror*; Kristeva, *Revolution*; Reineke, *Sacrificed Lives*.
7. Reineke, *Sacrificed Lives*.
8. Especially in Kristeva, *Powers of Horror*.
9. See World Council of Churches, *Baptism, Eucharist and Ministry* (Geneva: WCC Publications, 1982).
10. O'Grady, K., 'The Pun or the Eucharist? Eco and Kristeva on the Consummate Model for the Metaphoric Process', *Literature and Theology* 11 (1997), pp. 93–115, at pp. 104–5.
11. Monro, A., *Resurrecting Erotic Transgression: Subjecting Ambiguity in Theology* (London: Equinox, 2006).
12. Reineke, *Sacrificed Lives*, p. 111.
13. Reineke, *Sacrificed Lives*, p. 127.
14. Reineke, *Sacrificed Lives*, p. 127.
15. Reineke, *Sacrificed Lives*, p. 127.
16. Monro, *Erotic Transgression*, p. 121.
17. Monro, *Erotic Transgression*, p. 114.

18 Kristeva, *Powers of Horror*, p. 115.
19 Kristeva, J., *Hannah Arendt: Life Is a Narrative* (Toronto: University of Toronto Press, 2001); Kristeva, J., *Hannah Arendt, Female Genius: Life, Madness, Words*, Vol. 1 (New York: Columbia University Press, 2001).
20 Kristeva, *Life Is a Narrative*, p. 55.
21 Kristeva, *Life Is a Narrative*, p. 7.
22 Kristeva, *Life Is a Narrative*, p. 56.
23 Kristeva, *Life Is a Narrative*, p. 85.

Presiding from the broken middle

RACHEL MANN

Poetry, if it has any weight and value, does not need explanation. Nor does it especially benefit from theological justification. Poetry, as art and craft, lives in and for itself, even if we have the urge to put it to some utilitarian or theological use. Poetry is an end in itself. However, given that this is a book of theological and liturgical reflections and I've produced poetic responses to the nature of Eucharist and presiding, some account of the genesis of these poems is appropriate. The aim of this account is not to instruct the reader how to interpret the poems, which in any case would be a cheap and pointless move, but to help the reader locate the poems in a story and, thus, help them to find a place for the poems in this book.

When I was approached to contribute to this book I initially proposed writing a more or less conventional paper on what I called 'Presiding from the broken middle'. For any number of reasons this paper didn't emerge; a number of poems from the 'broken middle' did. In order to understand the context for these poems I need to say something about the concept of the 'broken middle' and my use of it. My first encounter with the term was in the difficult and profound philosophy of the late Gillian Rose. I do not propose to rehearse the main moves of her philosophy here; however I do want to acknowledge that her use of the term lay in her determination to reject the tyranny of binary opposites (e.g. totalizing 'modern' systems versus the fragmentation of the 'post-modern' *other*) as well as her desire to criticize the postmodern strategies which originally dealt famous mortal blows to such oppositions. Hers is a philosophy which resists the tyranny of extremes but also argues for the beauty, moral power and, in a sense, clarity of the broken middle. Her work on matters of law and ethics has a compelling beauty which recognizes the power and surfeit of competing moral claims and demands and yet argues for a sense of 'shalom' as justice which does not allow for the 'victory' of one claim over the other. Her famous autobiography, *Love's Work*, reveals that her commitment to inhabiting the 'broken middle' was not merely theoretical, but personal: theologically and personally she was resourced by both Judaism and Anglicanism, inhabiting a not always comfortable place between the two, resisting the temptations of ready answers and solutions to living. Famously, she uses Staretz Silouan's 'keep your mind in hell and do not despair' as the epigraph for her autobiography, a phrase which underlines Rose's determination to keep face to face with reality, especially as she faced death from cancer. She was determined not to take flight into a comforting vision of wholeness any more than she was prepared to be reduced to bitter atomistic selfishness by her disease.

Out of Rose's conception of the 'broken middle' emerges my own use. And this use focuses on one truth about me. Beneath the many and various truths about me – the fact that I am priest, the fact that I am poet, the facts that I can be selfish and generous by turns and so on – there is one truth which I rarely share and which is crucial. And it is this: I am a trans-woman. That is to say, I have, to use the vernacular, undergone a 'sex change' from male to female. The details of this change, while more or less interesting in themselves, are not directly relevant to what I want to say here; however, the basic *fact* of that change is. It is worth saying that changing gender has been a tremendously liberating, healing and wondrous experience, which has brought a level of personal integration and hope that I barely glimpsed in my childhood and teenage years. It is also worth stating that change has also been costly, difficult and at times downright painful. In many important respects I remain the person I was prior to the change – I still have a cheeky sense of fun, a need to show off and so on – but it is also true that I have become something new as well. As much as many things have remained the same, when one undertakes as great a personal change as changing gender, so much gets lost, obscured and is remade. Life is never simple for anyone who takes a moment to reflect, but can be especially complicated for the transgendered. It has taken me many years of honest and authentic self-reflection and living with God to become at peace with the simple unavoidable fact that some aspects of my past life are dissonant with where and who I am now. For me, the immense and joyous good news is that such dissonance, paradox and inconsistency is creative, thrilling and risky in the best sense of the word. The shalom in my self, which is very real, is not of a comforting and easily resolved kind. It is out of this creative dissonance that my poems and my use of the concept of 'broken middle' emerged. In terms of my private life, the notion of the 'broken middle' feels true, creative and fruitful. The concept gestures towards the truth that being a trans-woman is never simple and involves, for me at least, negotiating a reality that brings with it a facticity that has traces of being a boy and man as well as being a woman. And broken? Yes, but it would be lazy to assume that I take this word in a negative way. I, like all human beings, am broken. Perhaps I am more broken than most; I do not know. But I know also that my brokenness – which includes some aspects of my gender dysphoria, but is most certainly not defined by it – is also a place of creativity, hope and healing. This creativity is, I sense, an emergent property of forging wholeness out of pain and confusion, but crucially is a reflection of an essential and defining truth of the Christian faith: that it is out of woundedness and brokenness themselves that new life, shalom and creation come. But this is no shalom in stasis but the shalom in journey and transformation. Surely, Christ's wounds, the very wellspring of new hope, teach us precisely that.

I'm sure that what I've just said raises as many philosophical, theological and political questions as it may answer. I am always both amused and troubled by how trans-people can turn otherwise generous, reasonable people into security guards wishing to police the boundaries of religion, sexuality, gender and other concepts. I do not propose to wade into essentialist debates about gender or anything else, debates which struck me as tiresome even in the 1990s when I was active as a teacher of philosophy. However, it strikes me that, given that I wish to identify myself as a 'trans-woman', the following question has interest: 'what then does it mean to write, preside, or do anything as a trans-woman as opposed to someone identified simply as "woman" or "man"?' The working out of that question is worthy of a book, and there have no doubt been attempts;[1] given that I want my poems to be the main focus in this contribution, I simply want to offer the briefest thought. The difference between trans-woman and bio-woman,[2] say, centres for me on a lived-out orientation or, better still, 'way of being' which is signified by dissonant/alternative moments of experience. To try to explain this I find myself reaching, inevitably, for metaphor. The metaphors I want to use in addition to 'broken middle' are 'splinter' and even 'thorn in the flesh'. The notion of the 'splinter' in the self reflects a trans-truth: that though one may spend much of the time blithely, unselfconsciously and happily living one's life 'as a woman', which is how I mostly experience my life, one regularly becomes conscious of difference and discontinuity. Only a person who can fool themselves or who is determined to 'rewrite their story' can attempt to live otherwise. This 'thorn in the flesh' is a reminder of one's facticity – which is not just about the past but also about the present. When I claim to write or preside as a 'trans-woman' I am perhaps, at one level, offering a minimal claim: that in so far as there is distinctiveness, it lies in a simple subjective fact, a personal perspective which is both congruent and divergent from others' experience. At the surface level, the performed aspects of any activity I engage in may not be much different from anyone else – for example, when I preside at the Eucharist, say, I cannot say that I do it in a distinctively 'trans' way, whatever that might mean; but in terms of the lived, internal dimension, perhaps I am aware, in ways which many are not, of the dissonances, aporias, the splinters of presiding as someone living in the 'broken middle'. It is this distinctiveness I am exploring in poetic ways. Clearly trans-people are not alone in experiencing this 'splinter in the self' which reveals both how much one is in solidarity with others but also belongs to another way of going on; I sense that many 'queer' people would say that it is a key motif of their lives: that the experience of queerness is an experience of creative divergence. Indeed, I'm tempted to go so far as to say that this experience of being 'both of and not of' is a hugely common human experience, even if rarely acknowledged. In a society which, while unconsciously inscribing stereotypes on its members, increasingly makes clear that many aspects of gender, sexual and personal identity are 'performed' and in a process of flux and exchange, I anticipate a continuing queering of the field.

This then is the context of the poems I offer in this book: the perspective of a trans-woman who is also a priest, or of a priest who is also a trans-woman. Being a priest and being a trans-woman speak from and deeply into my core identity. That I am a poet lies in part in the interplays between both. These poems spring from those truths and seek to speak into them. Whether they are any good or if they succeed, I leave for you to decide.

Presiding from the Broken Middle

Lift up your hearts
We lift them to the Lord

Our hearts are wounded.
They are scarred by silence
injured by sneers. They have been torn
by the fears of others and sometimes
by our own need to feel safe.

But do not pity or feel sad.
Know that we too have received blessing,
know that ours is also a place of grace.

Our hearts are injured.
They do not pump safely like yours.
In the struggle to survive
so much has been lost.

We make a home in what remains.

Let us give thanks to the Lord
It is right to give thanks and praise.

And we shall speak a song God gave us
And we shall find bread in the stones we found
And we shall receive blessing when rejection is given
And we shall arise when we've been beaten down.

And we shall sing a song God gave us
And we shall break bread on holy ground

And we shall proclaim a blessing in a world that is riven
And we shall stand and know we are found.

And we shall roar a song God gave us
And we shall share bread among the lost and found
And God will heal from the broken middle
and with grace and hope and love astound.

Holy, holy, holy, Lord
God of power and might.

Not pure   not clean
not sound   not complete

And never   ever
what we were told we ought to be

But we have desired
have craved have hungered for
a taste of the holy

Not the holy of the pure
of the clean of the sound
of the complete

but the holiness of your bread.

Feed us now with your fragments.

Fragments which heal and break you
fragments which break and complete us.

Though we are many we are one body
Because we all share one bread.

Break the bread.

Break it now.
See what is revealed.

Are you surprised that from it, it is love which falls?
Are you surprised that through it, it is you unbound?

For we were told such lies.
You are outside. You are beyond.
In holy bread you will never be found.

But we too have shared the song of heaven
we too have offered our strange magnificent lives
we too heard God laugh from the broken middle
we too have bled, stayed standing, have cried.

God's bread is like broken glass in our hands:
it shines, it wounds, in the light of its queer mirrors,
it exposes us all.

Communion

We are not here to forget
those who were forced to hide in closets
those who were bullied into renouncing themselves
those who disappeared, were destroyed or abused.

We shall not forget cruelty and hate.

But we shall break bread.

This bread
breaks open the pain
tears the wound
exposes arteries and veins.
From this bread more than crumbs shall fall.

But in the fragments
something more than injury
something more than fury
something more than loss
shall be found.

The body shall not be ground into dust.

Song from the Broken Middle

'Keep your mind in hell, and despair not'.
Staretz Silouan

There are mornings
when we wake, throw off
the warm fur of the night
and see in the dance of dust in sunlight
a hint of a greater whole.

There are days
when the solitary singing of a blackbird
reaches deep beneath the regular
frequencies of our ears
and tempts us towards
an imagined heavenly home.

But this is not where we will ever truly be found.

Come. Down through the cracks, the gaps
through which the easy things fall. Come.
Break open your heart and receive the truth.

We are the citizens of a city
forever in flames.
Where women run through streets
screaming for their stolen infants.
Where no help ever comes.

We are exile's children.

Days may yet be coming when
you might watch coolly
as if from a distant moon
and dream that what we have is complete,
might pass for a satisfactory whole.
But that is never our view.

So come. Come to us now.
Receive our blessing.
Receive our truth.

Notes

1 See, for example, Bornstein, K., *Gender Outlaw: On Men, Women and the Rest of Us* (London: Vintage, 1995).
2 While I see that such a distinction does some work, is it simply my lack of seriousness which makes me want to laugh out loud at my own and other people's need for prefixes?

Receiving like a woman

NATALIE K. WATSON

Introduction

Having been asked to contribute to a book entitled *Presiding Like a Woman*, I began to wonder if this was a subject on which I, an Anglican lay woman, actually had something to contribute. Although I am aware that I am by no means the only lay person contributing to this book, I actually know very little about eucharistic presidency as such. Of course, the Eucharist is not only about those who participate in the role of presider. It is a celebration of the whole body of Christ, the Church in God's world. My own participation in the Eucharist is as a lay person as well as sometimes as a lay eucharistic minister, offering the chalice to the congregation while a priest distributes the bread that she or he has consecrated. Yet, does this mean that I as a lay person and a woman am once again relegated to being passive and receptive rather than active? There are of course those who do not want to see it that way. As I write, one of the English cathedrals is gaining notoriety by offering 'untainted wafers' to those who wish not to receive the elements consecrated by one of its priests, a woman. I have on several occasions experienced a member of the congregation refusing the chalice from me and other female lay eucharistic ministers with the words: 'We'll have it from a man.' This, in my view, is reducing the Eucharist to some kind of cheap magic, in which the person of the presider or even their sex or gender becomes more important than the gift of Christ himself and the participation in the life of God.

Receiving our humanity in the image of God

Yet, what does it mean to receive 'like a woman'? I would like to argue that in receiving the Eucharist, the body and blood of Christ, we receive not something alien to ourselves, but gain or regain the integrity to receive our own humanity in the image of God. We do so by participating in the incarnate nature of God. Such participation is an active process, as it involves the whole of our humanity, the whole of our womanhood in a way that is not reducible to culturally defined and conditioned femininity. Receiving the Eucharist is a profoundly sexual act as it invites us into ultimate intimacy with God, and such intimacy can only be achieved if we both

140

surrender and receive our own humanity as women (and men) made in the image of God. We are not merely included but actively participate in the life of God and the life of the Church.

The Eucharist is about God, about what God has done and is doing, with and to the world, with and to us. We are called to be people who live through and in response to the creative and redemptive activity of God in the world. This response is essentially one of thanksgiving, of Eucharist.

The Eucharist cannot be reduced to being a mere memorial of something Jesus once did with his disciples. To offer, break and share the body and blood of Christ is to participate in the timeless and yet embodied reality of God. Our celebration of the Eucharist takes place in a broken world. This means that we cannot celebrate the Eucharist apart from our own brokenness, our own memories of betrayal and of pain, and those of the world in which we live. We hear that 'the body of Christ has AIDS'. I would want to add that the body of Christ is being abused, raped, violated, denied dignity, where women experience such things. So, what does it mean to receive like a woman?

This is not an essay about posture. For women (and men) who have been abused and humiliated, be it sexually or emotionally, kneeling to receive bread and wine can conjure painful memories of their abuse and humiliation. Even if we kneel before God, the physical posture we are asked to assume can be reminiscent of having to make ourselves small before others, especially men. There can be no doing what we are commanded to do in memory of Christ without our own painful memories, and no breaking of the bread of heaven that simply glosses over our own brokenness. I remember, in working through times in my life when mealtimes had frequently been occasions of emotional and at times physical abuse, how it profoundly moved me that this meal was different: it was a meal from which I could never be excluded or sent away, as the host was one whose nature was love and acceptance.

Augustine of Hippo, not renowned for his positive attitude to women and seemingly traumatized by his overpowering mother, speaks of the mystery of the Eucharist as receiving what we are – we are the body of Christ as we receive the body of Christ.[1] Letty Russell speaks of the need to create a feminist spirituality of choice. She says that the choice we need to make is to be a woman and to receive our womanhood as part of God's good creation.[2] While the concept of choice is, in my view, overrated in modern Western consumer societies, the point which Russell makes is an important one. The Eucharist enables us to receive our own being as women, our female sexuality, in the context of a society and large parts of the Christian tradition which render women's sexuality, women's identity, as unclean and dangerous, or as something trivialized and objectified. It is thus that ultimate divine reality transcends magic. In receiving the body and blood of Christ we are not invited to become someone else but to become who we are. To receive the body and blood of Christ does not mean to accept that the male body which the second person of the Trinity assumed was superior to our own female bodies. This is Arianism at its worst, not incarnational theology. We may arrive stating that we are 'not worthy to receive you, but only say the word and I shall be healed', yet the Eucharist is not a magic ritual by which we receive enough healing to get through the coming week, but the word of healing that has already been spoken. It is the word of divine creativity that created humanity as male and female and concluded that 'it was very good'. This original divine creativity precedes and transcends all cultural assumptions made about femininity and masculinity and any hierarchical understanding of how they relate to each other.

The Eucharist: intimate and public

Receiving the Eucharist is both deeply intimate and essentially public. The two belong together and one is not possible without the other. Intimacy without the public dimension is secrecy that is open to abuse. Any public act that excludes intimacy is in danger of becoming abusive, of reducing the human body to material that can be traded and sold or rejected and thrown away. There are still parts of the Christian tradition that regard women's bodies and blood as unclean and polluting and on those grounds exclude women from both presiding at and receiving the Eucharist. In many Orthodox churches menstruating women are advised not to receive communion and some 'Catholic' traditions will not allow women between menarche and menopause in the sanctuary for fear of defilement. Such an understanding of women's bodies again reduces the Eucharist to a magic act that can somehow be impeded by forces present in God's creation. If a menstruating woman is capable of being the bearer of the incarnation, how can menstrual blood invalidate the power of the blood of Christ?

I have argued elsewhere that the use of body imagery in speaking of the Church can be a difficult one for women as women hear the body of Christ spoken about alongside the rejection of their own bodies.[3] They are told that they have to become part of someone else's body, the body of a man, in order to participate in God. Women come to the Eucharist with experiences of the goodness of their bodies, of their sexuality being denied, of being sexually abused and raped, of being told that their bodies are not good enough. Women are invited to feast on the body of Christ, while they live in a world where they are constantly challenged to diet so as to fit with the infamous cult of size zero, to make themselves sexually attractive to men and to be rejected if their bodies do not fit culturally defined norms of ideal body shape. Likewise, women are invited to drink the blood of Christ while their own blood is seen as polluting and dangerous, their own experiences of menstruation, childbirth and childlessness are regarded as embarrassing and to be concealed. To receive like a woman means to enter consciously into this space of contradiction.

The Eucharist is a space of disruption of the multiple and contradictory body discourses of the world in which we live. Augustine, once again an unlikely ally, argues that God will not save us without us. If this applies to women, we cannot receive the body and blood of Christ without receiving our own bodies as part of God's good creation and as the place where incarnation and redemption takes place.

In receiving like a woman at a public Eucharist we claim our place within the body of Christ in the image of God and as bearers of the incarnation. In doing so publicly, we state that there is no room for the structural sin of sexism in any church that celebrates the Eucharist.

The language and imagery of sacrifice has been used to exclude women from the Eucharist. Anthropologists identify sacrifice as a male substitutionary rite that establishes patrilineality, family identity through the male line, as a 'remedy for having been born of a woman'.[4] Some Christian theologians argue that because the Eucharist re-enacts the sacrifice of Christ on the cross, women are incapable of actively participating in it. If this is true, I want to ask why women would want to participate at all in a rite that by its very nature excludes them. Yet, if God is one creator and redeemer, creation and redemption cannot oppose each other, but are part of the same divine activity. Thus to celebrate the sacrificial self-giving of God by entering into the reality of suffering and death means to contradict such a separation of creation and redemption. The Christ whose sacrificial death on the cross we remember is Christ incarnate, born of a woman, who is part of the Triune God who created humanity. It has been said that women who become priests have to take on a male role, have to surrender their identity as women and thus their female sexuality. In contrast, women speak of the experience of being empowered by seeing a woman at the altar, and seeing something of their own salvation in a woman representing Christ at the altar.

Eucharist as converting ordinance

John Wesley spoke of the Eucharist as a converting ordinance, as a means of grace, as a sacrament that would draw souls to Christ.[5] For him this meant the conversion of individuals who were not yet believers to faith in Christ. Yet the Eucharist is also an act of conversion not only of the individual but of the Church as a whole, a conversion to God, to ourselves and to the world. Long before Wesley, the monastic father Benedict spoke of conversion as an essential trait of the monastic and essentially the Christian life. For Benedict, there is no turning to Christ away from his body, women and men who are bearers of the incarnation.

Such conversion is not merely a personal experience of the individual but a profoundly public one. Every Eucharist is not only a re-enactment of the past event of the death of Christ on the cross but a celebration of a new and different reality that transforms the world. Many feminist theologians have struggled with much of the language and imagery of the Eucharist, the language of sacrifice, of breaking the body and shedding the blood of Christ. I remember a lesbian friend saying in response to a paper I gave that she would not want to have to eat the body of a man. Women have experienced exclusion from the altar, be it as presiders through the ongoing misogyny of those who hold that women due to their impurity cannot be priests, or as menstruating women rendered unclean by the all-male hierarchy of so many churches.

Yet, I would like to argue that as members of the *ekklesia* of women, as full members of the body of Christ, we need to begin by reclaiming some of the central imagery used in the tradition. We need to begin with God and claim nothing but God in our reading of the Eucharist. Only that will help us to overcome the destructive discourses of ecclesial abuses of power and the trivialization of our experience. God gives godself to us in bread and wine. In receiving bread and wine, we become what we are: the body of Christ in our bodies. God the creator, the incarnator and God incarnate, crucified and risen, present among us in the Spirit, receives us into the being of God.

We come to the altar as women whose bodies are broken day by day, whose blood is rendered impure and dangerous and yet meaninglessly shed, be it actually or symbolically. Women are still frequently asked to sacrifice themselves, to forgo opportunities for the sake of their husbands or their children, to 'deny themselves', to be willing victims of domestic abuse and violence. It is in my view the height of blasphemy when women are asked to do so to follow the example of the suffering Christ, frequently by clergy to whom they have turned for help and support. This is truly taking the name of God in vain. The sacrifice of Christ on the cross which is re-enacted at the altar in the celebration of the Eucharist is the final and ultimate sacrifice which renders all other use of sacrificial language meaningless and calls us to a life of flourishing as part of God's good creation.

Yet, we come to the altar as broken people, with the pain and suffering inflicted on us by others and often by the Church and in the name of Christianity. At the beginning of the eucharistic liturgy, we are asked to repent from our sins and to receive forgiveness. While I think this is important and a central part of the journey towards transformation, I sometimes wonder if this is enough. Many sinful acts happen as a result of pain being inflicted on us. And that pain is frequently trivialized or overlooked. To name but one example, as a victim of adultery, I repent from the anger and hatred, from the desire to judge and condemn others, coming from that profound experience of betrayal by someone whom I trusted with my life. Yet, I also come to the altar bearing the pain of being told that 'these things happen', that it is in the nature of men to want to 'sow their seed', while women want stability they cannot have. I come as part of a church that often seems as though it does not want to know about the pain of people like me, that judges me for struggling to 'get over it'. I come with pain that 'dare not speak its name'. So I wonder if alongside repenting from our sins, we need to learn to name our pain. Alongside being told that our sins are forgiven, we may also need to be told that we have suffered and that that suffering is a wound in the body of Christ.

In celebrating the Eucharist, we remember and follow the commandment of Jesus who 'in the night that he was betrayed' took bread and wine and shared them with his disciples, among them the one who would betray him. As Jesus faced his betrayal, we no longer have to hide our experience of betrayal but can face up to it, we can encounter our experiences for what they are, and be transformed by a reality that is greater than that of our betrayal. Bread and wine are not magic potions to cure our pain, but the life of God given for us that makes us who we are, that enables us to receive anew the women we are created to be. They enable us to name our bodies and our blood as embodiments of the life of God, as parts of God's good creation. And it is there that healing and love become possible. We are worthy to receive the body and the blood of Christ.

In the celebration of the Eucharist, we recall and re-enter the story of creation and salvation, yet we do so as the people we are, as people who have been declared unworthy, as people who are caught up in the sinful structures of a fallen world. We reclaim what we are created to be, and as such we are worthy to embrace and to be embraced by the creative and redemptive love of God.

And this is true conversion: there is no conversion to Christ without conversion to the world to which Christ came, and to the people Christ loves, including ourselves. The grace to which the Eucharist is a means is not a quick-fix makeover like the ones women are asked to undergo to make themselves acceptable to a world that wants their bodies to be in a particular shape. It is the ultimate reality of God, creator, redeemer and sanctifier, God's shalom, the world as God intended it to be, that transcends and transforms the world as we encounter it.

In being called to participate in the life and the life-giving activity of God in the Eucharist, in receiving the body and blood of Christ and receiving ourselves anew as part of God's good creation, we are then called out to become part of God's life and creative and redemptive activity in the world. Tissa Balasuriya called for a eucharistic fast in which all celebrations of the Eucharist should be put on hold until the problem of hunger in the world had been solved.[6] While I hear the urgency of such a call, I do not agree with it. We celebrate the Eucharist in a space of contradiction. We are invited to feed on the body and blood of Christ in a world where many women, men and children starve for lack of food and others live in a world of abundance and are put under pressure to starve themselves to comply with cultural norms of body image. Jesus instituted the Eucharist on the night in which he was betrayed, and we too celebrate it in a world that constantly betrays the goodness of God's creation in all of humanity. Yet, in celebrating the Eucharist, we are reminded, we re-member, we celebrate that God is present and active in this world, that it is in this world, in this body that our salvation takes place. If we are eucharistic people, people who give thanks for what God has done and is doing, this will not stop at the end of the act of celebration. Our response of thanksgiving, of receiving God's body and ours, is to participate in the life and work of God in the world, to make present the reality of Christ's broken body and his blood in the world, to work that other bodies are no longer broken, that blood is no longer shed, to break cycles of suffering and violence.

Conclusion

To conclude: to receive like a woman is to live a eucharistic life of celebration and sharing the goodness of God's creation and redemption, of participating in the life of God incarnate in our own bodies that the world and the Church may be challenged to embody its creator and redeemer.

Notes

1 Augustine, Sermon 227.

2 See Russell, L., *Church in the Round: Feminist Interpretation of the Church* (Louisville, KY: Westminster John Knox Press, 1993), pp. 183ff.

3 See Watson, N. K., *Introducing Feminist Ecclesiology* (London: Sheffield Academic Press, 2002), p. 424.

4 Eisenbaum, P., 'A Remedy for Having Being Born a Woman: Jesus, Gentiles and the Genealogy of Romans', *Journal for Biblical Literature* 123/4 (2004), pp. 671–702.

5 See, for example, Westerfield Tucker, K., 'Table Etiquette: Means and Manners', <http://www.gbod.org/worship/articles/table.html>.

6 Balasuriya, T., *The Eucharist and Human Liberation* (Eugene, OR: Wipf & Stock, 2004).

Birthright or misconception?

GILLIAN HILL

In 1994, a few months after being ordained priest, I moved to a challenging inner-city area to become priest in charge. Faced with many requests to baptize the children of lone parents, I found myself increasingly drawn to a contemplation of the nature and meaning of baptism, especially for those living on the council-housing estates around the church. Most had experienced little or no contact with a church, many had heard horror stories of mothers being turned away or 'forced to go to church' and yet they demonstrated amazing persistence, especially when viewed against the backdrop of declining participation in formal religion found today in the UK. Six years later, after moving to a semi-rural benefice, I discovered that in my former parish this stream of lone parents had dried up and the subsequent (male) incumbent was now mainly baptizing children from families where there were two married parents. As the new incumbent was not operating a particularly strict baptism policy, the only conclusion was that somehow the presence of a woman priest had been a catalyst for change, enabling women who had previously felt excluded to bring their children for baptism.

While researching a PhD thesis, I set out to investigate why parents still seek baptism for their children when formal religion is in decline; to evaluate clergy attitudes towards mothers and the impact this might have upon their subsequent pastoral care; and to critically examine what bearing attitudes towards women in the Church might have upon the care of young mothers seeking baptism for their children. However, in the course of investigation the liturgy itself came under scrutiny as it became apparent that very little in the rite was connecting with the experiences of women being interviewed.

Baptism and Holy Communion are the pivotal sacraments of the Church, yet while much has been written about the Eucharist, there is less critique of baptism preparation or investigation of the baptismal liturgy itself. Personal exploration of issues surrounding inclusion and exclusion exposed differences in the way male and female clergy approach sacramental activity; and research-based interviews indicated that women clergy appear more sympathetic to the pastoral context in which they operate and empathize with the lives of the women with whom they come into contact.

Female presidency at the altar, and the embodied approach women bring to the sacraments, cannot be divorced from the pastoral and liturgical framework within which these activities take place. Without connection to experience, there is danger of rites becoming empty and meaningless for participants: 'Effectively the choice is between a model of stability and maintenance, against one of liberation and transformation.'[1]

There is a requirement for feminine models of pastoral care and liturgical practice to be evolved that do not view the struggles of women who face difficulties in raising their families, or a breakdown of relationship, as a 'problem' caused by female hormones, to be corrected with proper instruction, but that resonate with women's experience and offer a celebration of our participation in God's creative activity. Such models free women from feeling shame at being unable to cope with social pressures such as juggling work and family life and, it is hoped, may one day result in liturgies which are life-affirming and rich in symbolic reinterpretation.

Female clergy sometimes discover previously untold experiences of women during pastoral encounters. Issues such as violence, abuse of various kinds, abortion and a desire for a stable relationship may be revealed because the presence of a female pastor engenders empathy and trust. In one such story from the inner city, a parishioner told how her former husband had psychologically abused her and threatened her with death. When she approached her parish priest she was told that the sanctity of marriage was inviolate and should not be broken under any circumstances. It is time that such abuses of pastoral care are exposed and replaced with models that eradicate any notion that physical danger, repression or control is acceptable. Baptism is a sacrament concerned with new birth, life, death and pilgrimage, it resonates deeply with the experience of women, it raises a plethora of pastoral, liturgical and sociological issues, and for this reason deserves exploration in relation to female presidency and priesthood.

Liturgical hysterectomy

Insights emerging during the twentieth century include that of 'prophetic symbolism': a belief that throughout the Old Testament we find God's word being performed as well as spoken. For example, Jeremiah wore a yoke as a symbol of the coming subjugation of Judah to Babylon, and the prophet Hosea was required to take an adulterous wife to demonstrate Israel's unfaithfulness.

R. R. Osborn argued that these actions are sacramental in character, not just because they are symbolic, but because they actually enact the will of God and bring it into being; they are not only 'expressive' but also 'effective'.[2] Logically it could be argued that in order for the rite of baptism to be 'effective' the symbolism must resonate with the life of the enquirer, otherwise no connection can be made. So we find a need for liturgical expression to connect past and present experience for this generation and for symbols which have meaning in terms of everyday life.

After undertaking research into baptism it became clear that it is mainly women who request baptism for their children and pass on their beliefs to subsequent generations; men generally acquiesce but are rarely the initiators. Various theories abound as to why this is so, but most agree that women's proximity to birth and death gives them unique insight into life's most profound moments. These experiences seem to predispose women towards spiritual exploration and reflection upon the meaning of life. Given that this makes women guardians of faith for the next generation, it makes baptism all the more important, as it may provide the one opportunity for those having little or no connection with the Church to encounter the Christian faith in all its richness. Having identified the importance of enabling parents to make these connections, it seems all the more incredible that baptismal liturgy makes little mention of the rich symbolism surrounding procreation and birth. Parents have experienced the traumatic and life-changing experience of childbirth, so it seems extraordinary that there are just three references to birth in the baptism liturgy, and none at all to the womb – a symbol full of spiritual significance and meaning, which makes its absence all the more perplexing.

Exploration of this mystery revealed that in the first three centuries of the Church there were many references to the womb in relation to baptism. For example, Narsai wrote: 'The invisible Spirit opened again the womb by visible water, preparing the newly born fledglings for the regeneration of the font.'[3] Philoxenus spoke of the baptism of Jesus as turning the Jordan into 'the new wombs' heralding the beginning of the new creation and revealing the Trinity.[4]

It is significant that the model used for the baptism of proselytes during the first three centuries of the Church is based upon the account of the baptism of Jesus rather than his death. It was during the fourth century that the emphasis in early writings shifts to the death of Jesus as a universal experience. Kilian McDonnell theorizes that this was caused by large numbers of people turning to the Church in the second half of the fourth century and that a theology of death, which was a universal experience, would have more meaning to new converts than that of the Jordan. This theology called for radical outward conversion, which would have been irresistible to those faced with policing a large number of converts to the faith.

From a feminist perspective, the womb is a very powerful image, so the question must be asked, is the disappearance of the womb as an image of baptism linked to the suppression of feminine imagery in the Church? Do we have in essence a 'liturgical hysterectomy' where symbolism linked to women's procreative power has been excised in order to 'purify' the

Christian faith? It is surely no coincidence that the disappearance of womb theology coincides with a general suppression of women's ministry within the Church.

Mary Daly compared powerful professional males to gynaecologists ripping the wombs out of women and disagreed with those who have postulated theories of 'womb envy' to counterbalance Freud's misogynistic theories of 'penis envy'. These, she believes, focus upon female genitalia, thus colluding with male fantasies regarding women's creative powers. Rather, Daly believes that envy is more deep-rooted in the psyche, the clues being found in our language in such phrases as 'pregnant with meaning' or 'that's his baby'. Daly writes:

> Such deceptive powers provide clues to the deepest levels of deception. They suggest that procreative power which is really envied does not in fact belong primarily to the realm of mind/spirit/creativity. Yet this envy is not necessarily a desire to be creative, but rather to draw – like foetuses – upon another's (the mother's) energy as a source. Thus men who identify as mothers (that is super-mothers controlling biological mothers) are really protecting their own selves. The adequate and androcratic invasion of the gynocentric realm can only be total erasure of female presence, which is replaced by male femininity.[5]

At the heart of Daly's theory resides the belief that men have usurped the role of women, especially within the Church, by taking upon themselves the nurturing, protecting and creative roles, and then excluding women, relegating them to physical procreative activity that is then despised and undermined, out of envy.

The womb, the most powerful symbol of womanhood, has been totally eradicated from baptism liturgy; a liturgy which has at its heart a joyful message of new birth, emerging into the light from darkness and being 'born again'.

Jeanne Moessner-Stevenson echoes Mary Daly in her examination of the experiences of women who have undergone a hysterectomy and their feelings of bereavement and fears of becoming less feminine. She links the womb with the internal psyche of women and regards its loss as symbolizing women's anguish when they are robbed of their voices, their true identity, and their femininity within the Church in being forced to conform to a masculine image of what constitutes the 'feminine' – submissive and silent. Moessner-Stevenson's exposition of the woman at the well links the woman's physical thirst to 'an internal thirst of women', her water jar becomes a symbol of all that consumes her life. The well at Sychar 'replicates the anatomical well, the womb, the uterus, the gynaecological water pot'.[6]

For women the womb is symbolic, not just of procreative power, but of an inner desire to reproduce, to be spiritually creative and to give birth to all that wells up within. And it is clear from interviews with young mothers that giving birth arouses strong spiritual yearnings, sometimes for the first time, where their creativity becomes linked to the creativity of God. The rich womb imagery of the early Church would resonate with the experiences of young mothers today, yet it has all but disappeared from any liturgical expression, apart from references to the Virgin Mary where birth is effectively removed from any suggestion of sexual activity.

Una Kroll spoke of how, through contemplation of the womb, she 'rediscovered the womb of God through prayer'.[7] Kroll encourages women to focus upon their own bodies and experiences in order to explore the nature of God. Her own journey was from a childhood shaped by traditional images of God as Father to a new understanding of herself as a woman, both possessing a womb and also loved and nurtured as in the womb, and created in God's image.

The womb is a powerful symbol of femininity, and female clergy are ideally placed to recognize the life-changing nature of childbirth and the deep desire within women to receive blessing and affirmation at this important transitional stage of their lives. It is also recognized that requests for baptism may mask a deeper agenda which can only be revealed in an atmosphere of trust. As in all pastoral encounters there is value in being slow to dictate terms and conditions and being willing to journey with a person towards a deeper understanding of how Christ seeks connection with their lives. As an illustration two very different pastoral experiences are offered here.

The first concerns a young family who came to church because of their brain-damaged son. The mother wrote:

> I wanted J. baptised in church and not in a hospital ... so the baptism was on a Saturday afternoon with family and friends and then on Sunday in the normal church service he was welcomed by everybody. It was our way of enabling J. to belong to the church and just to know that whatever happened he would be looked after. We were bringing him as close to God as we could because we were beginning to know then how poorly he was and that we may not have him for very much longer and we just wanted to know that someone would be looking after him. There would be only one other person that would be there for him and that would be God and that's what kept us going through everything.

Each week the family would bring J. to church, connected to his oxygen and feeding tubes, and his presence in the service taught the congregation much about bringing the whole of human life, both the joys and the sorrows, into sacramental worship. Eventually little J. died, and his mother wrote:

> It is going to church that's given us that confidence and faith to carry on ... we know that J. is well cared for and he's well and that's all you ever want to

know when you lose somebody...we realise that J. was lent to us for a special reason and he brought us to church in the first place and without him we would never have had any of the people we have met and the friendships and contacts, being involved socially and spiritually or half the things we've done over the past year or so.

As a priest who has often encountered situations where devastating loss evokes deep feelings of anger towards God, it was very humbling on this occasion to see a family giving thanks for their son because through him they had come into the Christian faith. This encounter highlighted not just the benefits to the family concerned, but the benefit to the Church when we allow the suffering of others to break in and upset our carefully ordered worship.

In this case the request for baptism was initiated by dire need within the family, but it is not unusual to discover requests for baptism arising because a much loved grandmother is ill, or there is marital disharmony, or someone has recovered from an illness. It is possible to miss the unspoken pastoral need behind a request for baptism by the operation of strict inclusion/exclusion policies.

One example of this was a young mother who asked for a visit. She was very upset because she had prematurely given birth to twins who had been very ill and in hospital for three months. When they were allowed home she rang a local minister who came to see her. When he discovered that she was not a churchgoer, he gave her details of a church course, and left. She said: 'He didn't even say a prayer or bless my babies.' There was no recognition of the pastoral issues behind the request for baptism. The woman was seeking a way to express thanksgiving at having two live babies after a traumatic birth, not an invitation to a course. To divorce baptism from its pastoral context is to reduce it to a meaningless ritual which hinders people from making the necessary connections between their life journey and the Christian faith.

Church and household

The subject of children in church is outside the scope of this essay, but any investigation of baptism raises questions about the inclusion or exclusion of children and how families are viewed when they bring babies and young children to a service. There are also questions to be asked about the place of the household – where does it fit into our model of what constitutes 'church'?

Since being freed from the perceived tyranny of domestic life, women have fought for equal opportunities in employment and to break through the 'glass ceiling' denying them access to senior professional roles. The arguments surrounding the ordination of women are not new. Florence

Nightingale, founder of modern nursing, expressed her frustration at her restricted role within the institutional Church:

> I would have given the Church my hand, my heart. She would not have them ... She told me to go back and do crochet in my mother's drawing room; or if I were tired of that, to marry and look well at the head of my husband's table.[8]

Within the Church of England it is assumed that most sacramental activity will take place within a church building, suitably consecrated as a place of public worship. The ordination of women has often been viewed as an entering into, and occupation of, the traditionally male-dominated sacred activities taking place therein. The pain of women excluded from such rites was graphically summed up by Daphne Hampson in her essay 'Women, Ordination and the Christian Church'; after demonstrating for women's ordination at the Lambeth Conference, she wrote:

> It was shattering ... to watch the procession into choral evensong of four hundred Bishops and their advisors, all men, among them my friends, and to know that I was divided from them, irrevocably, by the fact that I was a woman. I felt entirely left on the sidelines – automatically, by definition.[9]

The sense of rejection experienced by women found its expression in protests against exclusion from the liturgical rites and sacramental acts of the Anglican Church; yet the idea that liturgical activity must take place inside a church building remains unchallenged. In Judaism, for example, worship is not confined to the synagogue, family meals and the household play a part in regular remembrance of God's saving acts. Hinduism also emphasizes the household as the place where religious tradition is passed to succeeding generations.

In the New Testament, alongside the thanksgiving taking place in synagogue and Temple, the importance of the household in worship is frequently mentioned. For example, Acts 2.46: 'Day by day, as they spent much time together in the temple, they broke bread at home and ate their food with glad and generous hearts.' Greetings to households are included at the end of several of the New Testament letters; for example in Colossians 4.15 we find greetings to Nympha 'and the church that meets in her house'. A question could be raised as to why worship is now so far removed from the domestic sphere, where women traditionally exercised authority, and confined to church buildings. Surely it is in our homes that we are most truly 'ourselves' and where Christ shares in the joys and sorrows of family life; the removal of worship from the household has perhaps encouraged a mindset where it is seen as acceptable to leave the true 'self' at the church door.

Richard Thomas explored the covenant community in the Old Testament where important festivals, such as the Passover, were celebrated within the home:

The transition of the central act of worship from the annual celebration of the Passover in the family home to a more frequent celebration of the Eucharist ... meant that the individual Christian's focus of belonging inevitably shifted with it. That strong feeling of a direct covenant relationship between the family and God was replaced with a sense of the individual belonging primarily to a local community of faith ... At the same time, the strong sense of the sacred household, fostered by what we might well describe as the lay celebration of Passover in the family home ... [gave way to a situation where] the family was effectively deskilled in the celebration of the central act of Christian worship.[10]

The concept that households should be at the heart of a Christian worship that is deeply rooted in normal family life has all but vanished in the regular practice of the Anglican Church. From the responses of those questioned for research purposes, much liturgical activity bears little resemblance to the everyday life of those not socialized into the mysteries of language and symbolism. There is a richness to be explored in encouraging families to 'play and pray' together in ways that incorporate a wholeness of life and worship. Perhaps the question should not be 'how do women preside?', but 'where?'

The case for change

Where does the embodied woman priest fit into the sacramental activity of a church where liturgy and tradition has been shaped by two thousand years of patriarchy? We tend to accept the concept that church buildings are where the gathered community, the people of God, meet together for worship to be encouraged by the faith of others, and it is wholly right for women to take their God-given place within the liturgical and sacramental activity of the Church. However, given the importance of women for the transmission of belief from one generation to the other, there are questions to be explored concerning the centrality of households as an integral component of that journey of faith.

Sacramental activity can be seen as part of a wider picture encompassing pastoral care rooted in a model concerned with the purposeful actions of a gathered intentional community.[11] Within such a framework both baptism and Holy Communion become both a gathering and an offering of the whole of human life, an acknowledgement that we are all on a journey of faith and come as broken and imperfect human beings. Those women priests with experience of birth may offer profound insights enabling bridges to be built with those in our communities who seek baptism or other services from the Church. Symbolism which connects past saving acts with present experience offers scope for liturgy to become enlivened with meaningful images from birth, death, and more importantly, the womb, as a potent symbol of new birth.

Stephen Pattison sees a need for the Church to move away from 'text-centred theologies'[12] which often regard practice as a poor second to the study of 'pure' theory. This is where women's experience and an embodied approach challenge any retreat into abstract ideas using procreation, life and death to force theologians into the 'discomfort zone'.

Research indicates that some pastoral care is rooted in fear: fear of change, fear of failure, or fear that cherished beliefs are being eroded in some way through lack of understanding. Clergy are all too human, and we are sometimes trapped by the belief that we have to be guardians of orthodoxy, rather than explorers travelling into the unknown, guided by a God who is more than capable of taking care of God's own reputation. It may be that, having touched the roots of our own humanity through participation in God's creativity, women instinctively try to draw others into an offering of the whole self and the profound experiences of human life at the altar and through the deep waters of baptism.

Notes

1 Graham, E. and Halsey, M. (eds), *Life Cycles: Women and Pastoral Care* (London: SPCK, 1993), p. 219.

2 Osborn, R. R., *Forbid Them Not: The Importance and the History of General Baptism* (London: SPCK, 1972), pp. 29–30.

3 From McDonnell, K., *The Baptism of Jesus in the Jordan: The Trinitarian and Cosmic Order of Salvation* (Collegeville, MN: Liturgical Press, 1996), p. 102.

4 From McDonnell, *Baptism of Jesus*, p. 103.

5 Daly, M., *Gyn/Ecology: The Metaethics of Radical Feminism* (London: The Women's Press, 1979), p. 83.

6 Stevenson Moessner, J., *Through the Eyes of Women: Insights for Pastoral Care* (Minneapolis, MN: Fortress Press, 1996), p. 330.

7 Kroll, U., from Parsons, G., *The Growth of Religious Diversity: Britain from 1945*, Vol. 11 (London and Milton Keynes: Routledge and the Open University, 1994), p. 98.

8 Nightingale, F., from Parsons, *Growth of Religious Diversity*, p. 207.

9 Hampson, D., from Pattison, S., *A Critique of Pastoral Care*, 3rd edition (London: SCM Press, 2000), p. 48.

10 Thomas, R., *Counting People In: Changing the Way We Think about Membership and the Church* (London: SPCK, 2003), p. 48.

11 See Graham, and Halsey (eds), *Life Cycles*, pp. 83–96.

12 Pattison, *Critique*, p. 219.

Presiding in the classroom: a holy work

NICOLA SLEE

Introduction

In what follows, I would like to reflect on my experience as a teacher to see in what ways this experience might offer insights into what it means to 'preside like a woman'. I will explore the notion of presiding to focus on the different ways in which teachers offer a mediating, enabling, priestly ministry within the classroom. I have chosen to broaden the perspective beyond specifically liturgical settings for at least two reasons: first, to affirm and demonstrate the claim that has been made in several places in this book, that women preside in a wide range of contexts, not only the ecclesial and liturgical; and second, to suggest that experiences of presiding outside the liturgical assembly might inform liturgical presidency, at the same time as allowing liturgical presidency to illuminate and inform leadership in other spheres. In doing so, I invite recognition of teaching as 'holy work', in every way as sacramental as liturgical presidency, and 'teachers as ministers of personal and social transformation', as Gloria Durka puts it.[1] Much of the history of women's teaching, like that of women's priesthood, has been hidden, and women's authority as 'teachers of the faith' denied or downplayed. Yet,

> For every woman
>> denied the voice to speak out her own religious truth,
>> refused the opportunity to teach her wisdom
> and ridiculed for her theological insights and ideas

we can and should celebrate every woman

>> who claimed her authority in vision, prophecy and dream,
>> who spoke out her truth in hymnody, verse and story.[2]

Starting with Mary, the teacher and priest par excellence,[3] Christian tradition is replete with a venerable tradition of women teachers, 'doctors of the Church' (even if not acknowledged as such) – from the unnamed Syrophoenician and Samaritan women in the Gospels who helped to form Jesus' mind to renowned theologians such as Hildegard of Bingen and Teresa of Avila; from mothers who nurtured and instructed the faith of their more famous offspring (not only Mary, but Monica and Macrina come to mind) to pioneering scholars (such as Elizabeth Cady Stanton in the United States and

Maude Royden in the UK) who paved the way for contemporary feminist scholarship.

Teaching is core to my own sense of vocation. It is in this context more than any other that I have the experience of 'sitting in front of the assembly', occupying the seat of authority, exercising superintendence, conducting and directing the company of learners, to call on some of the dictionary definitions of 'preside'.[4] Feminists have suggested a wide variety of metaphors that might articulate a feminist vision of teaching – the teacher as midwife, voice coach, contemplative artist and reticent outlaw, for example;[5] here I offer one more, the teacher as presider. While it is not usual to speak of the activity of teaching in terms of 'presiding', I suggest that this can be a helpful term for focusing on the ways in which the teacher manages, directs and shapes the processes that operate within the learning environment.

I am not thinking primarily here of lecturing, because, although the didactic delivery of material has a role to play in adult learning (particularly in the inspiration of learners), and although it has its analogy in liturgical presidency (the delivery of the sermon being analogous to the delivery of a lecture), it seems to me the least interesting form of teaching, from a pedagogical point of view, and the least potentially illuminating of the work and ministry of the presider. Rather, I am thinking about teaching situations in which learning is more participative and fluid, a shared enterprise between facilitator and learners, although no less formed than a good lecture is. I am thinking of a wide range of learning situations from my own experience: informal Bible study groups; postgraduate research seminars; residential courses and retreats in which the focus is on personal learning and where much of the learning takes place in groups; experiential workshops in which participants practise creative writing or work to put together an act of worship; and so on. In all these settings, I am working with adults, sometimes in formal academic settings but often not; sometimes in women-only contexts; almost always with very mixed groups of learners who represent a wide variety of educational, social, cultural, ethnic and ecclesiastical backgrounds.

Presiding as a commitment to liberative praxis

What is the work of the teacher in such settings? In what does 'presiding' consist? Above any specific function, the teacher's skill and her very being must be oriented towards education as the practice of freedom, and her teaching must be informed at every turn by a commitment to the liberation and empowerment of the students. It is this commitment which grounds and holds the teacher's work, channels her power and offers protection against the abuse of that power for her own self-aggrandisement. Feminist pedagogy is rooted in this commitment to education as emancipatory, transformative praxis, what Rebecca Chopp names 'saving work',[6] and what Brita Gill-Austern describes, simply, as 'pastoral care' – where the 'practice of teaching deepens authentic, just and life-giving connection in all spheres of life'.[7] Such teaching is, perhaps, modelled most clearly in Christian tradition by Mary: it is her secret work during the hidden years of Jesus' childhood which tutors him in prayer, in a sense of God and in the demands of justice which we see coming to full flower in his public teaching and practice.[8] Similarly, I would suggest that liturgical presidency, to be authentically feminist, must grow out of and be rooted in a fundamental commitment to Church as a community of emancipation and liturgy as the place where that freedom is enacted in embodied word, ritual, interaction and sacrament.

Rather than be focused on her own *teaching*, the feminist teacher is centred in and on the *learning* of those she seeks to enable, as Mary's teaching of Jesus demonstrates most powerfully. Simple as it sounds, this distinction is crucial. It is not that her own expertise is insignificant, but that it is always to be put at the disposal of the group's learning, and her own authority employed to release and bring to expression the gifts, knowledge and power of the group and of each individual within it, rather than to call attention to herself. This is not to say that the facilitator's role is not crucial; it is, and without it, the life and energies of the group are likely to become dissipated, disruptive and dysfunctional. Indeed, the group cannot function as what they are called to be – in this case, a learning community – without the teacher. There is a paradox in the work of presidency which means that, very often, the more effective it is in enabling the life of the group, the more inconspicuous and unselfconscious it will be. The effective group facilitator, like the effective priest, enables the group to claim its own learning and power, to know *itself* to be empowered and effective and to find her own satisfaction in that reality. This is to speak of the essential kenotic quality of all teaching, though it is important to use such language carefully so as not to reinforce the powerlessness of women, and to affirm that the exercise of self-emptying which lies at the heart of all Christian ministry is dependent on a strong and secure selfhood.[9] The teacher who seeks to enable learning as liberative praxis must exercise strong leadership, challenging power where it is misused, including the abdication of power or voice, teaching students to transgress, in bell hooks' suggestive phrase[10] (or what Gill-Austern describes as 'becoming partners in resistance'[11]), where compliance would mean a diminishment of their agency. It is the feminist teacher who can say to her students:

> Dare to
> declare
> who you
> are[12]

and model in her own claiming of voice the authority of a subject position authentically claimed.

The teacher works always for an enlargement of students' vision, imagination, potential and subject power, as does the person presiding in the liturgical sphere. Strong leadership is required for such teaching, but it is a leadership focused on the enabling of the learners rather than on the interests, needs or agenda of the teacher. Undergirding such teaching, such presidency, is a spirituality of profound attention – to the needs, gifts and wounds of the community in which the teacher serves; to her *own* needs, gifts and wounds, and the ways in which they must be cared for (requiring deliberate and intentional self-reflection), and attention to the *missio dei*, the gospel call to justice and freedom in which her own vocation and that of the whole *laos* are rooted.[13]

Presiding as the creation of safe and creative space

A first calling of the teacher is, simply, to gather the learning community and to create a space in which learning can take place – a space[14] that is safe, boundaried and clearly focused on the active pursuit of truth and freedom. The president does not *create* the community, but she is frequently the one to call the community together and to issue the invitation to the risky, adventurous process of learning. The president has the responsibility to make sure the space is safe and conducive to the activity the community is gathered to share. In learning situations this usually means paying attention to the physical space in which learning takes place and arranging that space in a way that will maximize learning,[15] allowing participants to introduce themselves and state their own hopes and fears for the event, setting clear boundaries around timing, roles, conduct, confidentiality and so on – effectively negotiating a 'contract' for the life of the group. All of this is necessary for individuals to have a sense of knowing who and where they are within the group, to feel safe in the knowledge that the facilitator will take care of these things, and to be enabled to take the necessary risks they will be called upon to take – for all genuine learning involves the risk of entering into the unknown, not only the unknown and unexplored territory of new knowledge but, more significantly, the unknown power and potential of the learners themselves, both as individuals and as a group. While the invitation to enter more deeply into one's own power and into the larger truth of God's reality is an ultimately liberating gesture, it is frequently also deeply disturbing – which is why learners often resist learning, or seek to inoculate themselves against deep change in all kinds of ways. Part of the work of the teacher is to keep the invitation to genuine transformation open to the students at each stage of learning, however often that invitation may be resisted, and to keep the space of the learning environment an open and clearly boundaried one in which students know that they will be supported and encouraged in their quest for truth. Both openness and boundedness are important in this creation of community; safety is necessary for genuine, transformative learning to take place[16] but there is always a danger of a learning community becoming too closed in upon itself, so the teacher has a right 'concern always to be expanding the circle of who belongs to that community', and 'bringing into substantive dialogue those who have been perceived to be on the margins'.[17]

Although such contracting of the boundaries of the group's life does not take place overtly when the ecclesial community gathers, this is part of what is going on, unconsciously probably, at the beginning of every act of worship, and it is part of what the president needs to attend to in gathering and greeting the assembly. Rather than being a mere formality, the opening greetings and prayers of the liturgy are essential for the community to sense and know who we are in Christ, why we are gathering and to trust that the president will 'hold' the space and time we have given so that each person may be welcome, may have a place at the table, may give and receive as they are able, and may participate in the conduct of worship. Much of this is conveyed subtly and unconsciously through the ordering of the physical space, the care and attention paid to the material objects and symbols in the space, and above all through the embodied being of the one presiding: through tone of voice, body language, eye contact and the sense they convey within themselves of being at home in their role as president and of welcome and inclusion. There must be a willingness to occupy the seat of authority, not in any controlling or authoritarian sense, but in the sense that the presider needs to sit comfortably and securely in their own selfhood, taking clear responsibility for the group, so that everyone can relax and let go into the work each one has come to do and claim their rightful authority within the group – rather than competing for power, as often happens in groups where there is no clear leadership. The presidency can be shared, can be passed from one person to another, in both liturgical and educational settings, and very often is in feminist liturgies as well as in feminist pedagogy; yet whether shared or exercised by one person, attention to the power dynamics within the group and careful management of those dynamics is essential if the community is to function well.

Presiding as an embodied holding, a work of form-giving

The presider holds a creative tension between the needs of the individuals, the dynamics of the group, and the purpose of the group's life. As a teacher, my work is to focus the group on the particular learning they have contracted to do and to maintain that focus, not allowing individuals or the group to deflect from task, continuing to hold the invitation and the challenges before the group. I do that in any number of ways: by presenting material to them in a variety of ways (sharing my expertise and knowledge, such as it is), by directing them to other sources of learning (books, articles, websites and so on), by encouraging and challenging them to engage actively with the material (asking questions, setting exercises, directing small group work) – but also, beyond specific 'teacherly' activities, in and through my own being as a learner myself: through my passion and enthusiasm for my subject, thus incarnating subject matter in ways that make the subject 'live' and that are potentially revelatory for the learners; through my demonstrable commitment to ongoing learning in the field (both through a commitment to research and publication but also to other forms of embodied learning, such as social justice or political engagement), and perhaps above all, through the intangible quality of my person as a learner and teacher. The teacher is almost certainly the one person least conscious of what this quality might be and how it communicates, because they inhabit it as a norm, but it is this intangible 'presence' which we hold before the group when we teach (as the priest offers her or his priestly presence to the liturgical assembly) and which calls out from the students an answering quality of being, as they discover themselves anew as learners, as those whose hunger for learning is reawakened, as those with the power to know and to shape their learning in life-giving ways.

This work of holding, enabling and shaping the learning process involves the co-ordination of many elements: the management of time and space, the encouragement of each person to participate fully as they are able, the gathering of the dispersed gifts of the community and offering of them so that each person is enriched by the gifts of all, and so on. When this is working well, there is a sense of organic development and dynamic flow which is both within and beyond the control of any one person, even though the presider may be the one 'holding' the flow. The learning has a shape and structure to it, one that is both spontaneous and scripted. Unlike a lecture with a set text, most of such teaching is a more spontaneous interaction between the teacher and the learners in the group. Far from being less prepared, the facilitator in such a setting needs to be *more* prepared, needs to know their material better, so that they can use it and adapt it according to the needs and interests of the learners. It is a skill to be able both to 'hold' the group to task and yet also be open to the dynamic energy and flow of the group itself, to allow someone to take the group off at a tangent, perhaps, or to play with what might at first seem a whacky idea offered by someone from 'offside', in order to discover some new insight or come to some new place that is only reached by following the unexpected diversion. In order for this to happen, the presider has to really trust and believe that the learning belongs to the group as a whole, rather than being her own sole possession. The teacher is one who can testify:

> I do not possess the truth
> but with others to witness to what they know
> I will be able to discern what is right.[18]

Sometimes this trust requires active intervention on the presider's part – inviting the quiet person to speak, encouraging the talker to desist from talking, say; sometimes it requires a more receptive letting go and letting be of whatever is emerging in the group. Whether active or passive, this is a truly a work of form-giving, as Maria Harris names it, an essentially aesthetic practice of finding an appropriate form for the learning that is emerging from the interaction between the learning subjects, the subject matter in which all are engaged, and the teacher. To speak of this theologically, this is 'the incarnation of subject matter that leads to the revelation of subject matter'.[19] This process requires profound attention on the part of both learners and teacher, each to the other, each to the subject matter in which they are engaged, and each to the interaction that is taking place within and among them. Good learning, like good liturgy, emerges from the life of the group which is more than the sum of its parts, which is the mysterious culmination of the shared hunger, knowledge, questing and offering of each member of the group interacting with the material and the other learners. This is why no two group seminars are ever the same, even when the material is exactly the same and even if the learners are the same individuals – just as no act of worship is ever the same, even when the script is identical.

Presiding as costly, transformative work

The work of presiding, either at the liturgy or in the classroom, is a costly work which often doesn't look like 'work' from the outside, because much of it is hidden and internalized. It is a bearing in the body of the presider of the life of the group, gathered and focused in time and space around a particular set of actions. It is a labour of praying the hungers of the community, sifting their stories, assuaging their desires, offering one's own knowledge, longings and presence as food to nourish the people.[20] Much of this work is unconscious as the gathered community projects onto the president their hopes, fears, angers at the Church (or the academy), frustrations, deepest longings, joys and griefs, and looks to him or her for healing, feeding, cleansing, renewing. Without needing to know the content of these hopes, joys and griefs, the president absorbs within her own body the weight of all these mixed and potent realities, and takes them into herself, lives them for the duration of the group's gathering, and mediates them, offers them back in the form of words, gestures, actions, looks, sighs even, which have the potential to meet the hungers of the community. At the same time, the president herself receives from the group; it is not a one-way process. Looking around, she sees the struggles and wounds of those gathered with her, she notices and absorbs the triumphs of learning, of the living and praying of individuals whose stories she may or may not know, the glory of relationships forged and celebrated, the gifts each one brings, whether hesitantly or confidently – and she is both blessed and burdened by that flow of life that comes towards her, meets within her and flows out again through her.

In the Eucharist, there is a mysterious exchange which takes place between the gathered assembly and Christ, as the offering of all this brokenness and potential is made on the table and the gifts of bread and wine offered back to the assembly, the same and yet not the same. Just this same kind of transformation and exchange can and often does happen in the classroom, as learners offer to each other the fruits of their costly learning and receive back from each other what they have offered and shared, mysteriously transformed in the interchange, mediated in and through the body of the teacher as presider. This is why Maria Harris speaks of teaching as a work of 'religious imagination' which requires both aesthetic and theological categories, as well as pedagogical ones, to explicate its potential for transformation. When teaching is conducted as 'an activity of religious imagination', when subject matter is incarnated authentically to lead to 'the revelation of subject matter', then learners discover that they themselves 'are the primary subjects of all teaching', and they 'discover themselves as possessing the grace of power, especially the power of re-creation, not only of themselves, but of the world in which they live'.[21] Such teaching and such learning are truly sacramental, sites of divine revelation and thus of profound empowerment, places where we make and know Eucharist:

> O come and eat, o taste and see:
> How good a feast.
> How rich a guest.
> How lavish a host.
> How ravished a hunger.
> I am met. I am meat. I am ate.
> I am full. I am fed.
> I am juice, I am joy, I am all golden peach.[22]

The gender question

Is there anything specifically gendered in this work of presiding I have been describing? I want to say both yes and no. No in so far as both women and men can, and do, exemplify this kind of priestly teaching, just as they exemplify eucharistic leadership in other contexts and vocations. Yes in so far as women are frequently those who have learnt, through socialization into roles of caring, nurturing and sustaining of relationships, how to exercise this kind of ministry of bearing and empowering of others in and through the bodies we inhabit – often in ways that are not recognized as priestly or authoritative, yet are. This is one part of the gift that women can bring to the exercise of priesthood, as well as to the vocation of teaching. Many feminists have spoken of the role of the priest or teacher as midwife,[23] and, while this is not the exclusive preserve of women, when women do such work – supporting, empowering, holding and directing the birth of the new, releasing and transforming incipient life – they bring to that work a particular character and skill that is rooted in their own gendered histories, embodiment and identities, and they mirror and reflect the *imago dei* in specifically gendered ways.[24] As others have suggested in this collection, women image forth the Christa, the female Christ figure, who does not have any one face or form, but is a new manifestation of the being and the passion of Christ in the world. When I preside in the classroom in such a way as to enable the liberative praxis of the community towards a greater justice, freedom and wholeness, I am, in that holy work, *in persona Christae*, holding before the gathered community the challenging, gracious, enabling presence of Christ/a as one who calls us to freedom – but so are they to me, and each to the other, as we each in our various ways respond to the invitation to the liberation and empowerment of one another, and as we incarnate for each other the call of Christ/a into ever new forms of freedom.

Notes

1 Durka, G., *The Teacher's Calling: A Spirituality for Those Who Teach* (Mahwah, NJ: Paulist Press, 2002), p. 1.

2 Slee, N., 'A litany of grief and gladness (2)', in *Praying Like a Woman* (London: SPCK, 2004), p. 85.

3 See my discussion of Mary as teacher and priest in *The Book of Mary* (London: SPCK, 2007), chs 6 and 7.

4 Chopp, R. S., *Saving Work: Feminist Practices of Theological Education* (Louisville, KY: Westminster John Knox Press, 1995).

5 Gill-Austern, B. L., 'Pedagogy Under the Influence of Feminism and Womanism', in Miller-McLemore, B. J. and Gill-Austern, B. L. (eds), *Feminist and Womanist Pastoral Theology* (Nashville, TN: Abingdon Press, 1999), pp. 151–9.

6 Chopp, *Saving Work*.

7 Gill-Austern, 'Pedagogy Under the Influence', p. 150.

8 See my poem, 'Mary teaching the child Jesus', in *The Book of Mary*, p. 66.

9 Feminists have strongly critiqued notions of sacrifice as they have been employed in Christian tradition to legitimize the powerlessness of women and other groups, although recent debate indicates some rapprochement and a more nuanced reclaiming of notions such as kenosis and sacrifice. See, for example, Ramsay, K.,

'Losing One's Life for Others: Self-Sacrifice Revisited', in Frank Parsons, S., *Challenging Women's Orthodoxies in the Context of Faith* (Aldershot: Ashgate, 2000), pp. 121–33.

10 hooks, b., *Teaching to Transgress: Education as the Practice of Freedom* (New York: Routledge, 1994).

11 Gill-Austern, 'Pedagogy Under the Influence', p. 165.

12 Slee, N., 'Conversations with Muse', in *Praying Like a Woman*, p. 60.

13 I have tried to spell out and exemplify something of what such attention might mean in the context of listening to women's narratives of faith in my study, *Women's Faith Development: Patterns and Processes* (Aldershot: Ashgate, 2004). The principles which undergirded the development of my research methodology in that study are similar to those I am articulating in this essay, and indeed, I see close analogies between the practice of feminist qualitative research and the practice of feminist pedagogy.

14 For a feminist analysis of the notion of 'space', see Graham, E., 'From Space to Woman-Space', in *Words Made Flesh: Writings in Pastoral and Practical Theology* (London: SCM Press, 2009), pp. 27–44.

15 Stevenson-Moessner, J., speaks of 'rearranging the furniture', both literally and metaphorically, as a way of translating feminist values from seminary to parish, in 'Feminist Values from Seminary to Parish', in Miller-McLemore and Gill-Austern (eds), *Feminist and Womanist Pastoral Theology*, pp. 211–21.

16 Safety will be particularly important for those who have been abused or wounded – thus Lakey Hess, C., speaks of the necessity of ' "safe-houses" for raising girls in families and communities of faith', in *Caretakers of Our Common House: Women's Development in Communities of Faith* (Nashville, TN: Abingdon Press, 1997), ch. 4.

17 Gill-Austern, 'Pedagogy Under the Influence', pp. 164, 165.

18 Slee, N., 'With others: a statement of interdependence', in *Praying Like a Woman*, p. 66.

19 Harris, M., *Teaching and Religious Imagination: An Essay in the Theology of Teaching* (San Francisco, Harper & Row, 1987), p. 167.

20 See my poem, 'Mary bakes bread', in *The Book of Mary*, p. 82.

21 Harris, M., *Teaching and Religious Imagination*, p. xv.

22 Slee, N., 'Word', in *Praying Like a Woman*, p. 117.

23 For example, Belenky, M. F. et al., *Women's Ways of Knowing: The Development of Self, Voice and Mind* (New York: Basic Books, 1986), pp. 217ff; Gill-Austern, 'Pedagogy Under the Influence'.

24 See Percy, E., 'Reverend Mother – How Insights from Mothering can Inform the Practice of Leadership in the Church', Parts I & II, in *Modern Believing* 44/2 (2003), pp. 33–44 and 44/3, pp. 24–36 for an exploration of similar themes, drawing on the experience of motherhood for an illumination of leadership.

In persona Christae: towards a feminist political Christ-( )-logy of presiding; or, how presiding with children trains us to challenge 'the powers that be'

ALASTAIR BARRETT

Presiding like a daddy?

Here's something that delighted me on many levels this morning (not able to be fully expressed in words) ... you holding Rafi as you celebrated communion! Incarnational, embodied: God imaged as father ... a picture of Jesus' humanity – a bit grizzly and a little wriggly as real babies are – against the backdrop of the reading, 'In the beginning was the Word ...' Rafi stretching out his hand towards the uplifted bread ...[1]

I can't write about 'presiding like a woman'. Or rather, I can write about '*like*', but not '*as*'. I *can* write, however, 'as a daddy', and 'as a feminist'. And 'as' those, at least, the email quoted above brought both encouragement and a whole host of questions. Do I *want* to image God as 'father' as I preside, or does that have too many echoes of centuries of patriarchal priesthood? Writing in a book called *Presiding Like a Woman*, do I risk falling back into designating 'caring for children' as 'women's work'? And excluding from my description of presiding those who are not parents?

With those questions, but with the encouragement of another 'host' too – an eclectic company of women, writers and priests – I will take the plunge, and seek to sketch one kind of 'feminist theology of presiding': a theology rooted in feminist conceptions of personhood and Christ-( )-logy,[2] and a practice of presiding, interacting, with little children in particular, that might just have the potential to empower us – *train* us, even – to challenge the (supposedly 'grown-up') 'powers that be' of our world.

A spirituality of presiding

Siobhán Garrigan, in her article, 'The Spirituality of Presiding',[3] traces her personal journey of growing and shifting understandings of the art of 'presiding' and her own place within it. Beginning with a focus on her *voice* as that which bears her 'presence', which in turn can bear God's word and God's spirit – or not – she guides us, via a small lump her doctor finds beside her uvula, to a broader, more full-bodied, conception of 'voice', finding herself 'pondering less the voice-bit and more the presence-bit': it is 'one's *presence*', she suggests, that 'speaks'.

Teasing out a tension between the linguistic roots of 'presiding' – in a 'sitting down', which is related at root also to 'walking' and 'yielding' – and the more common understanding of 'the one who stands up the front' or exercises some 'control or authority', Garrigan then throws the presider's cloak wider to include all those, in a multiplicity of roles within worship, from 'those who greet arriving congregants' to 'those who collect the offering', whose 'presence' is 'vital to leading others to accomplish something'.

But she pushes the definition further, to re-describe presiding not so much as 'multivalent', but as '*mutually constituting*' – not as present in 'a single acting agent', but as 'an *interactive* presence'. Drawing on the theory of Jürgen Habermas, she invites us to attend to 'presider' and 'congregation' together *in their interaction with each other*: 'we have to look not just at what was *said* but what was *heard*, not just at what was *offered* but at what was *received* or *refused*.' The question for presiding, Garrigan suggests, 'is how far one's interactions empower a full exchange'.

In her brief article, Garrigan has space only to offer hints as to what a *theology* of 'interactive presiding' might look like: of God's Spirit as 'an intrinsically mutual, relational reality' which 'only exists ... insofar as it *works with*'; and an understanding of collaborative, interactive presiding within the assembly as drawing the congregation into participation in the trinitarian life of God. In what follows, I want to turn Garrigan's practically won insights in a specifically *christ-( )-logical* direction: where, and how, might Christ(a) be incarnated in the liturgical space of interactive presiding?

A Christ-( )-logy in the 'between': two gospel interactions

Within the 'christological narrative' that is Mark's Gospel, there are a number of interactions between Jesus and others, 'transformative encounters', in which we cannot but attend, in Garrigan's words, not just to 'what was *said*' but to 'what was *heard*', not just to 'what was *offered*' but to 'what was *received* or *refused*'. Through tracing the shape of two – and, later, a third – of those interactions, I seek to sketch out a 'christ-( )-logical space' which might just prove hospitable to, and shape, practices of presiding.

Jesus and the Syrophoenician woman (Mark 7.24–31)

The first encounter takes us, with Jesus, to the very edge of the Gospel's geography, a 'point farthest out' from the narrative and political centre of Jerusalem – the rural northern region of Tyre (v. 24). A Syrophoenician

woman – an 'outsider' par excellence, 'Jesus' "other" ... not only geographically, but sexually, racially and religiously' – whose 'little daughter' is ill, has
'heard about' Jesus, and comes and bows down at his feet (v. 25), begging
him to heal her daughter (v. 26). What follows is quite a remarkable exchange.
Jesus responds with something between reluctance and racism, underlining
her inferior status and refusing her plea: 'Let the children be fed first, for
it is not fair to take the children's bread and throw it to the [little] dogs'
(v. 27). The woman then accepts his belittling of her, but in a 'deft phrase'
linking and valuing *both* 'human little ones' *and* 'canine little ones', and
anticipating Jesus' own teaching about the greatness of being least, she
'refuses his refusal by using its negative power to secure her own positive
purposes': 'Sir, even the [little] dogs under the table eat the children's crumbs'
(v. 28). At this, Jesus apparently changes his mind – 'For saying that, you
may go – the demon has left your daughter' (v. 29) – and the woman returns
home to her daughter (v. 30) and Jesus returns to Galilee (v. 31).[4]

Christ-( )-logical tactics, christ-( )-logical space

I want to highlight two aspects of this exchange that, for a 'Christ-( )-logy
of presiding' might prove both significant and unsettling. First, the woman's
tactics here. While we know next to nothing about her social status, she
negotiates the encounter by 'playing small' – bowing and begging, 'accepting'
her littleness – but comes out on top. Her 'performance' exemplifies what
queer theorist Judith Butler calls 'citational politics', 'that power of discourse
to produce effects through reiteration' – specifically here the 'reworking of
abjection into political agency'.[5] But it is also a stunning example of what
the discipline of theatrical improvisation calls 'status play'. Good actors, says
director Keith Johnstone, are not those who 'specialize' in a particular kind
of 'status role' – but those who can play 'high' or 'low' status at will, depending on the needs of the situation. Further, if anything an actor says or does
is an 'offer', and anything that prevents the offer from developing is a 'block',
then good improvisation, for Johnstone, is not about 'thinking up interesting
offers', but *assuming that an offer has already been made* and '*accepting*' it – taking
it on and developing it further. At its most creative, '*over*accepting' is the
capacity to receive anything one is given, however mundane or difficult, as
so much more than it appears, or was intended to be.[6]

In this 'edgy' encounter between Jesus and the Syrophoenician woman,
her humble, creative 'overacceptance' of Jesus' 'block' – her 'powerful redeploy-
ment of the terms of talk', as Perkinson puts it – achieves not just the
healing of her daughter, but, apparently, a transformation in Jesus too. 'Close
to the epicentre of change' in Mark's narrative, we see here Jesus not just
'turning around' and returning to Galilee, not just undergoing a kind of
'schooling' from this outsider in tactics he will soon deploy himself when

confronted with the powers that be, but also beginning a more 'inclusive' phase of his ministry – feeding a crowd of Gentiles (8.1–9) where previously he has fed a crowd of Jews (6.34–44) – and in the process, we might well say, 'repenting' of his initially dismissive attitude to the one who began as his 'other'. The word '*metanoia*' is not used in this passage – but is enacted quite visibly. He becomes, in an important sense, a 'disciple' of the woman.[7]

So where is Christ-( )-logy *located* in this exchange? This is my second point. For a start, as so often in Mark's Gospel, the 'word' about Jesus has clearly already 'gone on ahead of him' – here is the power of popular rumour that 'straddles national borders and transgresses individual authorship'. But more than that, in this encounter it seems clear that it is the woman's 'saying' – her '*logos*' – that has made the difference. Here, suggests Jim Perkinson, is 'a demonstration of messianic power ... wrested from the Christ by the word of the other'. Echoing Garrigan's reflections on presidency, we might well ask whether the 'saving word' here 'can be centred entirely within the speaking of Jesus alone', or whether, in fact, it has a certain 'undecidability' or 'hybridity' about it – issuing 'not so much from Jesus himself, as from *the open place between his words and the words of his others*'.[8]

The Syrophoenician woman's story 'de-stabilizes' and 'de-centres' our christ-( )-logical focus, but it also leaves me with critical questions: is Christology all about the 'demonstration of power', and the 'power of words' in particular? Does a focus on the woman's '*logos*' tie us in to what feminists have called a 'logocentrism' that privileges 'the speaking subject' above all other embodiments of humanity (and, indeed, God)? How can we move, with Garrigan, from a concentration on '*voice* as presence' to something more 'full-bodied'?

Jesus and the woman with a haemorrhage (Mark 5.21–34)

In our second encounter, Jesus is on the move again – heading for another sick girl, following her father, the synagogue-leader Jairus. A 'large crowd' are 'pressing in' on Jesus (v. 24), and in their midst is a woman who has been 'suffering from haemorrhages for twelve years' (v. 25) – and has been drained of her money in the process (v. 26). Like the Syrophoenician woman, she has 'heard about Jesus', but she chooses an even humbler approach: silently, invisibly even, coming up behind Jesus in the crowd and touching his cloak (v. 27). And here is the critical point: 'immediately' her flow of blood dries up, and she knows in her body that she has been made whole (v. 29). 'Aware that power ha[s] gone forth from him' (v. 30), Jesus then both looks around and asks 'who touched ...?' (vv. 30–32). It takes the woman, again, to take the initiative, to come 'in fear and trembling', fall down before him, and tell him 'the whole truth' (v. 33) – to which Jesus responds,

'Daughter, your faith has made you well; go in peace, and be healed of your disease' (v. 34).

As with our first passage, the flow of power here is presented as beyond Jesus' initiative or command – deconstructing the myth, suggests Graham Ward, of Jesus as 'the subject-in-control'.[9] But the tactic and the medium are different. 'It is the woman's *touch*', not her 'saying', 'that initiates the healing', that effects the flow of power. Jesus' announcement of her healing merely restates the 'truth' that she has proclaimed to him, and has already known bodily – known before he has even become aware of her, her touch, or the power flowing out from him.[10] And her touch, here, does even more than that. First, it *closes distance*: from first 'hearing' about Jesus from afar, the woman sees him amid the crowd, but it is her touch that finally brings her 'up close and personal'. Second, her touch introduces an *'economy of response'* between 'toucher' and 'touched': her deliberate action disrupts the relatively passive 'looking on' of the crowd, bridges the 'separation' and 'individualism' encouraged by the 'society of the spectacle', and attracts the attention of the person who was, until that moment, the focus. And third, in that attention, and his acknowledgement of her as 'Daughter' – 'of God', we might infer – the woman moves *from 'anonymity' to 'kinship'* with Jesus, children together of the kin-dom of God.[11]

Christ-( )-logy and Luce Irigaray

French feminist theorist Luce Irigaray has something important to say here. In Lacanian psychoanalysis, 'woman' is characterized by embodiment, wordlessness, and a 'hole' or 'void' – she is the 'Other', who can only enter into 'culture' through the masculine, 'phallic', structures of language. Irigaray, however, 'takes on' – we might say, 'creatively overaccepts' – this representation of 'woman' as she poetically crafts an alternative, 'gynocentric' symbolic. Touch becomes the primal, foundational sense (speech and hearing, after all, are dependent on the touching of vocal cords, sound waves, and eardrum), the 'hole' not an empty 'void' but – between the 'two lips' – a sacred space, the place of divine disclosure.[12]

The woman with the haemorrhage, then, might be re-figured not as one 'lacking', 'leaking', and in need; and not just, as some early commentators saw her, in her humility and faith, 'a figure of the Church'.[13] I want to suggest she might be a figure too of Christ(a) herself, a proper focus of the christ-( )-logical space which opens up between her and Jesus.[14] While Amy-Jill Levine sees in the woman's suffering and bleeding, her humility, silence and faith, an 'anticipation' of Jesus' own passion,[15] Irigaray would encourage us to 'frame' this encounter the 'other' way round. Seeing opened up in the body of the crucified Jesus, 'in the form of a wound, the place that, in women, is naturally open',[16] Irigaray begs a number of questions. Does Jesus, in some sense, become a 'follower' of this woman? Does *her* attention to *him* not simply 'interrupt' his flow but 're-direct' it – her touch inviting him to stop, turn, and seek her out and the 'truth' she bears in her body – 'schooling' *him* in attention to *her*, not as 'one of the crowd' but as a 'daughter' of God who incarnates God's 'kenotic', 'out-flowing' passion in a way that he will, later, seek to embody? Does 'Christ-( )-logy', here, find its place *within* 'discipleship',[17] rather than the other way round? That is, if we may understand 'discipleship' as that humble preparedness to attend to, and creatively 'accept', interruptions as 'offers' of divine epiphany, might we then locate 'Christ-( )-logy' – that space 'within which divinity is made manifest' – not simply 'in Jesus' (or, indeed, simply 'in the woman'), but (as Ward, following Irigaray, suggests) in that 'movement', that 'gravitational field', that 'economy of love' which the woman's attentive touch establishes *'between' her and Jesus*?[18]

'*In persona Christae*'? A christ-( )-logical space for presiding

When priest and feminist theologian Sarah Coakley presided for the first time, largely with her back to the congregation, at the stone altar 'fixed ... inexorably into the east end' of her Oxfordshire parish church, she was surprised to discover the experience 'curiously releasing', where she had expected to have her feminist sensibilities offended.[19] Tracing, through the theologically conservative work of anthropologist Mary Douglas and theologian Hans Urs von Balthasar, the gendered binaries, 'Christ/active/"masculine" – Humanity/passive/"feminine"', Coakley argues that, where the liturgical performance of the priest is seen as 'mediating' the Christ–Church relationship, it turns out to be 'impossible to "fix" the priest as "masculine" alone'. In the course of a traditional east-facing liturgy, and particularly in her reversals between 'facing Godward, representing the *laos*' and 'representing Christ, offering God to the people', 'the priest moves implicitly through these different roles [i.e. "Christ", "Church"], strategically summoning the stereotypical gender associations of each', in order to subtly destabilize them:

> What I here call 'the divine nuptial enactment' is that incarnational flow of the divine to the human, and the enabling thereby of the human response. What the priest does, and does well when appropriately and prayerfully disposed, is to allow the incarnational impact of this flow of divine desire to be made manifest through a playful 're-presentation' of both symbolic poles – Christ and the church – while implicitly questioning the 'normative' identification of one with 'masculinity' and the other with 'femininity'.[20]

The 'de-centred christ-( )-logical geography' which emerges from two interactions in Mark's Gospel, then, resonates with the discoveries of both Coakley and Garrigan, but it pushes them still further. It certainly 'de-stabilizes' the 'stereotypical gender associations' of the 'Christ–Humanity' binary, but it also points us beyond the 'normative' identification of the former with a single person – whether the man Jesus or 'the woman at the altar' – towards the 'christ-( )-logical space *between*' human persons, within which the 'incarnational flow of the divine to the human' is made manifest. Such a geography, however, sits quite uncomfortably with the familiar 'cardinal directions' of Coakley's longitudinal, hierarchically ordered parish church, which looks 'onwards and upwards' towards a 'lone monarch', 'away from here but represented here', and which places 'priests above deacons above cantors above lectors above doorkeepers or ushers above widows or other dominant women above the people above the outsiders'.[21] But neither does it fit neatly within the egalitarian 'worshipping circle', with which, I confess, I am more familiar. While the latter has the theological advantage of seeing 'one's fellow [congregation] members' not as 'an obstacle to worship' but as incarnations of divine beauty,[22] the danger, as Gordon Lathrop warns us, is that 'we can easily draw a line around our group' – identities and positions become fixed, the incarnational flow stemmed, the attention of the circle closed off from the 'outsideness' of the transcendent Other – thus reducing liturgy to mere 'ceremony', 'an unambiguous expression of a univocal idea', 'a world of our own closed projection'.[23]

In contrast, Lathrop reminds us, 'the one around whom we gather . . . is himself always also *away* from here, identified with those who are *outside* our circle, outside all circles, disassembled.' We avoid getting too 'unifocal' in our attention, Lathrop proposes, by nurturing the creative tensions produced by frequent 'juxtapositions' within the liturgy – and creating a liturgical space itself that has both 'strong and weighty centres' (word, table, bath) and 'wide and accessible doors'.[24] Remembering the two women of our de-centred Christ-( )-logy, we might say it like this: the christ-( )-logical space in which we gather is itself stretched out between 'here' and the 'point farthest out', between our 'centre of attention' and the disruptive initiatives of those most 'other' to our liturgical norms (whatever and whoever they may be). For a presider and congregation 'schooled' together in the christ-( )-logical tactics of improvisation, there will be a shared expectation that the initiative in any liturgical interaction might come from *anywhere* in the space – not only from the presider herself, but from among the congregation – or indeed from its '*outside*'.

The presider might well, therefore, as Coakley suggests, be the one who makes repeated reversals, but not so much between facing west and east, but between attending to the congregation – as 'the leader who serves', and who 'yields to other leaders' – and attending to the congregation's 'others', 'strangers' and 'margins'.[25] And rather than simply 'turning and turning about', as Coakley implies, she might seek never to occupy for long one of the 'foci' of the christ-( )-logical space (Lathrop's 'centres'), but, instead, to *move back and forth* across and to the very edges and doorways of the space (close enough to *touch* those who may be there and to establish genuine, reciprocal relationship with them), enabling and encouraging the movement of others, and, in the process, making visible and tangible the 'incarnational flow' within the 'space between'. Moreover, the 'yielding' of presiding may mean, at its most daring, an alert capacity – simultaneously both 'passive' and 'active', and, again, shared by both presider and congregation – for creatively 'accepting' and 'overaccepting' whatever 'offers' – however unconventional, unintentional and disruptive to liturgical 'flow' – might be made.

Anti-liturgy

Were the liturgy to be practiced in something like this way, it would be an antiliturgy in both possible senses. That is, it would contain within itself a critique of at least some of those inevitable concomitants of serious ritual, while maintaining serious ritual. And it would be like Ionesco's *antithéâtre*, an appeal for all comers to join in the action and resist becoming an audience.[26]

I had not heard of Ionesco, and I thought I had not heard of *antithéâtre* – but then I remembered Augusto Boal and *The Theatre of the Oppressed*. In Boal's 'Forum Theatre', actors repeatedly act out a problematic scene – usually one of oppressive relationships – until a member of the audience, a 'spect-actor', shouts 'Stop!', and takes the place of one of the protagonists in the scene. In the course of a single forum, many different 'endings' can be enacted, a wealth of 'knowledge, tactics and experience' pooled. Boal calls it a 'rehearsal for reality' – a way of *questioning* 'the world as it is' (hence *antithéâtre*) as well as catching glimpses of 'the world as it *could* be'.[27]

What if liturgy could embrace such an antiliturgical practice? Could we really stomach the kind of interruptions, questioning, and rearrangements that Boal's 'Forum Theatre' encourages? Would congregation members have the guts to shout 'Stop!', or presiders the humility and creativity to welcome and 'overaccept' such disruptive 'offers'? The beginnings of an answer, I suggest, might be found in the presence of little children.

'Antiliturgy' in church: presiding with little children

Little children can be, in my experience, within the space of moments both silent and noisy, attentively still and uncontainably adventurous, tearful and comedic, adorably cute and embarrassingly opinionated, entirely self-obsessed and touchingly caring. In short, little children are complex agents, just as are 'grown ups'.

They also, I suggest, have the capacity to be 'co-presiders'. But this is not where our liturgies generally 'place' them. As 'chaotic bodies', lacking the necessary language for making the 'correct' responses, or the necessary

173

direction for appropriate movement within the liturgical space, they tend to be marginalized to the 'crèche', the 'children's corner', or to the containing (and usually somewhat harassed) 'supervision' of their parents – perhaps just occasionally granted a stage on which to appear as a 'spectacle' for adult entertainment. They are liturgy's 'others', 'nobodies' – the comparison with the haemorrhaging woman of Mark's Gospel is not, perhaps, too far-fetched. In that Gospel, however, despite similar attitudes embedded within his own society,[28] Jesus is narrated as 'embracing' little children's interruptions (10.13), proclaiming them as figures of divine presence (9.37) and model citizens of the reign of God (10.14–15) – they are to be not just *welcomed*, but *followed*. Like the women we have encountered earlier, they too – par excellence, even – are a proper focus of christ-( )-logical space.

In the company of little children, then, presiders who, as Sarah Coakley suggests, are called to be 'beaters of the liminal bounds between the divine and human',[29] precisely through their creative embracing and 'overacceptance' of children's 'interruptions' of the liturgical flow might both stumble upon, and stretch out invitingly, that 'liminal space', both 'disruptive' and 'potentially transformative', with which parents of young children are all too familiar.[30] They will need to exercise that certain kind of 'attentiveness' – 'part instinct, part discipline, part gift' – with which philosopher Sara Ruddick characterizes 'maternal thinking': a patient, 'anticipatory openness' to a truth which is emerging from the child, even when one can make little sense of what one hears; a particular kind of 'looking' that is inextricable from 'activity, physical contact, direct touch, material response'.[31] And it will be by such attentive *touch* that presiders will christ-( )-logically reshape the liturgical space. When little children are brought to Jesus, and the disciples attempt to 'block' them with stern words, Jesus 'embraces' (10.13); where the disciples argue for the places of power, Jesus 'takes' and 'puts' the little child among them (9.36). With his touch he simultaneously acknowledges an intimacy, mutuality and kinship with them, and resites and reorders power within the space of interaction – presiding in the company of little children will do likewise.

But as 'co-presiders', little children have a liturgical and christ-( )-logical initiative all of their own. It is not just in their 'interruptions' that they question 'the world as it is' and gesture towards 'the world as it could be'. They also are adept at reshaping liturgical space, transgressing divisions and barriers, finding routes around, over and underneath, and freely walking across allegedly 'sacred' spaces. They will, given half a chance, touch those 'holy things' which are usually in only the presider's hands, and with unconstrained imaginations, reverence the most mundane objects as holy. They have a knack of reaching out to those who are at their most fragile, and infusing the most serious moment with surreal comedy. Within the last year, I have witnessed a little child 'preside' from behind a pillar in a rabbit costume, minister to each member of the 'communion circle' while clinging to the altar rail, comfort a tearful woman from the neighbouring pew, and absolve much of a congregation with delighted splashes of water.

'Antiliturgy' in public: presiding like a child?

On Friday 17 October 2008, a group of ministers-in-training from the Queen's Foundation, Birmingham,[32] with a few friends, got off a coach in the main car park of the Atomic Weapons Establishment, Aldermaston, and, despite police concern for our 'safety' and attempts to move us, gathered in a prominent position near the main gate. Framed by song and Scripture, sermon and prayer, surrounded by armed Ministry of Defence Police (including a very active police photographer), and bathed in bright sunlight, we engaged in three key symbolic actions: first, we received the sign of the cross in ash on our foreheads, lamenting our part in 'the guilt of nuclear weapons which turn life to dust and ashes'; second, we went forward to the forbidding perimeter fence and tied to it a mass of red and white poppies; and third, we joyfully shared the Peace – not just with each other, but also with several of the police officers 'guarding' and 'watching' us – a touching moment, making visible, making tangible, the peace of God.

We tend to imagine liturgy as a *'strategic'* activity: safe in 'our own place', we are gathered, shaped and empowered for 'managed' engagement with 'the world outside'.[33] Little children introduce us, however, to what Michel de Certeau calls *'tactics'*: opportunist, surprising, 'ad hoc engagements' within a space which we do not possess.[34] As a parish priest in an area of urban regeneration, Sam Wells discovered that 'the power of the church' lay not in the 'strategies' of the 'parent' – 'greater resources, more experience, greater physical strength' – but in the 'tactics' of the 'child' – 'stubbornness and doggedness, and the tendency to ask awkward or embarrassing questions ... still learning, potentially disruptive'.[35] What, then, if we were to perform our liturgies not 'strategically', but 'tactically'?

Presiders and congregations who seek to learn the way of discipleship by embracing, 'overaccepting', the interruptive initiatives of little children might, I suspect, be slowly but surely trained themselves in the childlike art of interrupting, and playfully, creatively, 'overaccepting' (rather than simply 'yielding' to), the 'liturgies' of the world: drawing attention to the 'holes, silences, inabilities' in the world's cosmologies that tyrannically claim comprehensiveness; and temporarily creating, or occupying, spaces which subvert the controlling gaze of the state, through an attentive, transgressive touching of the apparently 'untouchable'.[36] Like the children crying out 'Hosanna' in the Temple, we may well anger the authorities (in and out of church), but through such childlike performances the 'saving word' might just be heard, the 'incarnational flow from the divine to the human' be manifest.

Coda

This chapter, like McLemore's book, *In the Midst of Chaos* was written in the odd gaps between working as a parish priest and sharing the parenting of a 1-year-old. 'Sometimes,' admits McLemore, 'interruption is simply frustrating. It stops, it hinders, it breaks in.' But that, she reminds me, is 'the vocation of love and faith in family life' – and, we might well add, liturgical presidency – 'often, if not always, half-baked, partly unresolved, constantly interrupted, ever developing, changing, falling apart and coming back together again.'[37] Amen. So be it.

Notes

1 Lou Langford, personal correspondence, 4 January 2009.
2 I use the '-( )-' term, as will hopefully become clear, to allow for an undecidability of gender in our talk of 'Christ' or 'Christa', an open space in the middle of the term, in which God is becoming incarnate, and in which neither masculine nor feminine is assumed as 'normative'.
3 Garrigan, S., 'The Spirituality of Presiding', *Liturgy* 21 (2007), pp. 3–8 (my italics).
4 Perkinson, J., 'A Canaanitic Word in the Logos of Christ; or The Difference the Syro-Phonecian Woman Makes to Jesus', *Semeia* 75 (1996), pp. 65–9, 75–7.
5 Butler, J., *Bodies That Matter: On the Discursive Limits of 'Sex'* (London: Routledge, 1993), pp. 20–1.
6 Johnstone, K., *Impro: Improvisation and the Theatre* (London: Methuen, 1981), pp. 33, 97–101. See Begbie, J. S., *Theology, Music and Time* (Cambridge: Cambridge University Press, 2000) and Wells, S., *Improvisation: The Drama of Christian Ethics* (London: SPCK, 2004), for extended theological interpretations of Johnstone's work.
7 Perkinson, 'Canaanitic Word', pp. 75–8.
8 Perkinson, 'Canaanitic Word', pp. 65, 69–71, 80–1 (my italics).
9 Ward, G., *Christ and Culture* (Oxford: Blackwell, 2005), p. 60.
10 Ward, *Christ and Culture*, pp. 63–6. Ward notes that '*aletheia* ["truth"] in Mark's Gospel is [otherwise] reserved for the Christ alone' (p. 65).
11 Ward, *Christ and Culture*, pp. 63–9, 84.
12 Graham, E. L., '"Only Bodies Suffer": Embodiment, Representation and the Practice of Ethics', *Bulletin of the John Rylands Library* 80 (1998), pp. 265–9.
13 Ward, *Christ and Culture*, p. 84.
14 If geometry helps you, imagine Jesus and the woman as the two poles, or foci, of an elliptical christ-( )-logical space!
15 Levine, A.-J., 'Discharging Responsibility: Matthean Jesus, Biblical Law, and Hemorrhaging Woman', in Levine, A.-J. (ed.), *A Feminist Companion to Matthew* (Sheffield: Sheffield Academic Press, 2001), pp. 70–87, at p. 87.
16 Ward, G., 'Divinity and Sexuality: Luce Irigaray and Christology', *Modern Theology* 12 (1996), pp. 211–37, at p. 226.
17 As Levine reminds us ('Discharging Responsibility', pp. 84–7), Jesus is, in this story, already in the process of 'following' when the woman interrupts him.

18 Ward, 'Divinity and Sexuality', pp. 227–32.

19 Coakley, S., 'The Woman at the Altar: Cosmological Disturbance or Gender Subversion?', *Anglican Theological Review* (Winter 2004) <http://findarticles.com/p/articles/mi_qa3818/is_200401/ai_n9347132>, accessed 16/7/08.

20 Coakley, 'Woman at the Altar', n. 36. Rivera, M., in *The Touch of Transcendence: A Postcolonial Theology of God* (Louisville, KY: Westminster John Knox Press, 2007), arrives at a similarly resonant image, and one (helpfully) less heterosexually 'nuptial' than Coakley's: 'Like sap or placenta, what flows in and between us and nurtures us all is God among us, a living and dynamic, fluid envelope that both links – within and throughout – and subtends the space of difference and thus opens creatures to a relational infinity' (p. 137).

21 Lathrop, G. W., *Holy Ground: A Liturgical Cosmology* (Minneapolis, MN: Fortress Press, 2003), pp. 183–4.

22 Wells, S., *God's Companions: Reimagining Christian Ethics* (Oxford: Blackwell, 2006), p. 133.

23 Lathrop, *Holy Ground*, pp. 188, 192.

24 Lathrop, *Holy Ground*, pp. 65 (my emphasis), pp. 171–2.

25 Lathrop, *Holy Ground*, pp. 191–4.

26 Lathrop, *Holy Ground*, p. 195.

27 Augusto Boal, *Games for Actors and Non-Actors* (London: Routledge, 1992), pp. xxi, 20, 232.

28 See, e.g., Burns, S., *Worship in Context: Liturgical Theology, Children and the City* (Peterborough: Epworth Press, 2006), p. 104.

29 Coakley, 'Woman at the Altar'.

30 Miller-McLemore, B. J., *In the Midst of Chaos: Caring for Children as Spiritual Practice* (San Francisco: Jossey-Bass, 2007), pp. 98–100.

31 Miller-McLemore, *In the Midst of Chaos*, pp. 49–54 (cf. Ruddick, S., *Maternal Thinking: Towards a Politics of Peace* (London: The Women's Press, 1989), pp. 119–23).

32 For a fuller description, see Hull, J., 'Lamentation at Aldermaston', unpublished paper (Birmingham: The Queen's Foundation for Ecumenical Theological Education, 2008).

33 This, says Lathrop, is the mistake of the 'closed-circle distortion' of liturgy: Lathrop, *Holy Ground*, p. 192.

34 de Certeau, M., *The Practice of Everyday Life* (Berkeley, CA: University of California Press, 1988), pp. 35–7.

35 Samuel Wells, 'No Abiding Inner City: A New Deal for the Church', in Thiessen Nation, M. and Wells, S. (eds), *Faithfulness and Fortitude: In Conversation with the Theological Ethics of Stanley Hauerwas* (Edinburgh: T&T Clark, 2000), p. 123.

36 Lathrop, *Holy Ground*, p. 36; Wells, S., *Improvisation: The Drama of Christian Ethics* (Grand Rapids, MI: Brazos, 2004), p. 167. See also Ruddick, *Maternal Thinking*, p. 244; Wink, W., *Jesus and Nonviolence: A Third Way* (Minneapolis, MN: Fortress Press, 2003), p. 16; Hebden, K., 'Jesus, Gandhi, and Alinsky: Strategies for Non-Violent Resistance' (unpublished paper), 2009.

37 McLemore, *Midst of Chaos*, p. 100.

At the table of Christa

NICOLA SLEE

At the table of Christa

The women do not serve
but are served

The children are not silent
but chatter

The menfolk do not dominate
but co-operate

The animals are not shussed away
but are welcomed

At the table of Christa

There is no seat of honour
for all are honoured

There is no etiquette
except the performance of grace

There is no dress code
except the garments of honesty

There is no fine cuisine
other than the bread of justice

At the table of Christa

There is no talk of betrayal
but only of healing and hopefulness

No money changes hands
but all know themselves rich in receiving

Death is in no one's mind
but only the lust for life

No one needs to command 'Remember'
for no one present can ever forget

ND - #0045 - 270325 - C0 - 216/138/13 - PB - 9780281061860 - Gloss Lamination